Rethinking China's Rise

China's rise to power is the signal event of the twenty-first century, and this volume offers a contemporary view of this nation in ascendancy from the inside. Eight recent essays by Xu Jilin, a popular historian and one of China's most prominent public intellectuals, critique China's rejection of universal values and the nation's embrace of Chinese particularism, the rise of the cult of the state, and the acceptance of the historicist ideas of Carl Schmitt and Leo Strauss. Xu's work is distinct both from better-known voices of dissent and also from the "New Left" perspectives, offering instead a liberal reaction to the complexity of China's rise. Yet this work is not a shrill denunciation of Xu's intellectual enemies, but rather a subtle and heartfelt call for China to accept its status as a great power and join the world as a force for good.

XU JILIN is Professor of History at East China Normal University in Shanghai, and is one of China's most prominent public intellectuals. His many articles and books have focused on various aspects of China's modern intellectual history.

DAVID OWNBY is Professor of History at the Université de Montréal. He worked on the history of societies in *Brotherhoods and Secret Societies in Early and Mid-Qing China* (1996) and popular religion in *Falun Gong and the Future of China* (2008), before returning to an earlier interest in contemporary Chinese intellectual life.

T0384492

THE CAMBRIDGE CHINA LIBRARY

The **Cambridge China Library** is a series of new English translations of books by Chinese scholars that have not previously been available in the West. Covering a wide range of subjects in the arts and humanities, the social sciences and the history of science, the series aims to foster intellectual debate and to promote closer cross-cultural understanding by bringing important works of Chinese scholarship to the attention of Western readers.

Rethinking China's Rise

A Liberal Critique

Xu Jilin

East China Normal University, Shanghai

Edited and Translated by David Ownby

Université de Montréal

CAMBRIDGE
UNIVERSITY PRESS

CAMBRIDGE
UNIVERSITY PRESS

University Printing House, Cambridge CB2 8BS, United Kingdom

One Liberty Plaza, 20th Floor, New York, NY 10006, USA

477 Williamstown Road, Port Melbourne, VIC 3207, Australia

314-321, 3rd Floor, Plot 3, Splendor Forum, Jasola District Centre, New Delhi - 110025, India

79 Anson Road, #06-04/06, Singapore 079906

Cambridge University Press is part of the University of Cambridge.

It furthers the University's mission by disseminating knowledge in the pursuit of education, learning and research at the highest international levels of excellence.

www.cambridge.org
Information on this title: www.cambridge.org/9781108456586
DOI: 10.1017/9781108556965

Original essays © Xu Jilin 2013, 2011, 2010, 2015, 2014, 2015, 2015, 2004
English language translation © Xu Jilin and David Ownby 2018

First published 2018
First paperback edition 2020

A catalogue record for this publication is available from the British Library

Library of Congress Cataloging in Publication data
Names: Xu, Jilin, author. | Ownby, David, 1958– editor; translator.
Title: Rethinking China's rise : a liberal critique / Jilin Xu;
edited and translated by David Ownby.
Description: Cambridge; New York: Cambridge University Press, 2018. |
Series: The Cambridge China library | Includes index.
Identifiers: LCCN 2018007397 | ISBN 9781108470759 (hardback)
Subjects: LCSH: China – Civilization – 2002– | BISAC: HISTORY / Asia / General.
Classification: LCC DS779.43.X823 2018 | DDC 951.06/1–dc23
LC record available at https://lccn.loc.gov/2018007397

ISBN 978-1-108-47075-9 Hardback
ISBN 978-1-108-45658-6 Paperback

Contents

Preface

This volume is part of a joint research project entitled "Reading and Writing the Chinese Dream: Reinventing China's Tradition(s), 1980 to the Present." The project is funded as an Insight Grant by the Canadian Social Sciences and Humanities Research Council, and the lead researchers are Timothy Cheek of the University of British Columbia, Joshua Fogel of York University, and myself. It was thanks to Timothy that I first met Xu Jilin, the author of the texts translated in this volume, at a conference in Vancouver, and the seed for the idea that would eventually become this book was planted on the return flight from Vancouver to Montréal, as I read through a volume of essays that Professor Xu had given me, becoming increasingly impressed and enchanted. It was my first extensive exposure to the richness and diversity of intellectual life in reform-era China, a richness that is little known outside of China except to a handful of specialists. Our project, and this volume, are dedicated to the conviction that what these thinkers have to say is important to the world.

My thanks go first to Xu Jilin, who has been invariably helpful and generous with his time. The Chinese intellectual world is full of divas who can't be bothered to answer their emails; happily, Xu is not one of these. Thanks also to Timothy Cheek, who graciously allowed me to take over a project that he had hoped to accomplish one day. He also read through the complete manuscript, offering numerous suggestions for improvement. Joshua Fogel read several of the essays and made corrections and suggestions. Carl Déry read the manuscript and helpfully pointed out typos and other infelicities. Gloria Davies provided welcome feedback on the introduction.

I have given talks based on my work on Xu Jilin at Concordia University (Montréal), Meiji University (Tokyo), Monash University (Melbourne), and Columbia University (New York). My thanks to all those who offered comments and criticisms. The volume is better for them.

Thanks also to Lucy Rhymer and the staff at Cambridge University Press for their professionalism and efficiency.

Editor and Translator's Introduction

David Ownby

China's rise is perhaps the signal event of the twenty-first century, and is the subject of this volume of essays. China's rise is, of course, *celebrated* in China. More than thirty years of unprecedented economic growth has lifted hundreds of millions of Chinese out of poverty, reshaped the world economy, and allowed China to reassume its historic role as a great power. The relative decline of the United States, as evidenced by missteps such as the Iraq War, the financial crisis, and the election of Donald Trump, has produced a pride bordering on arrogance in many Chinese intellectuals, who are quick to offer China as a "model" of stability and "good governance" in a post-American world. The Shanghai historian Xu Jilin (b. 1957) is proud of China's rise as well. His adult life has coincided with China's economic transformation, and he has reaped the benefits in professional and personal terms. Yet despite his pride in China's accomplishments, Xu is also wary about certain less auspicious aspects of China's rise, and above all about the intellectual atmosphere that accompanies the cult of the state.

Xu Jilin is one of China's best-known liberal public intellectuals, but he is not a dissident. He is an establishment intellectual (or a "citizen intellectual," to use William Callahan's characterization[1]), and his writings are examples of opinions and arguments that could be openly defended in China between roughly 2000 and 2015 – and still today, to some degree. A professor of history at East China Normal University in Shanghai, Xu has devoted his career to the study of modern China's intellectual history, and has published dozens of books and hundreds of articles on topics ranging from the May Fourth Enlightenment movement (1919) to contemporary intellectual politics.[2] Prior to recent restrictions on the

---

[1] See William A. Callahan, "China's Strategic Futures," *Asian Survey* 52.4 (July/August 2012): 617–42.

[2] Xu's major volumes include: *Xunqiu yiyi: Xiandaihua bianqian yu wenhua pipan* (In search of meaning: transformations of modernization and cultural criticism) (Shanghai: Shanghai sanlian shudian, 1997); *Ling yizhongde qimeng* (Another kind of enlightenment) (Guangzhou: Huacheng chubanshe, 1999); *Zhongguo zhishi fenzi shilun*

Chinese blogosphere, Xu was also a very popular blogger, followed by some 650,000 readers,[3] and he continues to post frequently via WeChat, if to a smaller audience. The key to his popularity lies in a combination of an elegant narrative style, a deep understanding of history and historiography in China and the West, and a gift for linking historical issues to contemporary concerns.

The present volume offers translations of eight essays penned by Xu Jilin over roughly the past ten years that deal with various aspects of the evolution of the intellectual arguments concerning "China's rise" to great-power status. Xu criticizes statism and historicism as fanciful arguments whose wrong-headed origin he traces to a defense of Chinese particularism, the oft-repeated notion that "China is different" because of its long history and unique culture. He calls on China to embrace its great-power status with confidence, and to craft a new Chinese "universalism" that will contribute to a postmodern world of multiple universalisms. Xu selected the essays (although I omitted some and added others) with an eye toward the non-Chinese reader, meaning that he chose texts that address broad, general themes rather than narrow historical or historiographical concerns. I might add that the essays all

(Ten essays on Chinese intellectuals) (Shanghai: Fudan daxue chubanshe, 2003); and *Zhongguo, he yi wenming* (What civilization for China) (Hong Kong: Zhonghua shuzhu, 2015), among many others. As of November, 2017, many of his essays and interviews can be found at www.aisixiang.com/thinktank/xujilin.html. Previous studies of Xu's work include Timothy Cheek, "Xu Jilin and the Thought Work of China's Public Intellectuals," *China Quarterly* 86 (2006): 401–20, and Xu is discussed in more general studies of Chinese intellectual life such as Timothy Cheek, *The Intellectual in Modern Chinese History* (Cambridge: Cambridge University Press, 2015), and Joseph Fewsmith, *China since Tiananmen: The Politics of Transition from Deng Xiaoping to Hu Jintao* (New York: Cambridge University Press, 2008). For existing English-language translations of Xu's work, see: "The Fate of an Enlightenment: Twenty Years in the Chinese Intellectual Sphere," trans. Geremie R. Barmé and Gloria Davies, in Edward Gu and Merle Goldman, eds., *Chinese Intellectuals between State and Market* (London: RoutledgeCurzon, 2004): 183–203; "Reforming Peking University: A Window into Deliberative Democracy," in Ethan J. Leib and He Baogang, eds., *The Search for Deliberative Democracy in China* (New York: Palgrave-Macmillan, 2006): 245–58; "Social Darwinism in Modern China," *Journal of Modern Chinese History* (2012): 182–97; "Contradictions within Enlightenment Ideas," in Tian Yu Cao, Xueping Zhong, and Liao Kebin, eds., *Culture and Social Transformations in Reform-Era China* (Leiden, Boston: Brill, 2012); "May Fourth: A Patriotic Movement of Cosmopolitanism," *Sungkyun Journal of East Asian Studies* 9.1 (2009): 29–62; and "Historical Memories of May Fourth Patriotism, but of What Kind?" *China Heritage Quarterly* 17 (March 2009), www.chinaheritagequarterly.org/features.php?searchterm=017_mayfourthmemories.inc&issue=017.

³ Personal communication. Xu's main blog is found at http://blog.sina.com.cn/xujilin57. Other blogs, more or less active, are: http://blog.163.com/xu_jilin/, http://xujilin.blog.caixin.com/, and http://blog.ifeng.com/8359520.html.

address China's present and future, even if they are written from the perspective of a historian.

There are at least three reasons that these essays should be read by both China-watchers and those concerned with world affairs in general. First, Xu's essays offer a window into "what China thinks," a detailed portrait, crafted by a competent insider, of the world of ideas and politics in the age of Chinese President Xi Jinping (b. 1953). To Western eyes, the Chinese regime seems to be invariably "on message," and the Western media emphasizes the controlling nature of a government which, if no longer totalitarian, remains authoritarian. Xu Jilin's essays reveal the lively, complex debates that occur in spite of this authoritarianism, a sophisticated, cosmopolitan intellectual richness that the current regime has sought to control, but which continues to simmer beneath the surface.

Second, Xu's essays, while generally written in a tone of scholarly objectivity, also offer a liberal critique of and rejoinder to recent intellectual and political trends in China, a topic of considerable interest to those – in China and elsewhere – who continue to hope for the emergence of a democratic China. In many ways, Xu's liberalism is fairly typical, grounded in a belief in the rule of law and a constitutionalism that defines and limits state power. Yet liberals are on the defensive in today's China, as voices on the authoritarian left and the culturally conservative right currently find more favor with the regime. Consequently, Xu's criticisms go beyond slogans and table-pounding to engage writers and readers who do not necessarily share his views. Indeed, all of these essays are exercises in the use of history – both Chinese and global – to reach out to Chinese readers and remind them that China's rise is in some ways *not* unique, that the challenges, complexities, and dangers of China's current reality have appeared before, in China and elsewhere. His essays insist that *ideas matter*, that some are better than others, and that it is important to try to understand why we think the way we do.

The third reason to read Xu Jilin's essays is their extremely high quality, a quality that is in many ways the fruit of China's intellectual "globalization" over the past three decades. Many Chinese scholars have earned advanced degrees abroad; for those, like Xu, whose foreign-language skills are limited, a massive translation effort has made Western scholarship available in Chinese (as the footnotes to his essays richly illustrate). Traditional Chinese historical writing makes extensive use of citations, often to the point of obscuring narrative and argument. Scholars who wrote during the Maoist period (1949–76) strayed from the Party line at their peril, which meant that most texts were highly predictable. Xu, along with other writers of his generation, has been largely free to craft his own style, which emphasizes clarity of narrative and argument. Xu writes to be read, and I have attempted to convey that quality in my translations. To my mind, many of these essays are the Chinese equivalent of the sort of essays we might find in the *New York Review of Books*, the *Times Literary Supplement*, or similar publications, which seek to address the educated public at large. Indeed, most of the essays in this volume are more polemical, or perhaps educational, than scholarly.

Chinese Intellectuals in the Post-Mao Era

Xu Jilin's scholarship and style, like that of his fellow public intellectuals, is largely a product of developments in China since the 1990s.[4] The intellectual openness and independence that marks Xu's writings clearly would not have been possible under the Maoist regime, where all publications followed some iteration of the Party line, and intellectual debates occurred within Party forums. Things began to change after Mao's death in 1976, and accelerated in the 1980s, but the most important writings from the first post-Mao decade reflect either loyalist criticisms of the Communist Party grounded in a rereading of Marx – in the writings of Wang Ruoshui (1926–2002), Liu Binyan (1925–2005), and perhaps even Wei Jingsheng (b. 1950) – or a giddy, optimistic embrace of possible alternatives to the communist system, either in the guise of Western liberalism and science (embodied in translation and publishing projects such as Toward the Future and China and the World and perhaps in the television documentary, *River Elegy*) or in the guise of Chinese traditional culture (revived in another project entitled The Academy of Chinese Culture).[5] The suppression of the student demonstrations in 1989 and the conservative backlash that followed put an end to both the criticism and the giddiness.

The 1990s were less innocent and more complicated. The fall of communism in the USSR and Eastern Europe, followed by the collapse of the Soviet empire, came as a shock to many Chinese. Even liberals who might have been cheered by the failure of communism were sobered by the mixed results of the economic shock therapies prescribed by Western advisors for the post-communist era. Scholars often note that Chinese possess a particular fear of chaos (*luan*); in the 1990s, "chaos"

[4] See Xu's own assessment of the evolution of China's post-Mao intellectual scene, in "The Fate of an Enlightenment."

[5] For an insider's view of intellectual activities in the 1980s, see Chen Fong-Ching and Jin Guantao, *From Youthful Manuscripts to River Elegy: The Chinese Popular Culture Movement and Political Transformation, 1979–1989* (Hong Kong: Chinese University of Hong Kong Press, 1997); see also Wang Jing, *High Culture Fever: Politics, Aesthetics and Ideology in Deng's China* (Berkeley, CA: University of California Press, 1996).

took on highly specific meanings as Russia became an oligarchic klept-
ocracy and much of Eastern Europe fell into poverty and war. General
confidence in the West as a model or as a partner also declined in
China during this period, adding to the generally bleak atmosphere.
The American triumphalism that accompanied the Western "victory,"
aptly symbolized by Francis Fukuyama's writings on "The End of
History," rubbed many Chinese (among others) the wrong way. Some
suspected that the Tian'anmen demonstrations had been the result of
American machinations, which fed the notion that the United States was
working against China's development through international institutions
associated with the Washington consensus. All of this nourished the
rise of a paranoid, distrustful nationalism in China, and brought many
Chinese intellectuals closer to the state.

At the same time, Deng Xiaoping's success in refocusing China's energy
on economic reform, symbolized by his Southern Tour in December of
1992, eventually had another impact on Chinese intellectual life. Deng's
call to embrace markets, openness, and globalization meant that China
needed its intellectuals to help China compete with the outside world,
and this commitment translated into huge investments in university education and calls for Chinese universities to be competitive with other universities elsewhere in the world. The transformation, at least in the cases
of China's best schools, has been nothing short of astounding, as anyone
who spent time in China's universities prior to this transformation can
testify. China's best universities, like those of Hong Kong, Taiwan, and
Singapore, are now thoroughly professionalized and largely integrated
into global trends in knowledge production.[6] As a result, top-tier Chinese
intellectuals often spend large amounts of time in the West, and have
mastered Western methodologies in the humanities and social sciences,
as well as in more technical disciplines.

Changes in China's media landscape were equally important as
investments in education. Although Party control and censorship
remain important obstacles to the free exchange of ideas, the emergence of the Internet and social networks since the 1990s, the prolifer-
ation of magazines, journals, and publishing houses, and the embrace
of a consumerist popular culture have created a brave new world.[7] For

---

[6] See John W. Morgan and Bin Wu, eds., *Higher Education Reform in China* (London:
Routledge, 2001); Rui Yang and Anthony Welch, "A World-Class University in China?
The Case of Tsinghua," *Higher Education* 63.5 (May 2012): 645–66.
[7] See Daniel C. Lynch, *After the Propaganda State: Media, Politics and "Thought Work" in
Reformed* China (Stanford, CA: Stanford University Press, 1999); Johan Lagerkvist,
After the Internet, before Democracy: Competing Norms in Chinese Media and Society
(New York: Peter Lang, 2011); Chen Pingyuan, "Destiny and Options of Contemporary

intellectuals, there are now many outlets that will pay for their copy – provided that it will sell. For powerful ideas that do not find their place in consumerist popular culture, there is the Internet, whose presence in China is huge and – generally – less subject to the pervasive controls that continue to limit what can be published in China. As mentioned above, authorities have recently reshaped the structure of China's social networks so as to reduce their impact, for example by moving intellectuals away from wide-open blogs and toward smaller, group-driven formats like WeChat, which have less impact and are easier to control. Nonetheless, intellectuals eagerly exploit available platforms to exchange ideas and build followings.

Not all of these changes have been positive. Among other things, they have produced a fragmentation of China's intellectual world. Intellectuals on top-flight college campuses no longer have the leisure to reflect at length and in print on existential questions of moral responsibility; publish or perish is the new normal, and Chinese universities can be frighteningly competitive environments. In Timothy Cheek's apt characterization, China's intellectuals are no longer priests, but have become professionals.[8] There is of course safety and competence in professionalization; there may not be relevance, as American humanities professors can attest. The rise of a popular consumerist mass culture is threatening in other ways. To the extent that China follows a North American populist path toward *American Idol*, Oprah, and reality shows, elitist high culture – the foundation of the moral stance of the Confucian scholar-official, which remains important to Xu Jilin and to other contemporary Chinese intellectuals – risks being drowned out by the noise and the spectacle. Han Han, the author, race-car driver and singer who represented young China's first Internet generation, often sparred with the leading lights of the Chinese Academy on his blog, until recently a favorite among Chinese young people.[9] I suspect that Han Han's successors – like the current mass media star Papi Jiang[10] – will not bother, because they don't care about the academy. To the extent that contemporary Chinese intellectuals, who often see themselves as the conscience of the nation,

Chinese Scholars of the Humanities," *Contemporary Chinese Thought* 29.2 (Winter 1997–98): 5–28.

[8] Timothy Cheek, "From Priests to Professionals: Intellectuals and the State under the CCP," in Jeffrey N. Wasserstrom and Elizabeth J. Perry, eds., *Popular Protest and Political Culture in China: Learning from 1989* (Boulder, CO: Westview, 1992): 124–45.

[9] See, for example, Han Han, *Blogs de Chine* (Paris: Gallimard, 2012): 169–73.

[10] www.nytimes.com/2016/08/25/arts/international/chinas-viral-idol-papi-jiang-a-girl-next-door-with-attitude.html?_r=0.

lose out to consumerist-driven mass media, an important counterweight to state discourse is weakened and the voice of populism strengthened.

This "secularization" of China's culture in the post-Mao era, as well as the omnipresence and vulgarity of popular culture, are themes that Xu Jilin addresses in his essays. Here, the important point is to note the positive conditions that came together in the 1990s and 2000s to permit Xu – and other Chinese public intellectuals – to produce scholarship and commentary of a quality and richness not seen in China since the Republican Period (1911–49). These positive conditions – massive investments in China's best universities, international exchanges resulting in the globalization of Chinese research agendas, the transformation of China's media landscape, and relative political liberalization – have produced a series of exchanges and debates within the Chinese intellectual world concerning China's historical identity and her place in the world that are worthy of the world's attention.

How to Read Xu Jilin

That said, it is not easy for the Western China-watcher to get a handle on these exchanges and debates. We have tended to analyze the Chinese intellectual landscape by reducing it to three main groups: the Liberals, the New Left, and the New Confucians.[11] These divisions arose largely in the 1990s, after the shock of the Tian'anmen massacres had put an end to the heady liberal optimism of the 1980s and intellectuals debated the way forward, in exchanges that came to be increasingly acrimonious. Such labels are not without utility, and express some baseline positions held by members of the groups. At the same time, not all intellectuals self-identify as members of one of the groups, and the labels were in part created by critics of the "left" or of "liberalism" in attempts to tarnish their ideas via association with China's Maoist past or Western neoliberalism. The groups are not always particularly self-conscious nor organized, and what little they once possessed in the way of institutional identity (websites, journals, publishing houses) has been the target of suppression under Xi Jinping.[12] In addition, individual intellectuals are free to move in and out of groups, to change their position within groups, to be "liberal" on some issues and "Confucian" on others, or

---

[11] See Cheek, *The Intellectual in Modern China*, pp. 289–309; He Li, *Political Thought and China's Transformation: Ideas Shaping Reform in Post-Mao China* (London: Palgrave Macmillan, 2015). He Li also discusses neo-authoritarians and democratic socialists.

[12] A prominent example is the closing of the liberal magazine *Yanhuang chuqiu*. See www.nytimes.com/2016/07/28/world/asia/china-yanhuang-chunqiu.html.

to create new groups at the margins of the three main ones. In sum, the familiar division of Chinese intellectuals into Liberals, New Left, and New Confucians is useful as a handy first take on a complex situation, but does not do justice to reality.

For citizen intellectuals seeking to make a difference in China – or elsewhere, for that matter – life consists largely of their reactions to public events and trends that engage media attention. Debates and positions are crafted against the backdrop of one-time events like the US bombing of the Chinese embassy in Yugoslavia in 1999 or longer trends such as China's rise or the perceived decline of the United States, and are deeply engaged with state discourse on such events and trends. A member of the Liberals, or the New Left, or the New Confucians, may well seek allies among like-minded thinkers in trying to make his case and move state or intellectual or public opinion through the publication of a book, an article, or a blog post, but the ultimate goal remains to have an impact in a context where the Party-State is the major political actor (and also controls many of the resources that make intellectual life possible). Thus an accurate depiction of the life of public intellectuals in China would necessarily be historical, depicting a complex and interlocking series of debates in which the Party-State is a major actor.[13] While it is tempting to spend our time sorting intellectuals into their proper groups, or "mapping" the topography of intellectual life in China, to my mind the sociology of the exchanges between and among intellectuals and groups of intellectuals is a product of the larger history of intellectuals attempting to sway the Party-State, and of the Party-State regulating intellectual life. If we, as Western scholars, tend to reproduce the classifications used by Chinese intellectuals, it is largely because few of us have the time or the linguistic skills to read all of the books, newspaper and magazine articles, blog posts and WeChat "discover moments" necessary to keep abreast of what is happening.

Against that broader backdrop, I would suggest that there are several ways to read Xu Jilin.

One is as a Chinese intellectual engaged in research and reflection on the meaning of Chinese identity in the face of Western power, or perhaps simply in the face of modernity. In many ways, the questions raised by contemporary Chinese intellectuals like Xu are similar to those asked

---

[13] He Li, *Political Thought and China's Transformation* treats some of these debates – on democracy, economic reform, and regime legitimacy. Ma Licheng, a well-respected journalist in China, also attempts to historicize his discussion of the leading intellectual groups in his *Leading Schools of Thought in Contemporary China* (Singapore: World Scientific Publishing, 2016) (original Chinese-language edition 2013).

since China's fateful encounter with Western imperialism in the nineteenth century. What happened to us? Where did our civilization and our
power go? What do we have to do to catch up? What are the techniques
of pursuing wealth and power, and what will it cost us as a civilization?
What should we do about/with our tradition(s)? Although Xu is not an
intellectual whose primary role or goal is to explain the West to China
or to defend China against the West, readers of this volume will discover
that he spends a great deal of time talking about Western history and
what that history means to China's self-understanding and future. Of
course, as a professionally trained historian in the early twenty-first century, his outlook is more sophisticated than that of some of his intellectual predecessors, but Liang Qichao, Chen Duxiu, Lu Xun, and Hu Shi
would have little difficulty understanding Xu's arguments, because Xu
is in an ongoing dialogue with them, as well as with his colleagues and
peers in contemporary China.

At the same time, and paradoxically, we can also read Xu Jilin as a par-
ticipant in contemporary debates on the meaning of liberalism, not only
in China or East Asia, but in the world at large. I will not belabor this point
for want of detailed knowledge about the state of contemporary political
debate, nor am I sure to what extent Xu has theoretical ambitions at this
level. But the evidence of Xu's engagement with liberal authors is clear
throughout this volume. One text applies Charles Taylor's reading of the
"great disembedding" in European history to China, in a way that probes
both similarities and differences in the experiences. Elsewhere he recasts
many of the classical concerns of liberalism to reintegrate Confucianism
and other aspects of Chinese tradition with an eye toward creating a
"civil religion" along the American model but with Chinese content,
the hope being that Confucian values can fulfill the same function in
China as Judeo-Christian values have done in the United States, even
as both societies have secularized. Xu is hardly unique on this front
among Chinese liberals or Chinese intellectuals in general; the Chinese
New Left, in particular, grounds many of its arguments in texts from the
postmodern or post-Marxist West – although their goal is often to use
those arguments to defend China's particularity. Xu is perhaps innovative in imagining that China can evolve a liberalism that would make a
contribution to world civilization. This is not "liberalism with Chinese
characteristics," which insists defensively on China's particularism, but
rather a postmodern liberalism of which China could readily be a part.

A third, related, way to read Xu Jilin is as part of a Chinese rejoinder to
(or participation in) Western critical inquiry. This close reading of what
is often called the "Sinophone master narrative" has been brilliantly
realized by Gloria Davies in works like *Worrying about China*, where Xu's

writings appear frequently as objects of her analysis.[14] Here, the project is to understand the assumptions shared by Chinese intellectuals concerning the centrality of China, and China's salvation, to their work, as well as the authors' continuing (Confucian) commitment to the idea that proper thought is important and a part of self-cultivation as well as state service. One of Davies's important points is her discovery that, to the extent that contemporary Chinese intellectuals build their arguments on postmodern currents in the West, the Chinese *habitus* is in some ways wrong-headed, since Western postmodernists emphasize the difficulties of knowing the world in an effort to problematize and move beyond modernity, while Chinese intellectuals trust in the knowability of the world in the hopes of advancing China's interests. Xu's texts in this volume are of course grist for this mill, although my guess is that Xu thinks he has gone beyond the contradiction Davies notes in her study.

Since the present volume is a work of translation rather than analysis, I have not had to select or defend a particular strategy for reading Xu Jilin. I read him first as an engaged and engaging Chinese public intellectual seeking to explain the potentials and pitfalls associated with China's rise, a topic of some importance to all of humanity. Xu's essays also serve as an excellent example of the various voices assumed by Chinese citizen intellectuals as they attempt to influence the state, their peers, and the public at large. Only one of these texts (Chapter 7) is deeply academic and aimed chiefly at Xu's colleagues in history departments throughout China and the Sinophone world. Others (particularly Chapters 2 and 3) are highly polemical texts that draw on Xu's academic background but which seek to sway the opinion of public intellectuals like him. Yet others (Chapters 1, 4, 5, and 6) are written for the broader public, and some of these look more like op-eds than "serious" writing. One piece (Chapter 8) is a eulogy, and is thus emotional and expressive in ways not seen in other texts in this volume. I know of no means to measure Xu's impact in any scientific way. But these texts tell us something about the various strategies Xu employs to try to exert influence.

I should note at this point that in focusing on Xu and his writings, I run the risk of presenting him as more unique than he actually is. His voice is, of course, unique in the way that all voices are unique, but all of the essays translated here, and all of the themes addressed in those essays, are parts of debates and exchanges involving large numbers of Chinese authors. In other words, Xu is not the only author to compare China to Germany and Japan, to debate the value of a return to *tianxia*,

---

[14] Gloria Davies, *Worrying about China: The Language of Chinese Critical Inquiry* (Cambridge, MA: Harvard University Press, 2009).

to discuss the comparative utility of universal values and cultural consciousness. A methodology that focuses on the debates rather than on
individual authors has the virtue of elucidating the larger context, at the
risk of obscuring the role of individual writers. My choice has been to
explore the richness of one voice as a way of sharing with readers the
wealth of contemporary China's intellectual world.

China's Rise and Xu Jilin's Response

The effects of China's rise on China's intellectual sphere have been many,
and can be read as different efforts to provide contents for Xi Jinping's
embrace of the "China Dream" as a major propaganda point, although
in many cases their efforts preceded the launch of Xi's "China Dream"
campaign.[15] Energetic content providers include: various proponents
of the China model or the Beijing consensus; cultural conservatives,
including, but not limited to, the New Confucians; and authors from
the New Left who have embraced statism as a means to achieving "good
governance" while avoiding the perils and pitfalls of electoral democracy
as practiced in the West; nationalists and ultranationalists of a variety of
stripes, some of whom may also belong to other intellectual groups. For
those who follow China from afar, and only through mainstream media,
Xu Jilin's portrait of China's intellectual world will be eye-opening, and
the same may be true for China specialists who do not follow contemporary intellectual trends closely. When many in the West think about
Chinese intellectuals, they quite naturally think about dissidents such as
Ai Weiwei and Liu Xiaobo. Xu Jilin's discussion of Chinese intellectual
life – which of course cannot include discussion of Chinese dissidents
for reasons of censorship – illustrates how simplistic that Western focus
is, and plunges us into a complex world of debates in which genuine
intellectual opposition to Western democracy currently seems to have the
upper hand. Of course, some of this "genuine intellectual opposition"
is also politically motivated, but as Donald Trump's victory – fueled by
duplicity and demagoguery – further complicates the political future of
the world's leading democracy, it behooves us to read Chinese critics of
democracy more carefully. They may still be wrong from a Western liberal perspective, but at the same time convincing to those whose beliefs
in democratic politics are wavering.

---

[15] These discourses are deftly analyzed in Shaun Breslin, "The 'China Model and the
Global Crisis': From Friedrich List to a Chinese Mode of Governance?" *International
Affairs* 87.6 (2011): 1323–43.

For example, one figure consistently associated with the China model is Zhang Weiwei, a professor of international politics at Fudan University in Shanghai.[16] Zhang's original strength was his command of English; he was one of Deng Xiaoping's interpreters when Deng visited the United States in the 1980s and for the last few years, Zhang has traveled the world, presenting the China model to anyone who will listen – and there are many who listen.

Zhang's arguments begin with the basic data concerning the growth of China's economy since the 1980s, to which he adds personal impressions, comparing, for example the municipalities of Shanghai and New York, arguing that New York has been outclassed.[17] Anyone who has flown into the JFK and Pudong airports over the past few years would be hard put to disagree with Zhang, at least on a superficial level, and Zhang marshals further statistics on Shanghai's infrastructural advantages, the fruits of thirty years of intensive rebuilding, which, again, are not unconvincing. He extends his arguments beyond Shanghai and New York, noting that nowhere in the many cities and countries he has visited over the past decade or two has he found anything that compares to China. Again, if we constrain our conversation to the level of material progress, Zhang is hardly exaggerating.

On this basis, Zhang argues that China is a, or perhaps *the* world super-power (particularly if we measure such things according to purchasing power parity rather than GDP, as Zhang insists at some length[18]), and that the China model is available to inspire the rest of the world. China's exceptional characteristics, for Zhang, include: China's "super-large population, super-vast territory, super-long traditions, and super-rich culture," as well as her "unique language, politics, society and economics."[19] Of course, China possessed all of these in the nineteenth century as well, and they did not prevent her downfall.

Zhang's discussions of China's developmental model are perhaps more compelling. The features of this model include: "practice-based

---

[16] See Zhang's "trilogy": *Zhongguo zhenhan: Yige "wenmingxing guojia" de jueqi* (The China shock: The rise of a "civilizational state") (Shanghai: Shanghai renmin chubanshe, 2011); *Zhongguo chudong: Baiguo shiyexia de guancha yu sikao* (The China impact: Observations and reflections after visiting one hundred countries) (Shanghai: Shanghai renmin chubanshe, 2012); and *Zhongguo chaoyue: Yige "wenmingxing" guojia de guangrong yu mengxiang* (China's transcendence: The glory and dream of a "civilizational state") (Shanghai: Shanghai renmin chubanshe, 2014). The first volume is available in English translation as *China Wave: The Rise of a Civilizational State* (Hackensack, NJ: World Century Publishing, 2012).
[17] Zhang, *The China Wave*, ch. 1.1 (Kindle edition).
[18] Ibid., 1.3, 1.4 (Kindle edition).
[19] Ibid., 3.2 (Kindle edition).

reasoning, a strong state, prioritizing stability, the primacy of the people's livelihood, gradual reform, correct priorities and sequence, a mixed economy, and opening to the outside world."[20] However, as we read Zhang more carefully, we note that most of these features are simply mirror images of other models that Zhang seeks to denigrate. "Practice-based reasoning" is opposed to the highly theoretical economic models and theories, often associated with the Chicago School of Economics, which sought to grant overweening power to the market and dismiss the need for government regulation. "A strong state" is opposed to Reaganite or Thatcherite arguments that "the government is the problem." Zhang insists that government is a "necessary good" and not a "necessary evil." "Gradual reform" is in contrast to the "shock therapy" employed in the transition from a planned socialist economy to a market economy in the former USSR and much of Eastern Europe. Because of these stances, Zhang's debates with Western intellectuals often devolve into something resembling the thrust and parry of a typical internet comments section, where many participants simply talk past one another.[21] And Zhang Weiwei is but the tip of the iceberg. The China model or Beijing consensus has become a major theme in Chinese intellectual life, discussed by more respected, mainstream scholars like the economist Yao Yang and the political scientist Pan Wei, together with many others on the left and the right who embrace some version of Chinese exceptionalism.

New Confucians have a slightly different, if overlapping view of Chinese exceptionalism, and argue that China must return to its Confucian roots in order to create a lasting political legitimacy and to restore a sense of morality to a China adrift in cynicism and consumerism. Different New Confucian authors offer different visions. Jiang Qing, probably the best known of the group, suggests that a new Confucian order must necessarily be based on a combination of transcendent moral vision (embodied in the somewhat mythical "Three Dynasties" of China's pre-imperial history), the cultural and historical experiences of a people, and the expression of popular will.[22] Jiang thus addresses the concerns of many – in China and elsewhere – regarding the utilitarian nature of current democratic practices and their tendency to represent either well-organized

---

[20] Ibid., 4.2 (Kindle edition).
[21] See, for example, Francis Fukuyama and Zhang Weiwei, "The China Model: A Dialogue between Francis Fukuyama and Zhang Weiwei," *New Perspectives Quarterly* (Fall 2011): 40–67.
[22] See Jiang Qing, *A Confucian Constitutional Order: How China's Ancient Past Can Shape its Political Future*, ed. Daniel A. Bell and Ruiping Fan (Princeton, NJ: Princeton University Press, 2012); Daniel A. Bell, *China's New Confucianism: Politics and Everyday Life in a Changing Society* (Princeton, NJ: Princeton University Press, 2008).

special interests or the easily manipulated common denominator. And his calls for greater respect of morality and history cannot be rejected out of hand, again in light of the tenor of the 2016 presidential campaign in the United States and other recent elections in the democratic West. Yet Jiang's concrete, institutional proposals seem fanciful. He imagines a tri-cameral legislature with one house made up of "distinguished Confucians," another comprised of descendants from the Confucian family line, and a third chosen by popular election.

Another prominent New Confucian, Kang Xiaoguang, has proposed the adoption of Confucianism as China's national religion as a means of reconnecting China with its traditions, discarded and ignored since the early twentieth century. But Kang offers a wider range of possibilities than Jiang: a free press, which will keep the people informed and the politicians on their guard; an industrial corporatism that will represent the interests of the working class; and an "administrative absorption of politics" in which a technocratic meritocracy will deal with social and economic problems outside of the realm of politics.[23]

Xu Jilin is dismissive of Zhang Weiwei because he finds his arguments unpersuasive, and he lumps the China model proponents with "historicist" trends: nativist reactions to cosmopolitan incursions that date back to Germany's rejoinder to the imposition, by Napoleon's armies, of "universal" French civilization. Against French (and English) universal claims, German intellectuals crafted a counter-argument grounded in culture and nation, arguing that the universal does not exist, only the historical, which is embodied in the nation-state. Similar arguments have been repeated many times since – in Germany, Japan, India, Turkey, China, and elsewhere – when indigenous cultures have been threatened by the *mission civilisatrice* of cosmopolitan internationalism. As will be illustrated below, Xu believes that historicism is a false solution to a false problem. Xu is equally dismissive of the New Confucians, because he finds their arguments vulgar; as a historian who does his homework, Xu is scornful of the lack of grounding of many so-called New Confucians in the genuine texts and ritual practices of Confucianism. Of course, all traditions are "reinvented," but to Xu, many of the claims of the New Confucians are patently political and utilitarian, designed to catch the eyes and ears of China's leaders by offering a defense for continued authoritarianism: China's tradition. As we will see below, Xu makes his own attempts to reappropriate Confucianism and Chinese tradition within a refashioned liberalism.

---

[23] See David Ownby, "Kang Xiaoguang: Social Science, Civil Society, and Confucian Religion," *China Perspectives* 4 (2009): 102–11.

Most of Xu Jilin's concern is directed at the New Left, leading figures of which have also gravitated toward positions that endorse the
uniqueness of the Chinese experience and hence shore up state power.
As their name suggests, the New Left was originally grounded in concern
for the people – China's working class and China's peasants. Although
proud of China's economic and material development, they remained
wary of China's integration into the forces of global capitalism, and of
the new alliances struck between members of the Party-State and China's
new entrepreneurial elite. If the "New Left" was "new," it was because
its leading intellectual lights had studied in the West and developed an
interest in postmodern approaches to critical theory, fusing a nostalgia
for some aspects of Maoism with a creative and wide-ranging embrace of
socialist possibilities drawn from a wide variety of sources.

In Xu Jilin's telling, however, in the wake of China's rise, much of the
New Left has embraced statism, and in so doing abandoned the people.
For example, although Wang Hui, preeminent member of China's
New Left and China's best-known intellectual, once presented himself as a critical intellectual and viewed state power with great caution,
he has more recently argued that the CCP has been "nationalized"
over the course of the history of the PRC, so that the Party now fully
represents the interests of the people.[24] In other words, the Party-State
has somehow transcended the oligopolistic alliances linking it to – frequently corrupt – business practices so that it now suffers no conflict of
interest. There is of course no way to prove such an argument; Wang's
assertion is a statement of faith, or a bid for Xi Jinping's ear. Similarly,
Wang Shaoguang, another important figure on the New Left, now argues
that genuine democracy is not electoral democracy, which is more "electoral" than "democratic" because of the manipulations of candidates and
interest groups, but rather a "responsive democracy": "A government's
responsiveness to the people, meaning government policies that to
a high degree reflect popular needs, demands, and preferences, this
kind of democracy is the closest to the true meaning of democracy."[25]
If China does not yet fully embody this kind of democracy, it is closer
than other models, which continue to pursue the chimera of one person,

---

[24] Some of Wang Hui's work is available in English translation: Wang Hui, *China's New
World Order* (Cambridge, MA: Harvard University Press, 2003); Wang Hui, *The End
of Revolution: China and the Limits of Modernity* (London: Verso, 2009); Wang Hui, *The
Politics of Imagining Asia*, ed. Theodore Huters (Cambridge, MA: Harvard University
Press, 2011); Wang Hui, *China from Empire to Nation-State* (Cambridge, MA: Harvard
University Press, 2014); in addition to a number of articles.

[25] Wang Shaoguang, *Minzhu silun* (Four theses on democracy) (Beijing: Shenghuo, Dushu,
Xinzhi Sanlian Shudian, 2008), p. 78.

one vote.[26] Of course, when one abandons democracy for "good govern-ance," external controls over whether a government is indeed "respon-sible" largely disappear. Developing similar themes, another prominent New Left figure, Gan Yang, argues that China must find a way to "inte-grate the three traditions": the Confucian tradition, the Mao Zedong tradition, and the Deng Xiaoping tradition. Democracy based on indi-vidual freedom and constitutional rule do not figure in any important way in those traditions; "Chineseness" and Chinese traditions are more important than democracy in Gan's vision of China's future – although a younger Gan frequently insisted on the importance of mass democracy, expressed through elections.[27]

Particularly worrisome to Xu is the fact that some of China's younger public intellectuals continue to construct statist arguments on the basis of their Western education. The ideas of Carl Schmidt ("Hitler's crown jurist") and Leo Strauss figure prominently in the writings of intellectuals such as Jiang Shigong, who uses such sources to argue, for example, that the Chinese Communist Party possesses an "unwritten constitu-tion" whose writ goes beyond the formal written document.[28] Other intellectuals have, in Xu's words, "used the newly imported postcolonial theories of Edward Said to re-examine Chinese Enlightenment discourse since the May Fourth, and pronounced them to be a 'Western orien-talism' colonialized in China. They proclaimed that modernity in China was over, and that it should be replaced with a 'Chineseness' informed by native consciousness." In Xu's biting summary:

These scholars are not insiders sucking on the teat of Marxism-Leninism, not fundamentalists whose thought is stale, but most are rather modern intellectuals who have received a systematic education in the West … These historicist intellectuals work at first-tier universities inside and outside of China like Beijing University, Qinghua University, Hong Kong University, etc., and hold themselves to be independent intellectuals, although they maintain an ambiguous relation-ship with the state, sometimes close and sometimes distant. What is propping up their proposals is not dogmatic Marxism-Leninism but instead faddish Western theories.[29]

---

[26] Wang Shaoguang has published widely in English and Chinese. His most recent book is *Zhongguo: Zheng-dao* (China: The way of politics) (Hong Kong: Chinese University of Hong Kong, 2016).

[27] See Gan Yang, *Tongsantong* (Unifying the three traditions) (Beijing: Shenghuo, Dushu, Xinzhi Sanlian Shudian, 2007).

[28] On Schmitt and Strauss, see Kai Marchal and Carl K. Y. Shaw, eds., *Carl Schmitt and Leo Strauss in the Chinese-Speaking World: Reorienting the Political* (Lanham, MD: Lexington Books, 2017).

[29] Xu Jilin, "The Specter of Leviathan: A Critique of Chinese Statism since 2000," translated below, Chapter 2.

The result of all of this has been to produce a great "China chorus," as Xu calls it, a series of intellectual claims concerning China's unique path to wealth and power, claims that elevate the state to new and frightening heights.

Xu Jilin sets out to refute these arguments, but the great virtue of his essays is less to point out the individual inconsistencies in the arguments of his intellectual opponents in polemical terms, and more to place all of these arguments in a much broader historical and cultural context. Instead of accusing his opponents of intellectual inconsistency or sucking up to state power, Xu analyzes their positions in terms of themes such as statism and historicism, in essays such as "The Specter of Leviathan: A Critique of Chinese Statism since 2000," and "Universal Civilization, or Chinese Values? A Critique of Historicist Thought since 2000."

As mentioned above, historicism is the notion that there are no universal values, that everything is determined by history and all history is ultimately national. Those who insist on China's unique cultural heritage usually base their arguments on a kind of historicism, a claim to identity that seeks to brand universalistic and abstract discussions of human rights or political accountability as "outside interference in China's sovereign affairs." Sovereignty and statism are clearly linked, and in many ways are the product of historicism. Historicism's linkage of culture with nation – again, a product of the German nationalism emerging from the Napoleonic invasion – defines people first as members of a nation and second as individuals. The individual finds meaning not in himself but in the state, and the state has every reason to hold the individual to that tenet. And if statist symbols, rituals, and propaganda are insufficient to retain individual loyalty, the state must identify enemies, either within the state or outside, so as to reinforce citizen identity to the state and state projects. In this process, all values other than those of state sovereignty and state power are eclipsed. Without arguing directly that China is on a path toward fascism, Xu suggests that the consequences for China of the rise of these discourses go far beyond unpleasant arguments among public intellectuals.

At the same time, Xu suggests that all is not lost. In essays such as "Two Kinds of Enlightenment: Civilizational Consciousness or Cultural Consciousness," and "What Kind of Civilization? China at a Crossroads," he traces the histories of what he calls "civilizational consciousness" and "cultural consciousness" in China over the course of the twentieth and twenty-first centuries, in effect comparing China's reaction to the arrival of the West with Germany's reaction to the French invasion in the early nineteenth century. Here he finds an alternance between openness and a return to nativism, a cycle fueled by China's internal and external history. In the early twentieth century, Liang Qichao, among others, advocated openness to Western values, in opposition to previous reformers who were open only to wealth and power. After World War I, however, Liang, and others, sickened by the violence of the war, returned to a posture of protecting China's "national soul" against the excesses of Western materialism and individualism. At the same time, a younger generation of intellectuals, represented by the likes of Chen Duxiu and Hu Shi, once again displayed a "civilizational consciousness" in Chen's openness to French civilization and Hu's fondness for American pragmatism. Chen and Hu sparred with Du Yaquan and others who argued that civilizational consciousness compromised China's cultural agency. Ultimately, this complex and multi-faceted debate was subsumed by the anti-Japanese war, and the thirst for enlightenment by the necessity of national salvation. Mao's sinicization of Marxism-Leninism was, in Xu's terms, the triumph of cultural consciousness over civilizational consciousness.

The cycle began again in the post-Mao era, the 1980s being marked by an openness to the outside, followed by a nativist reaction since the 1990s, a reaction which has intensified with China's more recent rise. Xu belabors this point for two reasons. First, he wants to illustrate that the theme has a history, which presumably is not over. Thus the fact that statists and historicists are in the ascendant today does not necessarily mean that they will be so in ten years. External and internal events impact such attitudes, and China has embraced globalization. Second, Xu belabors the point because he wants to question the premise of the opposition between civilizational consciousness and cultural consciousness. For Xu, a proud native of Shanghai, the idea that "China" and "the West" can be separated from one another in such a manner as to allow polemical arguments about universal civilization and native culture makes little sense. China cannot "return to its roots" in any meaningful sense because of the history of modernity. The West, in the form of wealth and power, science, technology, ideas, and political philosophies, has been part and parcel of China for a century and a half, and if China perhaps approached economic autarky during the era of high Maoism, exchanges with the West – and with the rest of the world as well – have only accelerated in the reform period. That Western-trained Chinese public intellectuals use the "foreign" ideas of Carl Schmitt and Leo Strauss to build historicist paeans to China's uniqueness is, on the face of it, absurd.

Yet Xu Jilin's argument is not that China's intellectuals should simply accept the fact of global modernity/universal civilization and move on. Not for him the total Westernization of Hu Shi. In fact, his argument is considerably more subtle, and is aimed at the New Confucians and other cultural conservatives as well as the New Left, now in pursuit of state favor. His argument, developed in essays like "The New *Tianxia*: Rebuilding China's Internal and External Order," is first that there are different configurations of universal civilization, different ways of mixing commitments to human rights and liberty, economic growth and military power, Faustian striving with respect for nature. As a country with a long history based on one of humanity's original, axial civilizations, China – as a great power – has the responsibility to make its own claim to universal civilization, to defend, before other members of the global community, China's particular configuration of universal civilization. This is where Xu's argument differs from official Chinese White Papers on, for example, China's view of human rights. Xu is not arguing for cultural relativism, but for cultural relevance. If China wants to claim great-power status – and clearly Xu thinks China has that right – then she must consciously embrace universal civilization and make her own signal contribution. In other words, it does not work to say "I am a great power, don't meddle in my sovereign affairs on issues of human rights." China must not only explain her vision of universal civilization, she must convince the rest of the world, with arguments, not bluster.

To some extent, Xu Jilin is calling the bluff of the ultranationalists and the statists, illustrating the logical inconsistency in their posture. But he goes further, in a discursive move that illustrates a new wrinkle in his liberalism, a wrinkle aimed at reappropriating parts of China's past for the liberal cause in innovative ways. In his essay on the "new *tianxia*," Xu begins by exploring the effects of China's current culturalist-historicist-statist stance on foreign policy and minority policy issues, noting that China's rise has made China's neighbors very nervous, and that things have not gone smoothly in Tibet and Xinjiang for the past few decades either. On the basis of that observation, Xu goes on to discuss China's premodern universalism, i.e., the notion that China was the center of the known world, in the same context of foreign policy and minority relations. His goal is double. First, in an intellectual moment when Chinese thinkers are called upon to reappropriate Chinese traditions for nationalist and statist ends, Xu does the same thing but for different reasons and with a different outcome. Second, Xu hopes to demonstrate, through this reappropriation, exactly how China's uniqueness can contribute to universal civilization.

In a nutshell, Xu's argument is that China's premodern universalism, despite a certain arrogance and despite language distinguishing "Chinese" from "barbarians," was in fact an open, welcoming universalism. Barbarians could become Chinese and Chinese could become barbarians, which happened constantly in frontier regions. The categories were not racial, but instead cultural. The same logic applied to people from other countries, a logic incorporated into the well-known tribute system. Practical policies, particularly during the Qing period, built on these conceptions to construct a (sometimes) smoothly functioning system in which the Qing rulers adopted different standards for ruling peoples of different cultures, or for dealing with peripheral countries who wished to be part of the Chinese cultural world.

Xu's argument is that some of these practices – or at least the spirit behind these practices – should be revived. Chinese current minority policies, which consist of forced assimilation despite a formal discourse of mutual respect, reflect the brittle character of China's statist regime and the embrace, by that regime, of the goals of national wealth and power. A return to indirect rule through local control would surely work better, Xu suggests. As for relations with China's neighbors, an effort to modernize China's traditional sense of brotherhood with the sinicized world would surely work better than asserting ownership of vast swatches of the South China Sea, and building islands to police these waters.

I do not know if Xu intends these suggestions to be taken seriously or if he is simply being provocative. But what he calls China's "new *tianxia*" is a demonstration of the kind of contribution he would like to see China make to universal civilization, a contribution clearly reflective of China's unique history. A Chinese liberal thus reappropriates China's past for the well-being of humanity's future.

Xu's engagement with Chinese tradition does not stop with minority relations and foreign policy. To this point I have been dealing chiefly with Xu's responses to members of the New Left, but he has much to say to the New Confucians as well. As already mentioned, the New Confucians are part of a broader movement of cultural nationalism convinced that China's future must grow organically out of China's past, and connecting that past with the Confucian tradition. On the one hand, Xu seems to have little respect for the New Confucians, dismissing them as "grifters" and talking about the current generation of "vulgar Confucians." And it must be said that many of the self-proclaimed New Confucians are easy targets, having "reinvented" Confucian doctrine with considerable creativity. At the same time, Xu does not want to leave the Confucian tradition to the New Confucians, because he finds considerable value therein, as illustrated by his essay on "What Body for Confucianism's Lonely Soul?"

In part, this essay is meant to remind New Confucians (as well as Xu's readership) that Xu knows more about Confucianism than they do. Virtually all New Confucians write from a posture of partisanship, cherry-picking data so as to present Confucianism as a harmonious, seamless whole. Like his fellow liberal, Qin Hui, Xu asserts that imperial rule was more legalist than Confucian; Confucianism provided moral cover for the Machiavellian designs of emperors and prime ministers across the ages. Still, he acknowledges the value of Confucian state-craft, honed over years of competition with emperors and wily ministers, but wonders how this wisdom is to be employed in twenty-first-century China. He wonders if Confucianism might be revived in a democratic system, its moral and patrician dimensions perhaps serving to blunt the naked power-grabs of lobbies and other interest groups, an elitist counter-weight both to oligopoly and populism, but concludes that in the current regime it would serve only as less effective window-dressing than under the dynasties. He then goes on to explore the notion of a Confucian "religion," a possibility launched by Kang Youwei in the late nineteenth century and embraced by his contemporary followers. Xu is skeptical of this as well, finding that Confucianism really cannot compete as a "religion of the heart" with Buddhism, Daoism, Christianity and other rivals that speak the language of individual salvation. And he accuses Kang and his followers, of employing the notion of Confucianism as the national religion as a ruse to bring them back to power.

Xu is more open to the idea of Confucianism as a "civil religion," a term he borrows from American anthropologist Robert Bellah. Like many Chinese, Xu is deeply troubled by the moral vacuum at the heart of China's secularized, consumerist society, where any means toward the end of wealth and power seems to be accepted. He reinterprets Confucianism less as the lynchpin of the dynastic politic order and more as the skein of relationships and rituals that held China's little society together. Xu insists that China needs this, both as a positive good in its own right and because a liberal order without a moral consensus on basic values can easily lose direction.

Xu explores similar themes in another essay entitled "After the 'Great Disembedding': Family-State, *Tianxia* and Self," in which he employs Charles Taylor's notion of the "great disembedding" – the dissolution of the premodern world and the rise of the individual – to the Chinese experience. In a long discussion of self, family, state, and identity, Xu notes that a process that took several hundred years in Europe was compressed into merely a few decades in China, and was dominated by the rapid rise of the nation-state: "Contemporary China's deepest crisis is a crisis of the soul; society as a whole lacks a basic consensus on values and an ethical foundation. Once traditional Confucian values were rejected, the Chinese people lost their focus of identity, after which the nation and the state became secular objects for emotional catharsis."

In this text, Xu is not necessarily advocating a return to Confucianism, although he compares it to various modern communitarian visions which seek to revive social bonds in the face of the overweening power of the state, the market, and consumerism. But if Confucianism – or some other form of revived tradition – proves to be the glue that enables Chinese society to hold together, Xu is prepared to endorse it. In Xu's liberalism, freedom of individuals and markets requires a functioning civil society.

Xu further develops his thoughts on the pertinence of tradition in his eulogy to a recently deceased giant of the Chinese intellectual world: "Li Shenzhi: The Last Scholar-Official, the Last Hero." Li was a devoted Communist Party member for much of his life, and turned to liberalism in his declining years. Yet his liberalism is not what interests Xu in this book. Instead, Xu Jilin praises Li Shenzhi as the "last scholar-official," eliding Li's lifelong idealism (first for communism, later for liberalism), with the long tradition of engaged scholar-officials *and* with the early history of the Chinese Communist Party:

Those that flocked to Communist base areas like Yan'an were, like Li Shenzhi, the best of China's youth, the hot-blooded elite of that generation's scholar-officials. In the hopes of realizing their democratic liberation, they were full of the spirit of self-sacrifice and martyrdom. Li Shenzhi calls these CCP members "old-style CCP members."

And old-style is good! The old-style CCP members were the idealists of the CCP, twentieth-century scholar-officials who took spreading the Way as their personal mission. New-style CCP members enter the Party in pursuit of personal interests. The Party is a tool for them to climb official ranks and make money. But for old-style CCP members, the loves and hatreds of their lives were all poured into the Party. Their pride in the Party and fervor for their ideals are hard for later generations to understand. That they invested the feelings born of their red-blooded youth and their tragic love for their country is something that no one can disparage or deny. It was like cutting off their flesh to give to their mother; or taking out their bones to give to their father. Such devotion is indelible.

Elsewhere in the essay Xu compares Li to Wang Yangming and other similar Confucian figures in the late Ming, who believed that all people have the innate capacity to achieve sagehood. The portrait Xu offers of Li is stunning in its complexity; Li's simmering idealism embodied the best of the scholar-official, communist, and liberal traditions. Xu seems more impressed by his idealism than his liberalism. This is Xu's answer to Chinese intellectuals who use China's past to close doors, to limit future possibilities. I'm not sure Xu's is a liberal answer, and it is certainly not a secular answer, but Xu's tradition is rich with possibilities and contradictions, and is thus human and humane in ways that the brittle cult of the state can never be.

More than once over the past few years Xu Jilin has suggested, in private conversation, that he no longer sees himself as a liberal. I suspect that his reflections on traditions, continuities, and reappropriations are behind that remark, as his concern for China's moral vacuum has come to join his stances on the importance of individual freedom and rule of law. It is significant nonetheless that even as he explores the possibilities offered by China's modern history he does not feel compelled to create a "liberalism with Chinese characteristics," or to revive a liberal tradition in classical Chinese thought. The foreign origin of liberal ideas is in no way problematic for Xu; for him, one of the fruits of modernity and globalization is that all countries exist in a shared, if not homogenous, cultural space. It is that space that China must embrace if she is to fulfill her destiny and return to true great-power status. The essays in this volume offer the deep reflections of a mature Chinese patriot hoping to help his nation achieve that goal. China should join the world, but the world should also join China.

Translation Issues and Technical Tedium

I was first drawn to Xu Jilin's writings in large measure because of their readability, and I have tried to reproduce that pleasurable experience for readers in translating his essays from Chinese to English. This means that I have allowed myself considerable leeway as long as I felt Xu's meaning was preserved and the English text flowed smoothly. In other words, I have chosen not to litter the text with technical explanations of the literal meaning of Chinese expressions which, in a different setting, would surely be worthy of discussion. For similar reasons, where possible, I have added information identifying people mentioned and providing explanations that Xu himself might have added were he writing explicitly for a non-specialist reader in the text proper, rather than in translator's notes, without identifying brackets. In other words, where Xu's Chinese text says something like "the 'universal and homogenous state' feared by Kojève has already emerged," my translation reads "the 'universal and homogenous state' feared by the Russo-French philosopher Alexandre Kojève (1902–68) has already emerged." Of course, longer explications were sometimes required, and a certain number of translator's notes remain. There is also a glossary in which terms and concepts that recur repeatedly are defined and contextualized.

Xu Jilin quotes frequently from foreign authors in Chinese translation. In an ideal world, I would have liked to locate the cited passage in the original text, but this proved unduly time-consuming and thus practically impossible. Most of these Chinese translations are not available in libraries outside of China, which meant that I could rarely know which editions of the original work they worked from. In addition, some Chinese translators seem to take considerable license in their work, because even when I could locate what I thought to be the correct edition of a translated work, I could not find the exact passage from the original. So what the reader finds here in almost all cases is my translation of the Chinese text cited by Xu. In some ways this is better, because Xu did not read the original, and whatever nuance might have been lost in the translation from Western language to Chinese was lost to Xu as well. It might be fascinating to follow the changes in meaning as texts go from one language to another, to be used in different discursive contexts, but such was not my goal in the present project.

On a similar theme, when Xu cites a foreign text in a footnote, he of course cites the Chinese version, which is meaningless to the English reader. Hence, I have altered "Hengtingdun, *Disan bo: Ershi shiji houqi minzhuhua langchao*" to read "Hengtingdun (Samuel Huntington) *Disan bo: Ershi shiji houqi minzhuhua langchao* (The third wave: Democratization in the late twentieth century)," on the premise that the reader might like to know.

Like the Southern Baptist ministers of my youth, Chinese intellectuals repeat themselves a lot. Xu sometimes repeats himself within the same text, in a manner that must be persuasive to Chinese readers, but often seems tedious in English. In many such cases I have taken the liberty of dispensing with what seem to be needless repetitions. There are repetitions of similar themes and arguments across different chapters as well, which is of course normal; Xu has a number of important points that he attempts to make in a variety of different arguments and contexts. I could find no way to eliminate these repetitions without damaging the structural integrity of individual chapters, which would have been unfair to a writer who successfully strives for harmony and balance in his prose style. So I must ask for the reader's forbearance, and assume they know how and when to skim.

1 What Kind of Civilization? China at a Crossroads

Translator's Introduction

This rousing essay, published in 2013, serves as an excellent introduction to this volume and to Xu Jilin's work as a public intellectual. The broad theme addressed is that of civilization (in Chinese, wenming*), a concept which, in East Asia as elsewhere, has generally been associated with "Western civilization" in the modern era. An important part of the Japanese effort to modernize and catch up with the West in the last nineteenth century, for example, fell under the slogan "bunmei kaika" – "reform and enlightenment"[1] where "civilization" (bunmei) is rendered as "enlightenment," referring of course to the "advanced" civilization of the West. In the May Fourth period, iconoclastic Chinese reformers like Chen Duxiu preached the universal values of French civilization as a way of condemning Chinese obscurantism. And when enthusiasm for Maoist revolution waned in the wake of the Cultural Revolution, Chinese intellectuals relived the May Fourth movement and turned once again toward Western civilization as a solution to China's dilemma.*

China's rise over the past few years has muddied these waters, as China's economic and growing military might have nourished a renewed self-confidence that Chinese civilization has returned, that it is finally China's turn to fashion its own mission civilisatrice. It is this self-confidence that Xu Jilin hopes to challenge in this text, ranging widely in time and space in an effort to remind his readers that world leadership requires more than an impressive GDP.

Xu insists that "modern civilization" is made up of at least two dimensions: the pursuit of wealth and power (via military might, capitalism, etc.), and the defense of values – which may not be universal, but which must be defended, openly and convincingly, in universal settings. Xu dissociates "modern civilization" from the West, arguing that even if modernity's origins are indeed largely Western, by now it is simply a new "axial civilization" which has spread throughout the world, functioning in a variety of political and cultural settings.

---

[1] Originally published as "Hezhong wenming? Shizilukou de jueze," *Xinrui* 2 (2013). Also available online at www.21ccom.net/articles/sxwh/shsc/article_2013082990878.html (August 29, 2013). On the *bunmei kaika* movement in Japan, see Marius Jansen, *The Making of Modern Japan* (Cambridge, MA: Harvard University Press, 2000), ch. 14. For the influence of the movement on China, see Doug Howland, *Borders of Chinese Civilization: Geography and History at Empire's End* (Durham, NC: Duke University Press, 1996).

What China has so spectacularly mastered since the beginning of the reform era, Xu argues, is the "wealth and power" dimension of modernity, and if she has every right to be proud of her accomplishments, to have beaten the West at its own game, the larger game is not yet over. The larger game involves addressing the universal problems of modern civilization – excessive state power, income inequality, environmental degradation, and climate change – which are now as much China's responsibility as anyone else's. Instead of arguing that "China would be better if China were democratic like Western countries are," Xu instead insists that "as part of modern civilization, China must join the world, defend its values, and make its contributions."

Xu further sharpens his argument by highlighting the distinction between civilization and culture, a theme that appears repeatedly in this volume. Citing scholars of European history, Xu argues that civilization is universal and culture is local, civilization is about what is good and culture is about what is ours. When civilization – as wealth and power – runs roughshod over weaker countries, culture fuels a nativist reaction, as has happened in Germany, Japan, Russia, Turkey, China, and elsewhere. Yet Xu does not argue that culture should submit to civilization, but rather that culture should adapt universal values to local needs in such a way as to acknowledge the values of each. In this way, Xu manages to argue both that China must look inward to find the culture-appropriate values necessary to fill the current moral vacuum in Chinese society, and that the communitarian ethos that he hopes will emerge from that search can make a contribution to the variety of "universal" values that coexist in a multi-polar world.

Xu's text is breathtaking in its range, and his citation of Western authors, from Octavio Paz to Isaiah Berlin to Slavoj Žižek, suggests his engagement with intellectual currents throughout the world (even if Xu speaks no foreign language well). At the same time, Xu's grounding in Chinese history is obvious, and he manages to convey his erudition in a pleasing style that, to my American eye, reads like something out of the New York Review of Books *or the* Atlantic Monthly. *He also manages, in a feat of considerable diplomacy, to ask his readers to reconsider the implications of China's rise without dwelling overmuch on China's shortcomings.*

Beginning in the modern era, the Chinese nation has faced serious challenges from outside civilizations. Seventy years ago, the famous Chinese historian Lei Haizong (1902–62) made a penetrating remark to the effect that the outside enemies China had faced in the past either were like Buddhism, which had civilization but no power, or like the northern nomadic peoples, who had power but no civilization. Both of these, he said, were easy to handle. But the West that came with the Opium War possessed both power and civilization superior to those of China, which sparked an unprecedented civilizational crisis.[2]

China's civilizational crisis, which has endured for a century and a half, remains unresolved today. Although twenty-first-century China has

---

[2] Lei Haizong, "Wubing de wenhua" (A non-military culture), in Lei Haizong, *Zhongguo wenhua yu Zhongguo de bing* (Chinese culture and Chinese military) (Beijing: Shangwu yinshuguan, 2001), p. 125.

engineered a rise in wealth and power so that its overall national might can rival that of the West, China's civilization has yet to rise. While "the reforms have entered deep water," civilizational choices are still "crossing the river by feeling the stones."[3] And the worst is that we don't know where salvation lies. We are trapped in a civilizational maze, not knowing which flag to fly, which road to take.

In what direction will Chinese civilization develop? How will we rebuild the Chinese people's consensus on values and institutions? We will no longer find the answers to such questions by following an uncontested developmental strategy; economic development that detours around questions of civilization will only go around in circles, continuing to feel the rocks even in deep waters, while what we need is to identify our destination as soon as possible, and cross the great river of civilizational transformation.

Modernity: A New Axial Civilization

What is this great civilization that launched such a huge attack on China from the late Qing onward?

According to the Israeli scholar Shmuel Eisenstadt (1923–2010), a new kind of axial civilization gradually appeared in Western Europe in the sixteenth century, which we call modern civilization.[4] Modern civilization evolved out of two ancient axial civilizations: Christian civilization and Greco-Roman civilization. It appeared first in Western Europe, and later spread rapidly throughout the world, so that the countries and peoples of practically the entire world fell into its clutches. Like the Mexican poet and Nobel Prize winner Octavio Paz (1914–98) said: we are all "condemned to modernity."

What is modern civilization? Much research has already been done and many explanations already exist. In this context, I want to distinguish two important dimensions of modern civilization: one is a modernity that is value-neutral; and the other is a civilization guided by a clear sense of values. The first has to do with wealth and power, and the second is a set of value systems and corresponding institutional arrangements. In the late Qing period, both Yan Fu (1854–1921), the late Qing scholar

---

[3] Translator's note: "Crossing the river by feeling the stones" is how Deng Xiaoping pragmatically described China's transition away from a Soviet-style planned economy and toward an economy in which market forces play a more important role. The notion that "the reforms have entered deep water" means that they have moved away from the rocky river and into the deep sea; in other words, that great progress has been made.

[4] See Aisensetate (Shmuel Eisenstadt), "Maixing 21 shiji de zhouxin" (Toward the axis of the twenty-first century), in Aisensetate (Shmuel Eisenstadt), *Fansi xiandaixing* (Reflections on modernity), Kuang Xinnian and Wang Aisong, trans. (Beijing: Sanlian shudian, 2006), pp. 79–80. This appears to be a collection of essays edited and translated by the Chinese, and not the direct translation of an existing work by Eisenstadt.

and translator, and Liang Qichao (1873–1929), the late Qing reformer and founder of Chinese journalism, discovered two secrets about the rise of the West: one was wealth and power, and the other was civilization, which refer precisely to the two dimensions of Western civilization under discussion.

As for the modernity of wealth and power, this is expressed by any number of concepts: modernity, rationality, secularism, moderniza-tion, capitalism, etc. Even if the concepts are not the same, they share a common characteristic, a kind of value-neutral capacity and order that can produce the many types of modernity we find in today's world in alliance with different axial civilizations and ideologies. Concretely, the modernity of wealth and power can be divided into three dimensions. The first is the scientific techniques dealing with the material world. The wealth and power of domination created by the European sixteenth-century scientific revolution and the eighteenth-century industrial revo-lution swept away all obstacles and became invincible. In the twentieth century it took on new forms such as the revolutions in information technology, new energy technology, and biotechnology, all of which have advanced humanity's ability to transform and control nature and itself. The second dimension of modernity is rational order, or what Max Weber (1864–1920) called rational capitalism, impersonal systems of bureau-cratic management, double-entry accounting systems, etc. This modern enterprise management system, on an increasingly universal basis, has successfully "colonized" society, establishing universal rules governing the realms of economic, cultural, political and even daily life. The third dimension of modernity is a secularized spiritual pursuit, the Faustian spirit described by Goethe (1749–1832), embodied in the unlimited lib-eration and pursuit of humanity's desires and the adventurous spirit that emerged from this, the insatiable pursuit of wealth and power and the work ethic of scrimping and striving. This capitalist spirit, without values, without religion, soulless, has its own rules of survival, believing that the strong win and the weak lose, that those who adapt live on. Market com-petition and the victories of the strong forcefully push human society forward.

This kind of technological modernity, focused on the attainment of wealth and power, has become a universal strength in today's world. Its face is ambiguous, it doesn't believe in gods and souls; all it worships is its own invincible power. It can join together with any secularized axial civil-ization: in addition to the original form of Protestant capitalism, today we have Confucian capitalism, Islamic capitalism, socialist capitalism, etc. It can also graft itself onto any kind of contemporary ideology, producing liberal modernity, socialist modernity, authoritarian modernity, etc. The modernity produced by this neutral capitalism has become strong to the point that, as the Slovenian philosopher and social critic Slavoj Žižek (b. 1949) put it during the Occupy Wall Street movement: "You can criticize it, but you can't find a mechanism to replace it." In this world, where modernity and capitalism are everywhere, history has indeed come to an end from this perspective, and the "universal and homogenous state" feared by the Russo-French philosopher Alexandre Kojève (1902–68) has already emerged.

In addition to its core of modernity as wealth and power, modernity also possesses an even higher dimension, which is civilization. In the late Qing period, Yan Fu characterized it as "freedom in its essence, democracy in its function." At the heart of what we call civilization is a set of modern Enlightenment values, based on respect for freedom and equality, which developed to become a modern faith in universal brotherhood, democracy, rule of law, etc., that can rival ancient religions. This Enlightenment discourse exists not only at the conceptual level, but also possesses corresponding institutional arrangements, the three central ingredients of modern political order as identified by the American political scientist Francis Fukuyama (b. 1952): the modern state, rule of law, and accountable government.[5] The reason why modern civilization has been able to conquer the world is not merely a matter of the material and rational strength of modernity; behind that is an even stronger civilizational discourse and legal-administrative system. Together, the two make up a new axial civilization, possessing a greater universal valence than that of ancient civilizations like Christianity, Islam, Hinduism, and Confucianism. Modernity has become the discourse of mainstream civilization and the institutionalized form of civilization. Even if its origins are in the Christian civilization of Europe, in the process of its expansion, it has lost its exclusively European identity, and has become a universal civilization recognized by all secular civilizations, a world universal spirit that has transcended its original, particular civilizational background.

Yet modern civilization is not like iron. It is full of internal contradictions and tensions: rationalism versus romanticism, humanism versus technocracy, nationalism versus individual rights and dignity, developmentalism versus harmony, unlimited enterprise versus security and moderation … These conflicts and dilemmas within modernity suggest that this new axial civilization will experience divisions and fractures in the process of its internal development and external expansion, which has indeed been the case in reality. The divisions in modern civilization have followed two

---

[5] See Fulangsisi Fushan (Francis Fukuyama), *Zhengzhi zhixu de qiyuan* (The origins of political order), Mao Junjie, trans. (Nanning: Guangxi shifan daxue chubanshe, 2012), p. 16.

different axes: one is ideology and the other is axial civilization. The division of modern civilization into different ideologies occurred at the end of the nineteenth century: liberalism, socialism, and conservatism. After two centuries of conflict and struggle these three political ideologies, through internalization and mutual absorption, have now become three model forms: American liberalism, European socialism, and Russian or East European authoritarianism, in addition to which there are many mixed forms. And in the course of the history of the twentieth century, a number of failed "anti-modern modernities" also appeared: German fascism, Soviet totalitarianism, Maoist agricultural socialism, etc.

Another path of division within modern civilization has developed around axial civilization(s). Although twentieth-century Western civilization thoroughly conquered the entire world, trampling virtually every tribe, race and country underfoot, assimilating any number of lesser religions and civilizations and their national customs and local habits, nonetheless the conquest of ancient axial civilizations was less thorough, whether Islam, Hindu, or Confucian. Indeed, wherever Western civilization reached, it provoked an extreme resistance on the part of these great axial civilizations, so that conquest and anti-conquest, assimilation and anti-assimilation occurred together at the time of civilizational encounters. Modern Western civilization did greatly influence the ancient axial civilizations, forcing them toward secularization and Europeanization, but from another angle, those non-Western countries that succeeded in internalizing Western civilization also succeeded in separating modern civilization from its source, Christianity, and grafted it onto its own civilization and traditions, creating non-Western forms of modern civilization. As a result, in the latter half of the twentieth century, following the rise of East Asia, India's development, and the revolutions in the Middle East, many changes occurred within modern civilization, and modernity no longer belongs exclusively to Christian civilization, becoming instead a plural modernity that could be integrated with different axial civilizations, or even local cultures.

The plural nature of modernity did not change the unified state of modern civilization, which continued to exhibit the two dimensions mentioned earlier as universal characteristics – wealth and power on the one hand, and civilization on the other. The difference was that it existed no longer as a uniform, essentialized form, but rather in a form that recalls the philosopher Ludwig Wittgenstein's (1889–1951) "family resemblances." Universal modern civilizations are like members of a lineage, in that they look like one another, but do not share the same essence. By modern civilization we mean a set of values that includes wealth and power, rationality, happiness, freedom, rights, democracy, equality, universal brotherhood, harmony, etc. According to the views of Isaiah Berlin (1909–97), these values are not internally harmonious; there are frequently conflicts among them. Consequently one must choose among the various modern values. Different peoples, different individuals have different understandings about the priorities to accord to certain values. The reason that there are different modernities in the contemporary world is because they prioritize and understand values in different ways. England and America emphasize freedom and the rule of law. The European continent chooses equality, democracy, and social welfare, while East Asia emphasizes development, wealth, and power. Yet if we say that all are modern, it is because they have adopted most of the set of modern values, which means that they share this "family resemblance." Modernities thus differ in quality, and some are better than others. When a country's modernity accords too much importance to a particular value, for instance paying attention only to national wealth and power, so that citizens lack guaranteed basic rights; or if there is democracy but no corresponding legal order, so that corruption and bribery are rampant; or when society has achieved equality, but continues to struggle amid widespread poverty … None of these is a good example of modernity, or we could say that they are deformed sorts of modernity that lack the component of universal civilization.

So, what sort of modernity is symbolized in China's rise?

Will China Resist, Pursue, or Develop Mainstream Civilization?

China's rise since 2008 is a fact acknowledged by the entire world. The question is: what kind of rise is this? What kind of modernity has appeared? We have already mentioned the two secrets of Western civilization discovered by Yan Fu and Liang Qichao in the late Qing. In the eyes of many Chinese, wealth and power were most important and civilization could wait. So for a long period, wealth and power took precedence over civilization, and the attitude of Chinese people toward modern civilization was to pay less attention to universal civilizational values and the corresponding system of rule of law, and more to the technical side, the non-value-related aspects of science and technology, the rational order and the capitalist spirit. After a century and a half of hard work, the China Dream finally became a reality. But only half of the dream was actually realized, and China's modernity remained incomplete. Wealth and power "rose up," but civilization remains lost in a haze.

The secret of China's rise from a civilizational perspective was to "beat the foreigners at their own game," taking the skills of rationality and competition and the thrifty spirit of Protestantism, by now in decline Europe, and integrating these into China's Confucian secular statecraft tradition, thus developing an extreme personality type in which contemporary Chinese are more "Western" than Asian, possessing a Faustian, inexhaustible, enterprising spirit. The laws of competition of modern civilization have moved from Europe to East Asia. Chinese today are like nineteenth-century Europeans, bursting with ambition, industrious and thrifty, full of greed and desire; they believe that the weak are meat for the strong and that only the apt survive – they are vastly different from traditional Chinese, who prized righteousness over profit and were content with moderation. What kind of victory is this? A victory for Chinese civilization or for the Western spirit? Even when, in a not-too-distant future, China's gross domestic product surpasses that of the United States and China becomes the world's superpower, Westerners will just laugh: "Your power conquered us, but our civilization conquered you, and it was the obsolete, most detested nineteenth-century spirit that carried out the conquest!" So even when China controls the world, the final spiritual victory goes to the West. If we insist on talking about a victory for Chinese civilization, then it would not be the civilization of the Confucian literati, but rather that of the Legalists[6] with their lust for powerful countries and strong armies.

Even while China's GDP has grown ever greater, and China has become the world's factory with which no one can compete, her internal civilizational crisis has grown ever more serious. The people have lost their core values, society's ethical order is a mess, the political system faces challenges to its legitimacy, the government has lost its authority and credibility, the rule of law exists in name only … The crisis of civilization and the country's achievement of wealth and power make for ironic contrasts and leave the people dismayed. We're like Japan in the nineteenth century, and what we're seeing is the report card of a student that copied Western civilization. It's the report card of a seriously unrounded student.

Confronted with the reality of China, China's intellectual world has responded with two extreme, completely different points of view. One is that of "universal values," and the other is that of the "China model." From the point of view of universal values, our world has only one path

---

[6] Translator's note: The Legalists were a group of political thinkers on the eve of the establishment of China's first unified empire in 221 BC who stressed the utility and the power of laws to direct popular behavior to follow the desires of the ruler. Although later denounced by Confucians as immoral, Xu and many other modern historians argue that Legalist techniques of rule maintained their importance throughout the history of "Confucian" China.

toward modernization, that demonstrated by the West, the one correct path toward modernity proven by world history since the sixteenth century. From this perspective, China's current problem is that she has not studied the West sufficiently, and the reforms implemented to date are no more than those of the "Foreign Affairs movement," the half-hearted Westernization efforts of the late nineteenth century, which means that China needs to become completely Western in terms of universal values and political systems. The argument of the China model, the complete opposite of this, insists that China's success illustrates precisely that there is no need to imitate the West, that China can have its own path to modernity, its own civilizational values. China has a unique political system that accords with China's national situation, and China's rise will in the future serve as a model for undeveloped countries. Even if China abandons Western civilization, she will nonetheless achieve national wealth and power.

Hence we find ourselves before a very pointed question: in the context of modern civilization in today's world, will China resist mainstream civilization, or pursue it? Or is there a third road?

To answer this question, we must first make a conceptual distinction between civilization and culture.[7] The French philosopher Edgar Morin (b. 1921) pointed out that "Culture and civilization form two poles: culture represents uniqueness, subjectivity, individuality; by way of contrast, civilization represents transmissibility, objectivity, universality." Taking Europe as an example, European culture and European civilization are not the same: "European culture's unique heritage is based on Judeo-Christian values, on Greece and Rome, but after the spread of European civilization's characteristics of humanism, science and technology throughout Europe, it came to be rooted in places with completely different cultures."[8] In other words, civilization refers to the common values or nature of all humanity, while culture focuses on differences between peoples and the unique features of a group. The expression of civilization is comprehensive, and can be material, technical, or systemic, and also includes a set of universal values. Culture must in contrast be a spiritual state; culture is not interested in the abstract "person's" existential value, but instead in values created by a particular people or group. Clearly, from the point of view of civilization and culture, "universal values" versus "the China model" is a war between universal civilization and a particular culture. This war has already occurred many times

---

[7] Translator's note: Xu pursues this distinction in a more scholarly fashion in Chapter 7.
[8] Aidejia Molan (Edgar Morin), *Fansi Ouzhou* (Penser l'Europe), Kang Zheng and Qi Xiaoman, trans. (Beijing: Sanlian shudian, 2005), p. 31.

over in the course of the twentieth century, the two most representative examples being Germany and Turkey. The Germans hoped to use national willpower and a unique culture to resist the universal civilization of England and France, and the Turks sought to use Western civilization to replace Turkey's particular culture. These extreme examples provide us with deep historical lessons.

In the nineteenth century, when English and French thought arrived in Germany, the German intellectual elite used German culture to resist Anglo-French civilization. As Georg Iggers (b. 1926), the well-known German-American scholar of European intellectual history, has pointed out: "The cultural war between German *Kultur* and Anglo-Saxon *Zivilisation* enabled the German elite to fashion an ideology to consolidate their ruling power over the German masses. The German concept of '1914' is radically different from the French concept of '1789.'"[9] The "spirit of 1914" was the special expression in history and culture of Germany's decision to resist Anglo-French universal civilization. From Bismarck to Hitler, as Germany raced to catch up with England and France, the strategies employed consistently deployed the special character of German will to resist Anglo-French universal civilization. In their efforts to pursue national wealth and power, they were more English than the English, more French than the French, and in less than a century, transformed a divided, backward, feudal country into a unified, strong Germany capable of dominating Europe. However, the particular path that Germany pursued in opposition to mainstream European civilization was a path that led to war, and thus was a dead end with no future. After World War II and a period of painful national reflection, the German people decided to enter world mainstream civilization, combining Anglo-American/Anglo-Saxon political civilization with Germany's own Lutheran tradition and modern social democracy in the contemporary German model that successfully synthesizes divergent elements of Western civilization. At present, Germany is the sole exception to a European economy that is in deep recession, and the source of hope that might lead Europe out of the deep valley and toward new growth.

German history tells us that resisting mainstream world civilization is the wrong path, leading to self-destruction. If the proponents of the China model only want to imitate the West to obtain wealth and power, while in terms of civilizational values and institutions they cling to their own "unique" culture, then even if they succeed in creating a unique

---

[9] Geaoerge Yigeersi (Georg Iggers), *Deguo de lishiguan* (The German conception of history), Gu Hang and Peng Gang, trans. (Nanjing: Yilin chubanshe, 2006), p. 3.

Chinese path, it will only be a bizarre combination of universal capitalist utilitarian rationality and the East Asian authoritarian tradition. Will this be a new Chinese civilization 2.0? Or rather another short-lived Mongol Yuan dynasty (1271–1368), possessing only the material power to conquer, yet lacking the spirit necessary to create a new civilization? In the thirteenth and fourteenth centuries, the Mongol cavalry not only conquered the heart of China, but also swept across Central Asia and Eastern Europe, becoming a great continental Eurasian empire. But those Mongols conquerors knew only "shooting eagles, bow outstretched"[10] and possessed only military power. They lacked civilization, and their empire, without spiritual attraction or advanced governing institutions, could not last long, and in less than a century the once mighty Mongol empire fell apart and perished. In his *History of Philosophy*, Hegel (1770–1831) said: "The position that a people will occupy in terms of the developmental stages of world history is not determined by that people's external achievements, but rather by the spirit they embody. We must look at the stage of world spirit a people displays."[11] By world spirit, he meant mainstream modern civilization. China should not pursue a unique model in resistance to world spirit, but instead the universal path that adheres closely to mainstream civilization, which it can develop and project, pushing it to new spiritual peaks.

So should we do as the proponents of universal values suggest, and set our sights on the West and transform China into a completely Europeanized country? On this question, Turkey is the opposite of Germany, as Turkey used civilization to replace culture. Turkey's former incarnation was as the Ottoman Empire, but early in the twentieth century there occurred the Turkish Revolution, led by Kemal Atatürk (1881–1938), whose objective was complete Europeanization. Not only did he separate church and state, he also carried out a thoroughgoing secularization in which the formerly mainstream Islam was excluded from all public spaces, henceforth existing only in the form of individual belief. Turkey followed this path in which civilization replaced culture for roughly one hundred years. Although Turkey did achieve modernization, it was unable to restore the former greatness of the Ottoman Empire. The American political scientist Samuel Huntington (1927–2008) argues that Turkey became a divided, uncertain state, with a system whose top half possessed a modern civilization like that of Europe, while the lower half

---

[10] Translator's note: The reference is to the poem "Snow," by Mao Zedong.
[11] Pan Gaofeng, ed. and trans., *Heerge lishi zhexue* (Hegel's historical philosophy) (Beijing: Jiuzhou chubanshe, 2011), p. 58.

remained a world dominated by Islam.[12] This also means that civilization could not overcome culture and instead resulted in national disunity.

In the twenty-first century, Turkey initiated efforts to leave this modern dilemma behind. The ruling moderate Islamic party (AKP) sought internally to integrate universal modern civilization with the special characteristics of Turkish culture and Islamic civilization. While continuing to maintain the modern tradition of separation of church and state, Islam nonetheless was to return to the center of society, serving not only as a "religion of the heart" that can save the individual soul but also as a "religion of order" defining the ethics of the whole society. In this context, the late Ottoman thinker Ziya Gokalp (1876–1924) has resurfaced. The subject of Gokalp's reflections was how, in this time of great historical transformation, Turkey could simultaneously accept Western civilization and maintain its own cultural identity. From his perspective, with the arrival of modern civilization the original Islamic civilization took a step backward, becoming Turkey's particular national culture. Universal civilization could not replace or supplant a particular national culture, because this was the source of a people's self-identification and the way in which a people maintained its specificity.[13] What today's Turkey is putting into practice is precisely Gokalp's past prescriptions, in which the country as a whole displays a new attitude in which it belongs to mainstream civilization while at the same time revitalizing its own cultural traditions.

The conclusion we can draw from German and Turkish histories is that neither using culture to resist civilization, nor using civilization to replace culture, is the proper road for national revival. China should take a middle path between the two extremes, neither resisting world mainstream civilization, nor pursuing it – instead China should develop modern civilization, following world trends and at the same time employing her own cultural traditions to make her own contributions to the development of universal civilization. But to get to this point, China must first rejoin the peoples of the world, and having achieved wealth and power, return to the pursuit of civilization. Once China has adopted universal values and institutions it can set sail to navigate its way out of the narrow gorges of history.

[12] See Saimouer Hengtingdun (Samuel Huntington), *Wenming de chongtu yu shijie zixu de chongjian* (The clash of civilizations and the remaking of world order), Zhou Qi, trans. (Beijing: Xinhua chubanshe 1998), p. 159.
[13] See Zan Tao, "Gekaerpu de Tuerqi zhuyi lilun" (Gokalp's theory of Turkism), ch. 4 in Zan Tao, *Xiandai guojia yu minzu jiangou: 20 shiji qianqi Tuerqi minzu zhuyi yanjiu* (The construction of modern states and peoples: Studies in early twentieth-century Turkish nationalism) (Beijing: Sanlian shudian, 2011), pp. 166–94.

Unifying the Three Traditions, Civil Religion, and
Constitutional Patriotism

Civilizations aren't sketched on a blank sheet of paper, where you can draw whatever pleases you. Building civilization requires respecting China's cultural traditions, because even if some of these are by now brilliant ruins, some are still resources that can be mined, and some are ancient legends waiting to be brought back to life. Contemporary China possesses three important cultural traditions: China's historical cultural traditions, with Confucianism at the center; a tradition of modern civilization represented by the Enlightenment movement from the May Fourth period forward; and a nearly century-long socialist tradition. In the early twentieth century, Confucianism lost its institutional and social base and fell apart, existing only in a fragmented way in the daily lives of the Chinese people. Modern civilization imported from the West has, over the past hundred years, experienced many twists and turns, and as of today has completed half of its mission – the rational capitalist order – while the rule of law and accountable government have yet to be achieved. As for the equally long socialist tradition, it too followed a tortuous path during the Mao Zedong period. Still, in its opposition to capitalist hegemony and its pursuit of the ideal of equality it retains its place in China's general psychology as well as its capacity for social mobilization. Liberals, socialists (both the old guard and the New Left), and Confucian conservatives hold conflicting attitudes and standpoints concerning these three existing cultural traditions, but whether they like them or hate them, the traditions are there, and there is no choice but to confront them and take them seriously.

The New Left scholar Gan Yang (b. 1952) was the first to discuss unifying the three traditions, the idea of bringing the Enlightenment tradition, the Confucian tradition, and the socialist tradition together as the basis for China's new civilization. Unifying the three traditions is not only desirable, it is also possible. From a historical standpoint, Chinese civilization was unlike Western monotheistic civilization and accepted many gods. Monotheism pursues unity; polytheism searches for harmony, and Chinese civilization existed for more than 2,000 years as a pluralistic state. On the spiritual dimension, Confucianism and Buddhism coexisted without difficulty as the religion for the elite, while the masses' beliefs were a combination of Confucianism, Daoism, and Buddhism; Confucius, Laozi, and Buddha were all worshipped. The political order was a mix of hegemonic and benevolent rule. Confucianism provided legitimacy for the universal monarchy, while activist Legalism and non-action Huang Lao Daoism, a strain of Han dynasty Daoism with an overtly political dimension, alternated in providing the technical nuts and bolts of ruling. But while Confucianism maintained a dominant, mainstream position in both the religious and political orders, unlike monotheistic Judaism, Christianity or Islam, Confucianism did not exclude other gods, but rather secularized foreign religions and popular beliefs, adding Confucian ethical values to the teachings of these other religions. The situation was similar in the political realm. Francis Fukuyama has argued that China was the first to develop into a strong country with a unified, centralized monarchy, a bureaucratic control system, and an examination system for elite recruitment. This rationalized state capacity was developed in common by Confucians and Legalists. Li Ling (b. 1948), a well-known scholar of Chinese intellectual history, has noted that "Europe only had religious unity, not national unity. China is exactly the opposite, and its particularity is that it insists on national unity and religious plurality."[14] In historical Europe, we note one religion and many countries, while in historical China we find one nation and many religions. This means that unifying the three traditions is the common state of a Chinese civilization where the many reside in the one.

But we cannot simply stop at the level of a slogan like "unify the three traditions," because whether we're talking about ancient Chinese civilization or modern civilization or the socialist tradition, their contents are extremely complex, multi-faceted, and there exist all sorts of contradictions and conflicts. Within Chinese civilization we find five traditions – Confucian, Daoist, Mohist, Buddhist, and Legalist – and even within Confucianism there is the cultivation wing with its emphasis on morality and the practical wing with its emphasis on statecraft, there is the humanistic trend that takes people as the base and the authoritarian tradition that sees the emperor as the key link. Within Western civilization, even remaining within the Atlantic world, there are important differences between the American model and the European model. As a new continental power, the United States lacked the aristocratic traditions of the Middle Ages as well as Europe's modern social movements, which shaped its heroic tradition of worshipping individual struggle. Americans harbor great mistrust of the government, and individual liberties and rights are sacred, untouchable natural rights. America is also a country of the Puritan ethic, full of religious feeling, and independent individuals are also possessed of a group spirit, which has led

---

[14] Li Ling, "Huanqiu tongci liangre: Wode Zhongguo guan he Meiguo guan" (The same warmth and cold throughout the world: My views of China and America), originally given as a talk on October 12, 2011, at the Jiusan xueshe, one of China's small, legal democratic parties. It is available online at www.douban.com/group/topic/35402627/.

them to construct a thriving civil society. In comparison, European secularism is more thorough and religious sentiment weaker, and democratic socialism, the product of important modern social movements evolving out of liberalism's internal changes, has become the European mainstream. Unlike Americans, Europeans do not believe that capitalism is a given, and are more willing to use state intervention to bring about social equality and justice. As Jürgen Habermas (b. 1929) and Jacques Derrida (1930–2004) have said: "In European society, secularism is quite mature. Europeans believe in state organization and management, and are suspicious of the capacities of the market. They have an acute 'dialectical Enlightenment' consciousness, and do not place naïve optimistic faith in the development of science and technology."[15] As for the socialism that developed from Marx's work, as everyone knows, there are different traditions in the West and in the East. The Western European socialist party traditions created by Eduard Bernstein (1850–1932), the German political theorist and politician, and Karl Kautsky (1854–1938), the Czech-Austrian intellectual and politician, which advocate socialist ideals in the context of the constitutional framework of modern civilization, have today become the European mainstream. Eastern socialist practice from Russia to China, over the course of the last century and more, has made great achievements but has also declined, and at present has an uneasy, contradictory relationship with modern civilization.

Because of the complexity and multiplicity within traditional civilization, modern civilization, and socialist civilization, the question is not whether to unify the three traditions, but rather which "three traditions" we might seek to unify? It's like a bartender's competition producing different modern cocktails from different recipes where the tastes differ greatly, one from the other. If we choose "rich country and strong army" from the Legalists, together with the strength and power of capitalism from modern Western civilization and the nationalist despotic tradition of Eastern socialism, then when we unify the three traditions, the monster we create will be a nationalist authoritarian aristocratic capitalism or perhaps a bureaucratic Legalist socialism. And if we select Confucian paternalistic and humanistic traditions, liberalism's emphasis on freedom, the rule of law, and democracy, as well as the ideals of socialist equality, when we blend them together this unity of the three traditions will bring

---

[15] Habeimasi (Jürgen Habermas) and Delida (Jacques Derrida), "Eryue shiwuri, Ouzhou renmen de tuanjieri: Yi hexin Ouzhou wei qidian, dijie gongtong waijiao zhengce" (February 15, or, What binds Europeans together: Plea for a common foreign policy, beginning in core Europe), in Dannier Liwei (Daniel Levy) et al., eds., *Jiu Ouzhou, xin Ouzhou, hexin Ouzhou* (Old Europe, new Europe, core Europe), Liu Bohuan, trans. (Beijing: Zhongyang Bianyi chubanshe, 2010), p. 30.

together the wisdom and essence of all civilizations past and present, Chinese and foreign, and the path will be paved for a new blossoming.

From a certain perspective, China's rise is also the result of some version of unifying the three traditions, but in a way that we cannot continue, a way that is unhealthy. When we shift from "wealth and power" to "civilization" we need to change the recipe for "unifying the three traditions," shifting from the Legalist pursuit of a rich country and strong army to the Confucian posture of taking care of the people, taking modern rationalism a step forward to achieve the civilizational rule of law and democracy, and from the Eastern socialist authoritarian tradition shift to the respect for freedom and equality that we find in the original Marxist classics. Even if we are still borrowing from the Western experience, our gaze should shift from learning from the United States to learning from Europe. Whether we're talking about national histories or cultural traditions, the differences between the two great countries that are China and the United States are too important. As Henry Kissinger (b. 1923) said, Americans and Chinese both view their civilization and philosophy as belonging to different exceptionalisms: "China and America both believe they represent unique sets of values."[16] By comparison, China and the European continent are closer; for example, China and Europe are both homes of ancient axial civilizations, and these civilizations contain complexity and multiplicity. Like France, China has a great tradition as a bureaucratic country, and like Germany at one point fell behind and faced the necessity to catch up with the advanced countries, producing tensions and conflicts between civilization and culture. China, like Europe, has been much influenced by Marxism, and has a deep socialist tradition, its religious coloration is rather weak, and its level of secularization quite thorough. The development of a country's civilization cannot simply erase existing traditions and start over from scratch.

Civilization is both a political-legal system and a common culture. The American legal scholar Harold Berman (1918–2007) said: "Law must be believed, otherwise it serves no purpose."[17] The soul of law and systems is that all citizens believe in and identify with the values expressed therein. This set of values can be divided into the two dimensions of political values and religious values, expressed separately as constitutional patriotism and civil religion. Constitutional patriotism is a fairly thin kind

[16] Ji Xinge (Henry Kissinger), *Lun Zhongguo* (On China), Hu Liping et al., trans. (Beijing: Zhongxin chubanshe, 2012), preface, p. 2.
[17] Bo Erman (Harold Berman) *Falü yu zongjiao* (The interaction of law and religion), Liang Zhiping, trans. (Beijing: Sanlian shudian, 1991), p. 28.

of national identity, an identity with the political values represented by the constitution and with common political culture. Civil religion is much thicker, and includes the people's common history, culture, and traditions as well as moral and ethical values and the understanding of the transcendent sources of these values.

Constitutional patriotism emerged after World War II as a means to bring together the German people after the ghost of Nazism had been exorcised. And after the unification of the two Germanys, it became the commonly shared standpoint of the peoples of East and West Germany who had different religions and ideological backgrounds. This clearly has significance as a reference point and a model as we attempt to resolve the nationalities question in China. While Han Chinese make up more than 90 percent of the large family of the Chinese people, there are still fifty-five minority groups, such as Tibetans, Muslims, Mongols, and other peripheral frontier groups that have, like the Han, long histories and well-developed religions: Tibetan Buddhism and Islam, for example. And since the 1990s, Protestant and Catholic believers have increased. In contemporary China, world mainstream civilizations have already been internalized, and religions associated with these civilizations have become Chinese religions. The five big religions of Confucianism, Daoism, Buddhism, Christianity, and Islam all coexist, and have become an unchangeable plural fact. As Fei Xiaotong (1910–2005), China's pioneering sociologist, once pointed out, the Chinese people are in fact many peoples in one body. Not only are there many nationalities, there are also many beliefs – how could we combine all of this into a single unified modern country? The "five peoples' republic"[18] of the early Republican period was a legal-political solution, but did not really resolve the underlying problem of the common culture needed to unify the country. Almost a century later, the Han are still trying to assimilate the minority peoples into their own mainstream culture, for example taking Han belief in Confucian culture as the basis for a public religion or even a national religion. With the help of secularized modern power, Confucian culture really has assimilated many cultural groups who possessed only popular culture and beliefs, but it cannot assimilate Tibetans and Muslims whose religion is on the same level as that of the Han. Instead, efforts at forced assimilation incite a sort of cultural backlash. This means that no religion (including Confucianism, Daoism, Buddhism, Christianity, and Islam) can serve as the national religion

---

[18] Translator's note: The notion, put forth by Sun Yat-sen (1866–1925) and the Nationalist Party, that the Chinese Republic was made up of five dominant ethnic groups: the Han, the Tibetans, the Mongols, the Manchus, and the Moslems (Hui).

supporting a legal-political system, nor can it become the common belief of the Chinese people. Culture, ethics, and religion must give groups with different beliefs sufficient space to govern themselves, while the political community relies on existing basic political values – freedom, equality, rule of law, constitutional rule, division of church and state, accountability of government, etc. This has nothing to do with whether the religion and ethics in question are "good," but rather establishes the norm for what is "right" in the political territory of a common political culture that transcends the five big religions and at the same time publicly recognizes different religions, philosophies and ethical views, and provides institutional identity and legal guarantees in the clear establishment of a country's constitution. The five religions are plural, while constitutional patriotism constructs one body; this formula of pluralism in unity will allow us to rebuild the national identity of the Chinese people.

Yet constitutional patriotism remains weak in the final analysis. It is solely a political identity with no relationship to cultural identity. Its function is confined to the political sphere, and not only does it not address private religious beliefs, it also has nothing to do with society's common spaces that are not political or individual. But the public life of citizens, in addition to the political realm, contains two important spaces: the social and the cultural. This is what Habermas called the "lifeworld" that exists outside of the "systems world." In the public worlds of society and culture there needs to be a civil religion with stronger values, not just political values, but extending to ethical values and moral values that have evolved from historical and cultural experience, and even religious experience. At this point we should identify two different kinds of religion: "religion of the heart" and "religion of social order." The religion of the heart saves the individual soul, it provides the soul of believers with a sense of belonging and the meaning of life. A religion of social order only provides basic moral and ethical rules for public life, even if behind these we find a transcendent source for the values.[19] When we are talking about civil religion, we are not talking about the religion of the heart that deals with the individual soul, but with the religion of order that sustains the social public order. In thoroughly secularized Europe, notions of civil religion are fairly weak, but in the United States, with its rich religious tradition, there has always existed what American sociologist Robert Bellah (1927–2013) has called "civil religion." The American values such as freedom and equality affirmed in the Declaration of Independence all have their transcendent sources in the will of the creator. But this

---

[19] See Ha Qiesen (Richard G. Hutcheson), *Baigongzhong de shangdi* (God in the White House), Duan Qi et al., trans. (Beijing: Zhongguo shehui kexue chubanshe, 1992), p. 40.

idea of God is abstract, and doesn't necessarily mean the Christian God; it can be understood as the transcendent god of another religion. The true point of civil religion is not love of country but rather belief in the values respected by that county. It is not worship of a specific deity, but rather support for the values symbolized by the community in question. Even if in his private space each individual can have his own religious beliefs, in the common space of the community of that people and that nation, there is a civil religion – common political values and ethical values that embody a country's core values. Civil religion has to do with transformation through education and not with religion as such. It is not the national religion, even if it is one with the country and the people. It is separate from the political order, even if it is recognized and affirmed by the country. Civil religion is the historical experience shared by the people of a country, it is the commonly appreciated national culture and the measure of common values, even if it might come from different gods, moralities, and philosophies.

In that case, what form will China's future civil religion take? Traditional Confucianism, or a new public culture combining Confucianism, Daoism, Buddhism, Islam, and Christianity with liberalism, socialism, and other modern ideologies? Clearly this is a question worth taking seriously. Whether the Chinese people become a unified people, whether China's national construction can succeed, depends on whether China can emerge from its current vacuum of core values, and conceive a civil religion that the entire country can affirm. This civil religion must both follow mainstream civilization, containing the universal values of all humanity, and at the same time must contain elements from China's own historical culture. One might say that the day that China's civil religion is born is the day that Chinese civilization will be re-established. Compared with institutional construction, this clearly is a much more difficult civilizational transition.

"For the road was so far and so distant was my journey" ... Yet civilizational construction requires only patience and a clear sense of direction, so that we no longer follow the tortured path.[20]

---

[20] Translator's note: The quotation is from Qu Yuan's "Lisao" (On encountering trouble), a famous poem from ancient China's Warring States period. The translation is from David Hawkes, *The Songs of the South: An Ancient Chinese Anthology of Poems by Qu Yuan and other Poets* (London: Penguin Classics, 1985), p. 30. The poem recounts the travails of a righteous Nobleman, wrongly banished by the king, as he searches for redemption and eventually chooses suicide. The poem has overtones of intellectual dissent, or independence, as the author of the autobiographical poem remains true to himself, even in death. Here, Xu Jilin seems to be saying "We've got our work cut out for us, so let's get to it."

2   The Specter of Leviathan: A Critique of Chinese Statism since 2000

Translator's Introduction

The concern addressed in this impassioned text is that China's rise to superpower status has been accompanied not only by the rise of the state, without which no nation has achieved superpower status, but also and more importantly by a cult of state power. The precise manifestations of the cult of state power are only alluded to; a detailed and balanced discussion of these manifestations, which would include both praise for China's remarkable economic growth as well as questions about abuse of state power, is not possible under the restrictions of China's "directed public sphere."[1] Indeed, after attempting without success to publish his essay in China, Xu finally chose the Taiwan journal Sixiang (Thought*), which publishes three or four hefty thematic issues a year, featuring authors from throughout the Sinophone world, under the editorship of the well-known Taiwanese liberal Qian Yongxiang. Following the original publication in 2011, the piece was republished in China's blogosphere, with surprisingly few changes (indicated in the translation below), illustrating the greater latitude accorded to the Web in China, at least at that time.*

Instead of focusing on the dimensions of state power or the nature of the cult of the state, Xu examines the intellectual arguments offered by mainland intellectuals that support what he calls "statism." There is no argument of cause and effect; Xu does not say that in the absence of these arguments, the Chinese state would behave differently (if anything, the impression he gives is that to a greater degree the thinkers he reviews follow the state). Instead, he takes great pains to place these arguments in a variety of contexts: intellectual debate within China since the beginning of the reform era; intellectual debate within China since the Opium War; intellectual debate in the world at large since the European Enlightenment. This approach reflects Xu's discipline – Chinese intellectual history – but is also consistent with what Gloria Davies has identified as the penchant of Chinese intellectuals to "worry about China" and to focus on the role of ideas, and correct thinking, as keys to understanding the present and shaping the future.[2] At a more

---

[1] Originally published as "Liweitan de youhun: 2000 nian laide guojia sichao pipan," in Qian Yongxiang, ed., *Sixiang* (Taibei: Taiwan lianjing chubanshe, 2011), no. 18. Also available online at www1.guancha.cn/XuJiLin/2011_07_10_60973.shtml. See Timothy Cheek, *The Intellectual in Modern Chinese History* (Cambridge: Cambridge University Press, 2015), pp. 260–61.

[2] See Gloria Davies, *Worrying about China: The Language of Chinese Critical Inquiry* (Cambridge, MA: Harvard University Press, 2009).

basic level, Xu is also reminding his readers – in this case China's educated elite – that despite the novelty and excitement of China's rise, "statism" is not new to twenty-first-century China. It has reared its head at various times and places in the modern era, with dire consequences.

Xu begins by critiquing China's New Left intellectuals – chiefly Wang Hui and Wang Shaoguang – for having endorsed the rise of the state cult. These criticisms are unusually vehement for Xu, who attempts to avoid the "spittle wars" that have characterized Chinese intellectual debates since the 1990s, but they are not ad hominem *or partisan. Instead, as a Rawlsian liberal with concerns for social justice, Xu is disturbed that these intellectuals have abandoned or at least diluted their former defense of China's "little people," who, until recently, they depicted as the victims of China's state capitalism, in favor of an embrace of the capacity of the Party-State to magically represent the interests of the Chinese people as a whole. He explores their arguments in some detail – indeed, as a critical summary of recent New Left thought in China, one could do worse than this essay – and exposes what he sees as the contradictions in their arguments: behind the New Left's calls for "responsive democracy" (instead of "representative democracy") and "good governance" lies a mystical faith in a union between state and people that recalls the Maoist "mass line."*

Xu further discusses the rise of a new generation of New Left scholars, represented notably by the legal scholar Jiang Shigong, who use the ideas of "Hitler's crown jurist" Carl Schmitt to build seemingly sophisticated arguments justifying statism and state power. In part, such arguments point to the importance of identifying common political enemies so as to rally the "people" around the state. In addition, Jiang and his colleagues seek to "divinize" state power, to suggest that the institutions of liberal democracy are unnecessary distractions because the state, properly conceived, protected by an "unwritten constitution," can effortlessly represent Rousseau's general will.

Xu offers rebuttals of these arguments, including a long and nuanced disquisition on how Weber dealt with issues of power and responsibility that was removed from the mainland version of the text (noted below). These arguments are convincing, at least to those who share Xu's liberal viewpoint. But the strength of the text is its illustration of the degree to which statist ideas have penetrated Chinese discourse, at both the elite and popular level, as well as Xu's pointed reminders that ideas have consequences. Germany and Japan, both of which followed the statist route in the lead-up to World War II, are mentioned more than once. In all, this is a trenchant internal critique of Chinese statism by a major PRC Chinese intellectual.

A statist wind is rising in China, directed toward sweeping away the camps of the New Left and the conservatives. In the current situation in China, statism has developed out of nationalism, yet is more extreme and more political, and places more emphasis on the exalted, core position of the state in all realms of social life. Since the state is seen to represent the comprehensive interests of the nation and the people, it is also seen to be able to resist the penetration and interference of private interests in political processes. Chinese statism is not another iteration of traditional imperial autocracy or a return to totalitarianism; its legitimacy calls on populist theories and it has a kind of half-convincing basis in the popular will, as if it will realize its authority democratically. It is a kind of populist essentialist authoritarianism. Against the imposing backdrop of China's rise, China's statism hopes to prove itself as a political path and a model, unlike those of the West, possessing Chinese characteristics, an institutional renewal sufficient to challenge the universal nature of Western democracy, and at present it is using the people's interests and the sacralization of Chinese civilization to construct a state fetishism.

Where did this new wave of statism come from? What are its theoretical antecedents and its basic demands? Where is it headed? We have to understand this. Statism is not only popular in Chinese intellectual circles, but is increasingly gaining support in mainstream official ideology, and in certain areas where they "sing red to attack the black"[3] it has wide-ranging potential in practice. The 1930s history of Germany and Japan illustrates that once statism holds sway, it can launch the entire nation into disaster. We must take it seriously.

From the Left to the Right: Two Strands of Statism

Most important figures in today's statist thought came out of the Enlightenment camps of the 1980s, or were influenced by the Enlightenment in the 1990s. The core demands of the New Enlightenment movement of the 1980s were human freedom and liberation, and even if building a modern state was one of the internal goals of the Enlightenment, this nationalism harbored a consensus that universal modern values were primary, and compared with the enthusiasm for individual liberation, nationalism was not a central focus. In the 1990s, nationalist thought began to emerge. This nationalism was a complex intellectual current, including moderate cultural nationalism, which sought to realize the cultural identity of the Chinese nation on the precondition of having identified with the universal ends of modernity. There was also an extreme ethnic anti-Westernism, whose goal was to oppose all Western hegemonies so as to arrive at a place where China "could say no" and "be unhappy";[4]

---

[3] Translator's note: A reference to Bo Xilai (b. 1949), who served as Communist Party chief of the western municipality of Chongqing between 2007 and 2012, before being removed from his posts and eventually put in prison, presumably as part of factional struggles at the top level of Chinese politics. "Singing red to attack the black" refers to Bo's revival of some aspects of Maoism while ruling in Chongqing: promoting the singing of Mao-era songs as part of a campaign against criminality.

[4] Translator's note: The reference is to two books published during this period as part of the ultra-nationalist current: Song Qing et al., *Zhongguo keyi shuo bu: Lengzhanhou shidai de zhengzhi yu qinggan jueze* (China can say no: Political and emotional choices in the post-Cold War era) (Beijing: Zhonghua gongshang lianhe chubanshe, 1996); and Song Xiaojun et al., *Zhongguo bu gaoxing: Da shidai, da mubiao, ji women de neiyou waihuan*

and finally there was a liberal nationalism, which saw the construction of modern universal civilization as its basic mission. Following the United States' "mistaken bombing" of China's embassy in Yugoslavia May of 1999, China gradually worked itself into a nationalistic frenzy, which reached its climax during the run-up to the 2008 Olympics when the Olympic flame made its way around the world. Against the great backdrop of China's rise, nationalism turned political and conservative. The emergence of statism was the product of a combination of nationalism, romanticism, and historicism. Nationalism seeks the rise of the nation-state, this much is clear. Yet statism is different; it puts the state front and center, and takes the building of state power and state capacity as the central objectives of modernity. Under statism, the state is no longer a tool to realize the interests of the citizens, the state itself is a good, and has an autonomous state rationality. The state is an end in itself.

China's rapid economic development since the early 1990s translated into a qualitative elevation of the state's financial capacity, mobilizational capacity, and control capacity. China now has the strength of a superpower, and can compete with the United States and Europe in terms of international relations. Is such a frightening Leviathan a blessing or a disaster? The intellectual world is divided. Classical liberals think that a country lacking modern democratic institutions can be a frightening oppressive power. They advocate the continued development of society, so that a mature civil society and public space can constrain the autocratic power of the state. Within the liberal camp, in recent years there has emerged a standpoint that hopes to blend statism and liberalism into a statist liberalism. The contemporary Chinese legal scholar Gao Quanxi (b. 1962) argues that liberalism has two sides, one to guarantee human rights and constrain state power, and the other to build a modern state: "Let's first build a modern state, a Leviathan. We'll only have modern citizens once this is accomplished."[5] He emphasizes: "A truly mature liberalism pays the most attention to state interests. One can say that liberalism is individualism plus statism."[6] But speaking more broadly, Chinese liberalism has lacked a comprehensive argument concerning statism: in the historical process of the rise of the nation, what role should the state ultimately play? Can the state represent the

(China is unhappy: A great era, great goals, and our domestic and foreign dilemmas) (Nanjing: Jiangsu renmien chubanshe, 2009).

[5] Gao Quanxi, "Ziyou zhuyi yu minzhu zhuyi" (Liberalism and nationalism), available online at www.aisixiang.com/data/7006.html.

[6] Gao Quanxi, "Lun guojia liyi: Lun yizhong jiyu Zhongguo zhengzhi shehui de lilun kaocha" (On state interests: A theoretical investigation based on Chinese politics and society), *Daguo* 2 (2004), available online at www.aisixiang.com/data/8054.html.

totality of the national interest? Does it have its own state rationality? Statism rushed in to fill these gaps in liberal territory. Statism built on recent crazes for arguments concerning the modern state by Machiavelli (1469–1527), Hobbes (1588–1679), and the German jurist and political philosopher Carl Schmitt (known as "Hitler's crown jurist") (1888–1985), and responding to a "crisis of hunger and thirst for the state," stirred up a whirlwind of interest in the topic.

In the Chinese intellectual world, statist thought has two different genealogies and origins. The first is the extreme left wing, which has collectively turned to the right, and the second is Schmittism, which has appeared over the past decade.

The move toward conservatism by the radical left is a recent occurrence in the intellectual world that has surprised many. The original nature of the left wing was to sympathize with the lower-class masses, and to oppose the power of capital and politics. This is the source of the charisma of the radical left wing. In China there is an old left wing and a new left wing. The old left wing upholds the fundamentalist ideology of orthodox socialism. They are part of the existing political system, and we might call them a fake left wing which is in fact conservative. The New Left wing is an intellectual force rising up out of the great debates between the Liberals and the New Left in the 1990s. Their chief concern has been the "capitalist" China emerging in the 1990s. They identify problems arising from China's reforms, from political corruption to social inequalities, as being calamities caused by Western neoliberalism, and they hope that China will rise above the Western capitalist road to take the path toward institutional innovation. In addition to many Western left-wing theories, the intellectual resources of the New Left include positive values that they have themselves creatively rehabilitated from the Maoist socialist tradition. The New Left holds two basic positions: one is to sympathize with and praise the lower-class masses; the second is to bitterly denounce capitalism and its democracy. When, in the 1990s, they felt that state was trailing behind the New Left and harming the interests of the lowest rungs of society, the New Left's critique of power was trenchant. But in the twenty-first century, when they discovered that the state will was moving gradually from "incorrect" neoliberalism toward "correct" socialism, the New Left began to move to the right and a near-complete embrace of the state, and the extreme left wing was transmuted into a conservative statism. When the People's Republic of China celebrated the sixtieth anniversary of its founding in 2008, a number of representative figures from the New Left joined in the chorus of public opinion singing the praises of "the great sixty years." Using the mechanism of selective memory, they came to see the first thirty years and the second thirty years of the Chinese socialist model as a consistently successful experience.[7] The Hong Kong-based political scientist Wang Shaoguang (b. 1954) published a piece in the authoritative journal *Chinese Social Science* arguing that China's development over years was the result of upholding the socialist direction, concluding that "as long as we maintain the socialist direction, then the future path will grow ever wider."[8] Wang Hui (b. 1959), literary scholar and best-known member of the New Left, summed up the sixty-year experience as China's having a "relatively independent and complete sovereign character." This independent sovereignty was realized through the practice of the ruling party; as Wang said, "since the Chinese ruling party and state have an independent character, they have evolved a set of self-correcting mechanisms."[9]

Left and right, radical and conservative were never absolute poles. Under certain conditions they can undergo mutual transformation, or even bizarrely combine into a whole which seems left but which is actually right. The bottom half is a left wing that sympathizes with the lower classes, while the upper half is a right wing that embraces authority. The Chinese New Left had a tendency toward statism from the very beginning, and indeed has been loath to separate itself from state authority. As early as 1996, the New Left scholar Gan Yang (b. 1952) noted that China should "move toward political maturity," avoiding the situation of a strong economy and a weak state. His concrete proposal was to use direct national elections to overcome the problem of burgeoning local interests, thus allowing the state to obtain legitimate authority directly from the people and to build a strong state on the legitimate basis of "mass democracy."[10] Gan Yang is a radical democrat, but is also a conservative statist, and his dream is precisely the democratic authoritarianism of Max Weber (1864–1920). This kind of democracy has two functions: it can both grant political sovereignty to the citizens and also

---

[7] Translator's note: Chinese liberals, as well as many Western China-watchers, tend to separate China's recently history into two discrete blocs: the Maoist period, from 1949 to 1979, and the era of reform and opening, which has followed.

[8] Wang Shaoguang, "Jiangshou fangxiang, tansuo daolu: Zhongguo shehui zhuyi shijian 60 nian" (Maintain the direction and search out the path: Sixty years of socialist experience in China), *Zhongguo shehui kexue* 5 (2009).

[9] Wang Hui, "Zizhu yu kaifang de bianzhengfa: Guanyu 60 nian lai de Zhongguo jingyan" (The dialectics of self-reliance and opening: On sixty years of Chinese experience), *21 shiji jingji baodao*, 2009, special National Day issue. Later, Wang Hui published a more systematic version of his interview remarks in "Zhongguo jueqi de jingyan jiqi mianlin de tiaozhan" (The experience of China's rise and the remaining challenges), *Wenhua zongheng* 2 (2010).

[10] See Gan Yang, "Zhongguo heshi chengwei yige 'zhengzhi minzu'" (When will China become a "political people"), available online at www.aisixiang.com/data/19117.html.

strengthen the legitimate foundation of state authority, consolidating authoritarian rule. The democracy that Weber appreciated was the instrumental function of the latter. Authoritarianism is not opposed to democracy, but it prefers the style of democracy in which "authority is delivered once." Weber once said to German General Erich Ludendorff (1865–1937): "In a democratic system, the people elect the leader in whom they themselves have confidence, and if this leader then says 'Shut up and do what I say!' then the people and the parties can be comfortable with doing what he says." Ludendorff was pleased, replying: "I really like this kind of democracy!"[11] The radical democracy of China's New Left at the outset was a Weber-style democratic authoritarianism whose goal was the construction of a strong state.

Beginning in the early 1990s, Wang Shaoguang and his fellow New Left scholar Hu An'gang (b. 1953) published a report on "strengthening China's state capacity" which provoked intense debate.[12] The report clearly described state capacity as "the capacity of the state to realize its own will," which was concretely expressed in terms of extractive capacity, regulatory capacity, legitimacy capacity, and coercive capacity. The New Left's collective turn toward the right was not a bolt from the blue, but instead has its own internal intellectual and historical logic. An essentialist democracy that rejects parliamentary democracy must establish individual or oligarchic authority within the state structure on the basis of democratic legitimacy. While China's New Left strongly opposes power, in its heart its real enemy is Western neoliberalism. When the state and neoliberalism make common cause, the New Left is the critic of the state, but once the state distances itself from the "erroneous" neoliberal line, and returns to the "correct" socialist path, then in the eyes of the New Left the state is transformed into the hope of the people. In the late 1990s and early 2000s, Wang Hui, positioning himself a "critical intellectual," sharply criticized the "apolitical politics" of global capitalism and bureaucratism. Yet more recently, in summarizing the independent experience of China's sixty-year rise, Wang Hui has affirmed the "nationalization of the ruling party" which now represents the universal interests of the people.[13] These abrupt changes of direction seem to point to the

---

[11] Bisemu (David Beetham), *Makesi Weibo yu xiandai zhengzhi lilun* (Max Weber and the theory of modern politics), Xu Hongbin, trans. (Taibei: Guiguan tushu gongxi 1994), p. 261.

[12] Wang Shaoguang and Hu An'gang, "Zhongguo zhengfu xiqu nengli de xiajiang jiqi houguo" (The decline of the extractive capacity of the Chinese government and the consequences of that decline), *Ershiyi shiji* 21 (1994).

[13] See Wang Hui, "Zhongguo jueqi de jingyan jiqi mianlin de tiaozhan" (The experience of China's rise and the remaining challenges).

New Left's important readjustments in political strategy under new political conditions: when calls for "direct elections by all of the people" or "grassroots democracy" are quashed, leaving no way forward on this front, then the politics of the New Left switches from support for social movements to trust in the state will, from "enlightening the people to carry out the Way" from below to "carrying out the Way on behalf of the ruler" from above.[14]

Schmittism is another part of the intellectual genealogy of statism. Ever since the Chinese scholar Liu Xiaofeng (b. 1956) introduced the thought of Carl Schmitt to the Chinese intellectual world, we have seen a wave of enthusiasm for his work in the fields of legal studies and political science that has now lasted for nearly a decade. And this wave of enthusiasm planted the seeds of statism wherever it traveled. The preeminent representative of Schmitt's thought in Chinese political arguments is Jiang Shigong (b. 1963), a well-known legal scholar at Beijing University. In 2004, when Ukraine and other countries launched their "color revolutions," Jiang Shigong was preoccupied by the fact that the government of Ukraine, constrained by its liberal constitutional ideas, and lacking a basic understanding of the nature of politics, missed the opportunity to forcefully suppress the opposing groups, and finally submissively handed over political power. In a Schmitt-like tone, Jiang talked up the lessons that China should draw from this: "The crucial questions in politics are not questions of right and wrong, but of obedience and disobedience. If you do not submit to political authority, then 'If I say you're wrong, you're wrong, even if you're right.'"[15] "The most important question in politics is making a clear distinction between friends and enemies. Between friends and enemies, there is no question of freedom, only violence and subjugation. This is the reality of politics, a reality that liberals often do not dare to face."[16]

For the past decade or so, a body of academic theories of state rationality, with Schmitt at the center but also including Machiavelli and Hobbes, have been all the rage among certain intellectuals, whose understanding of the state is full of the worship of German romanticism. For them, the state is no longer a tool to carry out the people's interests, but is an end in itself, with its own rationality and functions. State power

---

[14] Translator's note: The "Way" refers to the traditional Chinese view of proper governance, involving harmony between the cosmos, the emperor, and the people, and the expressions in quotation marks are often found in traditional Chinese political discourse.

[15] Jiang Shigong, "Wukelan zhuanxingzhong de xianfa quanwei" (The authority of the constitution in a Ukraine in transformation), *21 shiji jingji baodao*, December 8, 2004.

[16] Jiang Shigong, "Wukelan xianzheng weiji yu zhengzhi jueduan" (Ukraine's constitutional crisis and political decisions), *21 shiji jingji baodao*, December 15, 2004.

no longer requires the necessary evil of restraints, but is its own good that represents the comprehensive interests of the nation and the common will. The state should no longer be constrained by religious or ethical values, because it has its own autonomous rationality and its sovereign will which is indivisible, non-transferable, supreme. Basing himself on Western constitutional theory, Jiang Shigong carried out a systematic study of the legitimacy of China's political system, arguing that the will of the Chinese state was the will of the Party-State, and that modern China's revolutionary tradition meant that in addition to the formal state constitution, there was an unwritten constitution of the will of the Party. The Chinese Communist Party represents the supreme sovereign power of the basic interests of the people. It's like the theory of the two bodies of the king in Western medieval political theology: the Party is the soul, and the state is the body. The chairman system of the "trinity" of Party, government, and army is China's unique constitutional system.[17] During the celebrations of the sixtieth anniversary of the founding of the PRC, all sorts of praise for China's unique political model made the rounds, and as Zhang Weiwei (b. 1957) summed it up: "Government is a necessary good. In the long flow of China's history, prosperous eras were never separate from relatively enlightened and strong governments. Unlike the American proposition that 'Government is a necessary evil,' China's transformation is led by an intelligent government committed to development."[18] Pan Wei (b. 1960), the Chinese scholar of international relations and nationalist thinker, was even clearer:

The most basic feature of China's political model is that it possesses an advanced body that controls the government. The Chinese Communist Party (CCP) is the political group leading China's modernization efforts. This group proclaims that it represents the entire people as we advance toward the blessings of modernity. It is devoted to the public interest and not to private interests, it is disciplined and united, providing a strong core of political leadership to the dispersed and free Chinese people.[19]

These conservatized New Leftists and Schmittists are not insiders sucking on the teat of Marxism-Leninism, nor are they tired fundamentalists; instead, most are modern intellectuals who have

---

[17] See Jiang Shigong, "Zhongguo xianfa zhong de buchengwen xianfa – lijie Zhongguo xianfa de xin shijiao" (The unwritten constitution within China's constitution: A new way of understanding China's constitution), available online at www.aisixiang.com/data/34372.html.

[18] Zhang Weiwei, "Zhonggong chenggong beihou de bage linian" (Eight concepts behind China's success), available online at http://theory.people.com.cn/GB/10158261.html.

[19] Pan Wei, "Zhongguo moshi: Renmin gongheguo 60 nian de chengguo" (The Chinese model: Sixty years of success of the People's Republic), *Lüye* 4 (2009).

received a systematic education in the West. Inspired by "China's rise," and starting from the notion that "what is real is rational," they expound on the "rational real" from every possible angle. Historicist thought is not a unified intellectual community, yet even if their theoretical resources and political propositions are not completely identical, they nonetheless share a common value standpoint, which is worship of the highest sovereignty and national will, a belief that the state represents the comprehensive interests of the people, and that only through the ruling capacity of the Party and the government will China be able to realize its political rise. These historicist intellectuals work at first-tier universities like Beijing University, Qinghua University, Hong Kong University, inside and outside of China, and hold themselves to be independent intellectuals, although they maintain an ambiguous relationship with the state, sometimes close and sometimes distant. Behind their proposals is not dogmatic Marxism-Leninism but instead faddish Western theories from the left and the right. In my view, what deserves serious treatment are not the historicist propositions, but the theoretical justifications behind the proposals, these theories that appear to be true but are false and seductive, attracting many intellectual students yearning for China's rise.

"Responsive Democracy" or "Responsive Authority"?

China's reforms have followed a path different from those in Russia; economic reforms have led the way while political reforms have lagged. As China enters the twenty-first century, calls from within for China's democratization continue to be heard. "Democracy" is the sacred concept of our age, like "revolution" in the past. No one dares openly oppose democracy, but there are divergences concerning the kind of democracy we want.

The democracy proposed by Chinese liberals is a program of constitutional democracy. They want to build the state's legitimacy on the basis of constitutional democracy, establish the constitution as the basic principle of the state's political life, separate the Party from the government, achieve a limited balance of power within the system, and construct a complete civil society and public arena, bringing about a social autonomy on par with that of the state. These moderate reform demands by the Liberals were influential in the late 1990s and early 2000s, but in recent years have retreated as a result of the pressure of outside events. Another democratic option is the social democratic program, which hopes to take Western Marxism as its point of departure, and blend socialist demands for equality and public ownership with the Western social democratic system, bringing about a democratic socialist ideal. This democratic program at one point generated a lot of enthusiasm, but was quickly marginalized. With the emergence of historicist thought in the past few years, the Schmittists talk little about democracy, and are concerned solely with the absolute capacity of the highest sovereignty. Still, the New Left has its own radical democratic ideals.

In New Left circles, Wang Shaoguang is the thinker who has addressed the question of democracy most systematically. His 2008 book, *Four Theses on Democracy*, is a quite distinctive democratic program. By "distinctive," I mean when compared to the democracy of competitive elections. In the historical evolution of Western democracy, Ancient Greece and Rome practiced classical direct democracy, in which citizens directly participated in and decided on the public affairs of the political community. Modern democracy is indirect, procedural democracy in which the people choose elites through competitive elections who will rule indirectly as their representatives. This procedural democracy, as defined by Joseph Schumpeter (1883–1950), has been broadly adopted in modern democratic practice; the American political scientist Samuel Huntington (1927–2008), for example, used this criterion to evaluate whether a country is democratic, proposing his theory of "third wave democracy" occurring in the late twentieth century.[20] Wang Shaoguang fiercely criticizes modern representative democracy, accusing it of being "electoral" without being democratic, saying that it "restricts the opportunities for democracy to directly participate and make policy," "limits the opportunities for the majority to participate in politics," and that there is "no way to reform the 'aristocratic,' 'oligopolistic' nature of the elections."[21] Even if these criticisms are overstated, we must admit that they contain a certain degree of truth. The flaws in electoral democracy with competing powers at the center have long been deeply analyzed and criticized by contemporary Western civic republicanism, communitarianism, and radical democracy. All of these have pointed out that these flaws reduce citizens' political participation and spirit, that elections are easily manipulated by the power of money, that they lead to the bureaucratization of everyday political life. Thus these critics of representative democracy have proposed a variety of solutions such as consultative democracy, participatory democracy, and the politics of the

---

[20] See Hengtingdun (Samuel Huntington) *Disan bo: Ershi shiji houqi minzhuhua langchao* (The third wave: Democratization in the late twentieth century), Liu Jinning, trans. (Shanghai: Shanghai sanlian shudian, 1998), ch. 1.

[21] See Wang Shaoguang, *Minzhu silun* (Four theses on democracy) (Beijing: Shenghuo, Dushu, Xinzhi Sanlian Shudian, 2008), ch. 1.

common good, as correctives to the internal flaws of representative democracy. Nonetheless, these democratic proposals do not seek to replace or overturn representative democracy with its competitive elections, but rather to use the classical democratic spirit to repair the insufficiencies of modern democracy.

But what Wang Shaoguang wants to do is to put forward a different democratic program to replace representative democracy with what he calls "genuine democracy," a "democracy where the people are the masters, not a democracy where they are castrated and rendered harmless."[22] On the face of things, it looks like Wang Shaoguang wants to restore the classical tradition of direct democracy, and to hand over these democratic powers to the people who are dear to the hearts of the New Left – the grassroots masses. This is fine as theory, but the problem is that China is not an ancient Roman city-state, but instead a huge country with a sprawling territory and a massive population. How are we meant to carry out direct democracy? After Wang has laid out a number of participatory mechanisms such as open information flows, listening to the people's opinions, soliciting the people's wisdom, carrying out the people's decisions, he simply and frankly plays his final card: his so-called "genuine democracy," which is Mao Zedong's (1893–1976) old "reverse participation model: the mass line" in which the Party purports to synthesize and represent the will of the people![23]

The democracy of Ancient Greece and the "mass line" may both look like direct democracy at first glance, but the two are glaringly different in nature. Citizens were the political masters in the ancient Greek city-states, while the political masters in Mao Zedong's mass line were the rulers. The concerns of the ancient Greek city-states were who was going to rule; while those of the "mass line" were how to rule effectively. Yet from Wang Shaoguang's point of view, democracy, rather than being a form of political power deciding "who will rule" is rather a form of government management deciding "how best to rule."[24] What is democracy? "When the masses express their wishes and the government responds, this is democracy."[25] Wang Shaoguang argues that while democracy has many shades of meaning, the most important is "a government's responsiveness to the people, meaning government policies that reflect popular needs, demands, and preferences to a high degree; this kind of

---

[22] Ibid., p. 242.
[23] See Wang Shaoguang, *Qumei yu chaoyue* (Disenchantment and transcendence) (Beijing: Zhongxin chubanshe, 2010), pp. 194–206.
[24] Ibid., p. 124.
[25] "Wang Shaoguang tan minzhu he 'xuanzhu'" (Wang Shaoguang discusses democracy and "electocracy"), *Dongfang zaobao-Shanghai shuping*, October 18, 2009.

democracy is the closest to the true meaning of democracy."[26] This kind of "responsive democracy" championed by Wang stealthily replaces the people with the rulers as the masters of politics, and for this reason the meaning of democracy has also changed. The meaning of democracy in ancient Greece was how to take the will of the ruled and make it into the common will, while the concerns of "responsive democracy" are merely how the rulers respond to, adopt, and represent the will of the ruled. Consultative democracy, Web-based public opinion, expert guidance, public consultation and other such proposals to achieve direct democracy can supplement representative democracy and become part of an enlightened authority. After Wang Shaoguang abruptly rejects the basic structure of representative democracy, the only variant of democratic practice he can imagine is the heritage left by Mao Zedong's populism.

In Wang Shaoguang's "responsive democracy" plan, everyday people achieve grassroots democracy through the ballot, discussions, public opinion, and participation. The people express their popular will in these ways, the government responds and adopts parts or all of what has been expressed, and the state collectively realizes the basic interests of the people. This authoritarian democratic model, combining mass democracy with response by the authorities, is clearly the spiritual inheritor of Mao Zedong's "democratic centralism," in which mass "democracy" is merely symbolic, while the "collective" nature of the rulers is the only truly decisive will. Yet the "democratic" part is not optional, as it supplies formal legitimacy to the "collective" deciding will. This model has a fatal flaw, which is that in between the grassroots masses and the higher-level authorities top and bottom are delinked, because of the lack of competitive elections and institutional oversight and accountability, and the people's interests and will cannot, through systemic guarantees, be efficiently transformed into the government's will. In the Western democratic structure, there is a legislative assembly that represents the electors and supervises the government, and a judicial branch that in the people's highest interests checks to see if the government has gone against the constitution. But in a "responsive democracy," governmental power need only proclaim that it is representing the people's basic interests and then it can harm the concrete interests of the citizens in an unrestrained, unobstructed, brazen manner. The many recent incidents of government usurpation of power in carrying out demolitions and confiscations of individual property, all in the name of the public interest, are the best examples of the vacuity of "responsive democracy."

---

[26] Wang Shaoguang, *Minzhu silun* (Four theses on democracy), p. 73.

As a simple matter of fact, "responsive democracy" is actually "respon-sive authoritarianism."You have "democracy" and authority, and through the rulers' response to the ruled's interests and desires you achieve the good name of "democracy," and thereby increase the ruling legitimacy of state authority. In this seemingly enlightened "responsive authoritar-ianism," political initiative remains always in the hands of the govern-ment: its response to and adoption of the popular will is an expression of the enlightened nature of the rulers; if they do not respond or adopt, then there's nothing to be done, as there are absolutely no systemic constraints. This kind of democracy is closer to traditional Confucian paternalism which claims to govern "for the people," yet the difference between "paternalism" and "democracy," even if it comes down to merely one character in Chinese, is huge in reality.[27] In democratic politics, the "people's decisions" are carried out through institutional competi-tive elections, which is politics for the people, the rulers "decide for the people" as the agents of politics. Although Wang Shaoguang proclaims repeatedly that he wants the people to decide, in his plan for "true dem-ocracy," the people finally wind up in a passive stance where they are "represented," "their proposals adopted," "responded to," and the ini-tiative to be – or not to be – democratic, remains firmly in the hands of the rulers.

There are different political concepts behind modern democracy and Confucian paternalism. On this point, Pan Wei sees things fairly clearly. He argues that: "After the Middle Ages the West evolved a 'rights-based' thought, while China's 'responsibility-based' thought has continued down to the present. The two notions of 'responsibility-based' and 'rights-based' sum up the basic differences in Chinese and Western thought, and these differences are at the origin of the differences in the Chinese and Western models."[28] The subject of "rights politics" is the citizen, who, under the protection of politics, has the right to protect his legitimate interests, as well as the right to oversee the officials that he himself has elected. The subject of "responsibility politics" is the ruler. According to the moral demands of Confucian paternalism, the official must belong to and serve the people, but this "people" is an abstract and symbolic totem without institutional supervision of the officials, so that the so-called "responsibility" is merely a weak moral constraint, and the

[27] Translator's note: The concept that I have translated as "paternalism," *minben*, a ruler's claim to be acting in the interests of the people, shares the character *min* with the Chinese word for democracy, *minzhu*.
[28] Pan Wei, "Gongheguo yi jiazi: Jiazi shentao Zhongguo moshi" (One sixty-year cycle in the life of the Republic: The search for a China model), *Kaifang shidai* 5 (2009).

actual object of the official's responsibility is not the people below, but his superiors above. Within a bureaucratic system, all levels are responsible to their superiors, and oversee their inferiors, a lovely example of politics with Chinese characteristics![29]

For the community of citizens, democracy is a question of self-rule by society, but for the government, it is a process by which the citizens confer power on the government. This conferral of power is not the type of single transfer that Weber wrote about, but instead is subject to the indirect supervision of the legislature and the judiciary and public opinion, or in a consultative democracy to the direct oversight of the public decisions of the people as a whole, who often examine the legitimacy of governmental policies. Because "responsive democracy" lacks an institutional conferral of power, relying merely on self-proclaimed representatives, the so-called response is a personal rule by an enlightened despot lacking objective standards and effective supervision. Consequently, "responsive democracy," from the beginning of its pursuit of democracy to its burial of democracy, does not permit the people to take charge, but instead allows the authorities to make decisions for the people, and finally is transformed into a self-denying, self-subverting "responsive authoritarianism."

The process of the transformation of "responsive democracy" into "responsive authority" is a political process of continual depoliticization, in which the will of the citizens who should be the subject of politics is continually represented and marginalized, while the question of "who will rule" quietly turns into the question of "how to rule." As a result, in recent years in China the question of whether we should democratize has turned into a question of good governance. While Wang Shaoguang, with his origins in the New Left, refuses to abandon the flag of democracy, other statists straightforwardly propose replacing the irritations of democracy with good governance or an able government. Zhang Weiwei frankly states: "Good government is more important than democracy. China rejects the hoary 'opposition between democracy and despotism,' and argues that the nature of a government, including its legitimacy, should come from its true contents, and thus be decided by good governance. It should be measured by what the government can provide for its people."[30] The Chinese political scientist Yu Keping (b. 1959), who once enthusiastically announced that "democracy is a good thing," has

---

[29] Translator's note: This is a humorous play on words, since the Chinese model is often dubbed "socialism with Chinese characteristics" in the Chinese press.

[30] Zhang Weiwei, "Zhongguo chenggong beihou de bage linian" (Eight concepts behind China's success).

begun to abandon democracy for pragmatic politics in the face of the difficulties in democratic reforms in China in the past few years, and has switched to talking about good governance, noting that: "In the contemporary period, political legitimacy has undergone a vast transformation, its origins are moving away from well-being, democracy and good government toward good governance, which is destined to become 'the most important source of political legitimacy for humanity in the twenty-first century.'"[31] In his explanation, good governance indeed contains many good things: the rule of law, participation, justice, transparency, responsibility, efficiency, stability, rigor ... But, as is the case with "responsive authority," the political subject remains the government, not the citizens, and politics is a matter of technique, and is depoliticized, as the political process becomes a question of government management in which the citizens are absent. And this government that is meant to carry out good governance is in fact an omnipresent and omnipowerful public power, lacking institutional supervision.

But from the point of view of the statists, Chinese state power, from ancient times to the present, has not been too strong, but rather too weak. They believe that the difference in real power between China and the West is not a matter of whether one has civilization, but rather the strength or weakness of state capacity. The Chinese philosophy professor Wu Zengding (b. 1971) argues that: "The reason that modern Western countries have very strong capacities to expand and subjugate, is because their states have high-level integrative and mobilizational power in all realms of society."[32] Historian Han Shuhai (b. 1965) has re-examined the past 500 years of Chinese and world history, and argues that "the fluctuations in world history over the past 500 years are essentially explained by 'state capacity.'" China's gradual decline is explained by its lack of a strong central government. He praises the post-1949 "great revival of the Chinese nation, which began at the outset with the Chinese revolution which, by building a base-level organization, greatly increased social organizational capacity and state efficiency."[33] Wang Shaoguang was the first to bring up state capacity, and in his view, in addition to

[31] See Yu Keping, "'Hefa yu zhili' guoji yantaohui juxing" (International conference on "legitimacy and governance"), available online at http://fudan.edu.cn/fudannews/2010/0712/25171.html. The entire reference to Yu Keping is omitted in the online version of the text published in China.
[32] Wu Zengding, "Chongtan xiandai Zhongguo geming de 'lishi biranxing' wenti" (Re-examining the question of the "historical necessity" of modern China's revolution), in "Gongheguo 60 nian: Huigu yu zhanwang" (The Republic at sixty: Review and future perspectives), *Kaifang shidai* 1 (2008).
[33] See Han Shuhai, *Wubainian lai shei zhushi?* (Who wrote the history of the past five hundred years?) (Beijing: Jiuzhou chubanshe, 2009).

paying attention to democracy as a form of political power, one must also take seriously the question of state capacity. Many democratic countries experience a long period of democratic decline and failure because they lack effective government power. "Only a strong state can bring about a high-quality democracy";[34] "the state is the largest, most effective organization of the people's power."[35] Only half of what Wang Shaoguang says is correct. It is true that a high-quality democratic country requires great state capacity, but a strong state is not naturally "the largest, most effective organization of the people's power." There are democratic countries like the Philippines which are unable to deal with problems like the Hong Kong hostages[36] and there are also totalitarian societies like North Korea that trample on the people's rights, but still play in the soccer World Cup tournament. Strong state power can do great good, but can also do great evil. At base, state power is like human nature: human nature contains both good and bad, and under good institutions can become an angel, while under bad institutions can become a devil. A strong state most needs democratic institutions and comprehensive constitutions and the rule of law, to prevent power from doing evil. A state with overweening power can both create economic miracles for humanity, but can also degenerate to the point of harming human rights and the world. Among Western countries, the reason why Britain and the United States have remained strong is that they possess reliable civilizational institutions which impose constraints. And the reason why Germany and Japan rose once and then ultimately failed is precisely that they blindly pursued the expansion of state capacity, and as a result betrayed the universal civilization of humanity.

In his *Four Theses on Democracy*, Wang Shaoguang distinguished between two concepts regarding the form of political power on the one hand and state capacity on the other: the former is related to whether the institutions are democratic, and the latter to the question of whether the state has controlling power.[37] We can understand it this way: the form of political power is related to civilizational values and their institutionalization, while state capacity is decided by the legitimacy of the political system. A legitimate political system will elevate state control capacity and ruling efficiency, for example by increasing economic competitiveness or more quickly freeing hostages, etc., but it can

---

[34] Wang Shaoguang, *Minzhu silun* (Four theses on democracy), p. 130.
[35] Wang Shaoguang, *Qumei yu chaoyue* (Disenchantment and transcendence), p. 114.
[36] Translator's note: The reference is to the Manila hostage crisis of August 2010, in which an incompetent police intervention resulted in the deaths of several Hong Kong tourists who had been taken hostage by a local man with a grievance.
[37] Wang Shaoguang, *Minzhu silun* (Four theses on democracy), p. 130.

also suppress human rights or carry out wild demolitions and illegal confiscations, etc. For this reason, whether the political form is democratic, whether it conforms to the values of universal civilization, appears to be extremely important. Setting aside democracy and engaging in wild talk about state power incurs the risks of great moral danger and political crisis When the New Left's "responsive democracy" becomes a mere enlightened despot exercising good governance, democratic constraints on authority become very weak. An enlightened authoritarian is a highly legitimate administrative power that can maintain the capacity for rationality and efficiently achieve the highest national interests. A rationalized authoritarian power bases its behavior on concrete policy objectives, which occupy a higher position than the values of universal civilization, and from an ethical perspective it is nihilistic and technocratic. By contrast, a good democracy must have values; its true meaning is not in the notion of "the people making the decisions" but in its ability to promote good and preclude evil, and embody the higher values of civilization.

By "good democracy," I mean democracy that can guarantee man's free nature. Speaking from the historical practice of democratic institutions, this means constitutional democracy, a democracy with constitutional norms that take freedom as the highest ethical principle. Wang Shaoguang dislikes embellishments of and limitations on democracy. In his view, "true democracy" is unlimited, a democracy where the people are directly in charge. Does this kind of pure democracy really exist? If it is not constrained by higher moral values, then even if it directly expresses the will of the majority of citizens, democracy can still degenerate into a frighteningly violent regime. Socrates was sacrificed to this kind of violent regime. Democracy is not limited to one form; it simply means that power is conferred by or agreed on by the people, otherwise democracy can be combined with all kinds of "isms": constitutional democracy, authoritarian democracy, or populist democracy. Democracy is not a self-evident institution, but always requires elaboration and fleshing out with higher values, be they the values of freedom (constitutional democracy) or the values of authority and order (authoritarian democracy), or the abstract will of the people as a body (populist democracy). The choice of a democratic model is in fact a choice of values, and democracies with different values are naturally different, some better, some worse. But from the standards of liberal values, what we call a good democracy is necessarily a democracy that can guarantee man's free nature and basic rights, and not a democracy with strong state capacity. And what we call a good government is not a government above the law, a hegemon with overweening power, but a government that conforms to ethical values, with checks and balances in terms of power, and with administrative efficiency.

The democracy preferred by China's New Left is in fact a mix of populism and authoritarianism. They believe in the highest will of the people, but also place great faith in the great authority of the government. Democracy and authority need not always be in conflict; in modern politics they often come together in paradoxical ways. Because democracy can supply a base of legitimacy to authoritarian rule, if modern authoritarian rule rejects the comprehensive will of the people, it has no other source of legitimacy. Thus democracy can join hands with authority to construct a strong state, or in the words of the New Left, "the grassroots joins with the elite to attack the middle." Here, the grassroots means the masses, and the elite means the central political authority, while the middle means local governments and their interest groups. Wang Shaoguang says: "Ancient emperors and kings all knew that they often had to join with the people at the lower level to contain the bureaucrats in the middle. It's the same in the United States, where the federal government circumvents state governments and joins together with African-Americans at the state level to force state governments to yield on questions of human rights."[38] Han Shuhai put it even more penetratingly: one should not think that democracy is a simple matter of "the officials against the people"; from the perspective of Chinese history, "the state and the ordinary people actually have common interests and common enemies, and these enemies are the powerful 'gentry.'"[39] There is no need for further proof: it is clear that the democratic platform of the conservatized New Left is in fact a populist-style authoritarianism, or in other words an authoritarian-style democracy. The New Left in the West also believes in the power of the people and in mass democracy, but they absolutely do not compromise with oppressive states or empires. For example, Michael Hardt (b. 1960) and Antonio Negri (b. 1933), the post-Marxist authors of *Empire*, dream of destroying oppressive powers and place their hopes in the organization of the globalized masses. By contrast, China's twenty-first-century New Left has abandoned its original demands for a social movement, and invested its hopes in the state for a response to popular wishes. Although they oppose the bureaucratic state, they do not have a natural fear of the state in the way that the

---

[38] Wang Shaoguang, "Heping jueqi yu guojia liangzhi" (Peaceful rise and good government), *21 shiji jingji baodao*, December 29, 2003.
[39] See Han Shuhai, *Wubainian lai shei zhushi?* (Who wrote the history of the past five hundred years?).

Western left does; quite the contrary, their hopes are invested in a populist state, a responsive authority that will rule in the name of the people.

Why does populist democracy finally turn into populist authority?
Because populist democracy contains internal contradictions that it
cannot resolve: on the one hand it opposes any representative or bureaucratic power, and hopes through direct popular participation in politics to carry out popular self-rule and self-management; but on the
other hand, it has no choice but to quickly and efficiently combine the
dispersed popular will into a unified popular will, and transform
the desire for political participation into the administrative will to rule.
As a result, populist democracy has only two options. One is a thoroughly
anarchist utopia, like the historical Paris Commune, or Hardt and Negri's
global league of the people, but such attempts at direct rule have never
succeeded; the other option is to hand over the popular will to a "great,
immortal law maker," and have a great man with a charismatic personality or a revolutionary elite political party represent the unified will of
the people and rule in their place. The Jacobin dictatorship during the
great French revolution, Soviet political power during the Russian revolution, Mao Zedong's Cultural Revolution – all of these were undoubt-
edly examples of authoritarian populism. Contemporary China's New
Left is attempting in a secularized, post-revolutionary period to carry
forward the spiritual tradition of this populist democracy, and create a
new model of "responsive authority." Democracy will take the road of
authority, which is not that far away. All they would have to do is to get
rid of all embellishments, do away with all covenants, and place their
democratic hopes in a responsive government that "serves the people,"
and democracy would become authoritarianism, while authority would
be delighted to call itself "democratic" or "good governance," and with a
happy smile take the great gift from statism, and achieve legitimate rule.

The Specter of Schmittism: The Absolute Power of the State

After more than thirty years of reform and opening, huge changes and
transformations have occurred in Chinese society. Many forces have been
freed from the totalistic control of the Mao Zedong era and the original
political community has begun to disintegrate, while a new political community has yet to be built, which has a created a deep communal crisis.
How to rebuild the political community? Two antagonistic currents have
formed in the Chinese intellectual world. One is a Lockean school of
limited government, and the other is a statist theory inspired by Hobbes
and Schmitt. The political community that liberals hope to build centers

on the society; the construction of civil society and public space will lead to a relatively autonomous social and ethical community. As for the political system, it will be a limited government with constitutional rule and the rule of law as central components. Such a government can be strong, but there must be a separation of powers. During the 1980s and 1990s, these liberal demands were partially realized in the practice of state reforms; such was the "small government–big society" reformist thought of Deng Xiaoping (1904–97) and his successors. After the beginning of the twenty-first century, however, the situation experienced a reverse, and the theme of "increase the Party's and the government's capacity to rule" quietly replaced the original "small government–big society," becoming the dominant mainstream ideology as well as political praxis. And what is the legitimacy of the new ruling line? Statist thought emerged at precisely this moment, hoping to comprehensively revise the reform direction of "small government–big society," in favor of a Schmittist political order in which the state possesses absolute authority.

The key points of a Schmittist political order are unity and representativity. Heinrich Meier (b. 1953), a German academic authority on Schmitt, notes that:

Schmitt proposes that the state rely on the people's unity – the people are a political unity constructed out of a national will which results from a division between friends and enemies, and relies on this politically united body to assure the representativity of the government ... It is very clear that Schmitt affirms mass democracy, but this democracy must embody authoritarianism which, through the two concepts of representativity and unity, will work to maintain consistency.[40]

As for a Schmittian political order, there are three points worthy of note. First, the most important thing about the political community is to maintain unity, a unity achieved through the exclusion of heterogeneous elements both inside and out. Inner heterogeneous elements include all private interests, and external heterogeneous elements are the enemies of the people. Second, while unity must rely on the form of democracy, it is ultimately embodied in a unified national will, and the representatives of this popular will possess a higher discretionary power transcending the constitution and the law. Third, the will of the state is absolute and unique and expressed in the form of a sovereignty that is exalted, indivisible, and

---

[40] Quoted in Yang Weierna Mile (Jan Werner Mueller), *Weixian de xinling: Zhanhou Ouzhou sixiangzhong de Kaer Shimite* (A dangerous mind: Carl Schmitt in post-war European thought), Zhang Mei and Deng Xiaoqing, trans. (Beijing: Xinxing chubanshe, 2006), p. 42.

untransferable. What Chinese statists want to build is precisely this kind of Schmittist political order.

So what statism first pursues is political unity. Unity is of course an important goal in modern politics, but liberals and statists have different ideas as to its meaning. Liberals admit the multiplicity of interests and values in modern society, and their goal is to bring about a common political life on the basis of maintaining reasonable differences; at the core of political unity are public rationality and constitutional government. However, Schmittist statists see politics as a division between self and the enemy, and the formation of "our" political community requires a common enemy. The unity of a people results from the expulsion of the other, and protection against private interests that might undermine or destroy the unity of the state. For this reason, although contemporary Chinese statist thought has different intellectual origins, all strains share a common enemy in the West, or more concretely Western neoliberalism and representative democracy. The imagined existence of a highly unified West thus becomes the exterior support statists require to achieve their own unity. Schmitt once said: "Tell me who is your enemy and I'll tell you who you are."[41] In the same way, the Chinese statists' definition of the China model also employs the antagonistic existence of the Western enemy. In their view, Western representative democracy allows private interests in society to enter the public political process through the competition of political parties, meaning that the legislative body becomes a field of competition lacking unified will and reflecting only private interests, especially those particular interests of the propertied classes[42]. Here, public and private, in the political process, have been split into two opposing extremes with public as the absolute good and private as the absolute evil. What all political parties represent is nothing but private interests, and the result of the private exchanges and compromises in the legislature can only form the majority interest. But the so-called public interest has a different representative – the state.

The ideas of private will, mass will, and general will were first raised by Jean-Jacques Rousseau (1712–78). The general will is a core concept in Rousseau's political thought, a concept that is related to, but different from, private will and mass will. In Rousseau's theory, the general will is always grounded in the public interest, while the mass will grows out

---

[41] Shimite (Carl Schmitt), "Huici" (Vocabulary), cited in Maier (Heinrich Meier), *Gujin zhi zheng zhong de hexin wenti: Shimite de xueshuo yu Shitelongqi de lunti* (Die Lehre Carl Schmitts. Das theologisch-politische Problem: zum Thema von Leo Strauss), Lin Guoji, trans. (Beijing: Huaxia chubanshe, 2004), p. 58.

[42] See Wang Shaoguang, *Minzhu silun* (Four theses on democracy), pp. 38–70.

of private interests and is nothing but the agglomeration of private, individual wills.[43] In other words, the mass will is the sum of private wills, and the general will is the subtraction of the private wills, the portion of the overlapping or intersecting common parts of all private wills. More than a decade ago, the political scientist and New Leftist Cui Zhiyuan (b. 1963) wrote an essay in which he re-examined Rousseau, and noted that "a thorough-going, democratic liberal cannot but be concerned by the general will."[44] Rousseau's theory of the general will is a core question in modern politics. A unified political community naturally needs a common will, which is but the secularized form of the transcendent will of God. But Rousseau has a fatal flaw, in that he pits the general will and the private will against one another as antagonists, and the prerequisite for the production of the general will is the vanquishing of individual wills. Consequently, in Rousseau's kingdom of the general will, individual will and private interests are completely illegal, which produced the reign of terror of the Jacobin dictatorship after the French revolution. Yet the path followed by the American revolution and nation-building was different. The Federalist Party, represented by James Madison (1751–1836), believed that politics is constructed on the basis of private interests, and that conflicts between private interests are inevitable, because human nature can be degenerate and because human rationality is fallible. "Dissent, debates, and mediation of conflicts, conflicts of interest, and continual factional struggles, all of this is inevitable. The reason for this is that the motivations for these phenomena are all 'deeply rooted in human nature.'"[45] Rousseau's and Madison's different standpoints on politics are based in different understandings of human nature. In Madison's view, human nature has a dark side, and is driven to seek after profit, but as long as there exists an appropriate distribution of power, evil will constrain evil and they will balance one another out, transforming evil into good, and private interests into the public interest. However in Rousseau's view, human nature is basically good, and the political process is a process of promoting good and eliminating evil; the key question deciding whether the general will could be produced came to be how to overcome private desires and approach the greater public good.

---

[43] See Lu Suo (Rousseau), *Shehui qiyue lun* (The social contract), He Zhaowu, trans. (Beijing: Shangwu yinshuguan, 1980), p. 39.

[44] See Cui Zhiyuan, "Lu Suo xinlun" (New discussions of Rousseau), in Cui Zhiyuan, *Dierci sixiang jiefang yu zhidu quangxin* (The second intellectual liberation and institutional reinvention) (Hong Kong: Niujin daxue chubanshe, 1997).

[45] Dawei Heerde (David Held), *Minzhu de moshi* (Models of democracy), Yan Jirong, trans. (Beijing: Zhongyang bianyi chubanshe, 1998), pp. 113–14.

Those among China's New Left who follow Rousseau's thinking similarly hate the market and private interests. Wang Shaoguang argues that "The market is necessary, but must be 'embedded' in society, and the state must play an active role in the market economy. We cannot allow, there cannot emerge a 'disembedded', completely freely functioning market economy."[46] Wang Hui also said: "When marketizing reforms become the mainstream, in the absence of the checks and balances provided by socialist forces existing within the state, within the Party, and in all realms of society, the state can be quickly captured by interest groups," and it has been precisely the tradition of socialism with Chinese characteristics that has kept the state from privatizing.[47] Although the New Left and the neoliberals they oppose are like oil and water, they share a basic premise: the market and the state are natural-born enemies. Neoliberals believe that the state is the culprit, and advocate for complete marketization, believing that marketization can save China. But the New Left prescription turns things upside down: the market is a bad thing, and only through the intervention of a strong state can the market be re-embedded into society, preventing a capitalist disaster. Both the neoliberals and the New Left are overlooking one thing: what has already occurred in today's China is precisely the mutual embeddedness of state and market! The state is not necessarily anti-market, the market is not necessarily against the state, and China's capitalism of power and nobility is nothing other than the freakish child of the private union of market and state.

The New Left hates the market, and also hates civil society. Over the course of thirty-plus years of reform and opening, China has produced a handful of NGOs, which have played their own unique role in protecting the rights of citizens, in public philanthropy, and in public service. Wang Shaoguang fairly early on undertook a systematic study of NGOs, but what his research findings proved was that "the 'civil society' praised to the skies by a few people in recent years is in fact nothing but a grab bag."[48] "Most of the so-called 'civil society organizations' are nothing other than interest groups pursuing their private interests or pressure groups."[49] Citizen organizations are voluntary, autonomous social

---

[46] Wang Shaoguang, *Minzhu silun* (Four theses on democracy), p. 77.
[47] Wang Hui, "Zhongguo jueqi de jingyan jiqi mianlin de tiaozhan" (The experience of China's rise and its remaining challenges).
[48] Wang Shaoguang, "Dazhuanxing: 1980 niandai lai Zhongguo de shuangxiang yundong" (The great transformation: China's two-way movement since the 1980s), *Zhongguo shehui kexue* 1 (2008).
[49] Wang Shaoguang, *Anbang zhi dao: Guojia zhuanxing de mubiao yu tujing* (The Anbang way: The goal and plan for national transformation) (Beijing: Sanlian shudian chubanshe, 2007), preface by Hu An'gang.

groups, including political, social, welfare, culture, entertainment, and sports organizations. They are not the result of government planning, but evolve from within society, and quite naturally are everywhere. The key is how we look at them. If our measure is that of "great unity,"[50] then NGOs really are a grab bag made up of all sorts of people engaged in all sorts of activities. But if our standard is that of a modern society, then NGOs are a sign of plurality, division, and activism. Wang Shaoguang divides the functions of NGOs into outer effects and inner effects. The outer effects include seeking independence from the state, and limiting the power of the government; inner effects are to cultivate the public spirit within social groups, and the exchange capacity to cooperate and build mutual trust. Wang Hui, who praises social movements, emphasizes the outer effects, and seeks to "prevent the state from becoming the captive of domestic or international monopolies through society's democratic control of the state."[51] But in Wang Shaoguang's view, apolitical, leisure, and entertainment NGOs are preferable to political citizen groups, and he hopes that all of society's NGOs can be depoliticized, smilingly moderate and obedient, maintaining harmonious relations with the government. He repeatedly emphasizes: "An effective state is the prerequisite of civil society ... When the state is strong and dynamic, civil society has greater chances to flourish."[52] What is ironic is that in today's China, when the state "is strong and dynamic," society is the loser, and we have citizens but no civil society or citizen organizations. A mass of people without autonomous social organization is a "pan of loose sand," in the words of Sun Yat-sen (1866–1925), and this unorganized mass is precisely the breeding ground for authoritarianism, because only a Hobbesian Leviathan can mold the disparate will of the dispersed masses into a comprehensive unified popular will. In the absence of autonomous civil society, when all social organizations have been stripped of their exterior functions of constraining the state, when all that's left are the inner effects of leisure and entertainment, then the state becomes a hegemon without restraints, dominating society. Although what statists attack is the market, their true enemy is society. While they appear to be directly opposed to the neoliberals, in fact they are more than ever united in their hatred for society: Neoliberals want to use the market to replace society, and statists want to use the state to suppress society.

[50] Translator's note: An ancient concept linked to notions of a state's or a ruler's legitimacy, or often to territorial unity. Here, Xu is being sarcastic.
[51] Wang Hui, "Wei weilai er bianlun: Zai Rineiwa luntanshang de jiangyan" (Arguing for the future: A talk at the Geneva Forum), available online at http://wen.org.cn/modules/article/view.article.php/704.
[52] Wang Shaoguang, *Qumei yu chaoyue* (Disenchantment and transcendence), p. 142.

Both the conservatized New Left and the Schmittist statists mortgage China's future hopes to a strong, omnipotent, supreme state body. In their view, no matter whether it is a question of political parties within a representative democratic system, or NGOs within a civil society, to say nothing of individuals pursuing their private interests, all represent the pursuit of private interests, and even if they waste their time putting together what they take to be a democracy, the best they will come up with will be a grab bag in the form of the will of the majority. Yet the true general will, the basic interests of the broad mass of the people, has nothing to do with private will or mass will, and only an all-knowing and omnicompetent government can be the true representative of the general will, and exercise decisive power that is sublime, indivisible, and untransferable. Wang Hui was originally a fairly critical intellectual, but has undergone a frightening change of direction in the last couple of years, and has abandoned his criticism of "apolitical politics" for praise of the Party-State that "represents universal interests." In his 2007 essay, "Depoliticized Politics: The Many Constructions of Hegemony and the Decline of the 1960s," he criticized the increased bureaucratization and depoliticization of modern politics, and trenchantly criticized the fact that "the functioning of contemporary China's ideological state apparatus is not the result of particular values or ideology, but instead follows a 'de-ideologized' or 'depoliticized' logic – even if it often resorts to ideological discourse." From another angle, he also argued that "the ruling party, in the process of ruling, has gradually become the subject of the state system, and as a result the ruling party is no longer acting in pursuit of a political idea or political practice, but is close to becoming a normalized state power, which, at a certain level, is a 'depoliticized' power apparatus."[53] This foreshadows the logic he employed two years later when he identified the Party-State with universal interests. In 2009, in the context of the PRC's sixtieth anniversary, Wang Hui was interviewed by *Twenty-First Century Economic Reports*, and later in the magazine *Wenhua congheng* published an essay entitled "The Experience of China's Rise and its Remaining Challenges," where he formally put forth his theory of "the Party-State representing universal interests." His argument is that the state built by the 1949 Chinese revolution represented the universal interests of the people from the very outset, but after the market

---

[53] Wang Hui, "Qu zhengzhihua de zhengzhi, baquan de duozhong goucheng yu 60 niandai de xiaoshi," (Depoliticized politics, the many constructions of hegemony, and the end of the 1960s), *Kaifang shidai* 2 (2007). For a simpler exploration of the same topic, see "'Qu zhengzhihua de zhengzhi' yu dazhong quanmei de gonggongxing" ("Depoliticized politics" and the public nature of mass media), *Gansu shehui kexue* 4 (2006).

reforms of the 1980s, and the penetration of disparate interests into the will of the state, the state found itself faced with the threat of privatization. Since the state was the director of market reforms, and was deeply embedded in society, the state started to fall prey to interest groups, with various organs of the state becoming representatives of different interest groups. "How to lead the state to become the representative of universal interests has already become an extremely pressing issue." He then placed his hopes for a representative of universal interests in the CCP: "The practice of Chinese socialism has led to the creation of a state that can represent the universal interests of the majority and the absolute majority, but the prerequisite for this is that the state or the government must break the hold of special interests." Because the CCP keeps its distance from economic activities, unlike in the West, where the government represents private interests, and represents the greatest number of interests of the greatest number of people, it can renew itself and serve as the backbone against corruption.[54]

Wang Hui's arguments are based on a belief that the modern state should be separate from private interests, the representative of the pure general will and universal interests. In the context of a market society, where the government is deeply penetrated by all sorts of diffused private interests, the only hope to save the state comes from a political party claiming to be the representative of the people's basic interests that will command the national will, and Chinese socialist practice happily provided just such a corresponding historical tradition. However, Wang Hui's thought contains a self-contradiction: on the one hand he has witnessed the Party's depoliticization, the fact that it no longer possesses ideological values, and increasingly practices a technical-bureaucratic politics. Wang hopes to restore ongoing political debates about certain political values, because the basic nature of politics is conflict. On the other hand, however, he also dreams that the Party can represent the unconflicted, common interests of all classes, but the public nature of this kind of dream can only be constructed on the basis of technical bureaucratic politics, which requires depoliticization as a prerequisite. Wang Hui's understanding of politics is an unbureaucratic mass democracy with direct popular participation. But this sort of radical left-wing politics cannot mesh with the bureaucratic personality of the state. Like Wang Shaoguang, Wang Hui, having eschewed modern representative

---

[54] Wang Hui, "Zhongguo jueqi de jingyan jiqi mianlin de tiaozhan" (The experience of China's rise and its remaining challenges). See also, Wang Hui, "Zizhu yu kaifang de bianzhengfa: Guanyu 60 nian lai de Zhongguo jingyan" (The dialectics of self-reliance and opening: On sixty years of Chinese experience).

democracy, can only find a way for the will of the grassroots masses to manifest as state will at the state level by investing his hope in a political party that can supposedly represent universal interests. But whether in theory or in practice, Wang Hui cannot provide a convincing argument for this, so he winds up resorting to the illusory ideology of the historical tradition of socialism: "Because socialist countries take the representation of the interests of the majority of the people as their basic mission, under market conditions, they are better able than other types of countries to distance themselves from relations with interest groups. Only in this sense can we say that a socialist government is neutral."[55] Modern politics is naturally representative politics; the problem is that there are different modes of representation. In the framework of democratic institutions, both the government and the political party must have the power of representation; first the electors must confer the power on them. As the American political theorist Sheldon Wolin (1922–2015) pointed out, "the basic nature of the power of representation is a process of conferral of power."[56] Without this conferral, how is representation possible? Yet Wang Hui's theory of representation clearly comes from a Leninist "vanguard" theory, which lacks an institutional, orderly conferral of power, and is merely an ideological value statement, a self-conferral to which those who are to be represented have not agreed. And when Wang Hui argues that there is a "neutral state" that represents the universal interests of the people, he has clearly abandoned his radical left-wing critical standpoint and moved toward a conservative Hegelianism. From the standpoint of the radical left wing, politics is the arena of conflicts of interest, and the state is only a dominating force with its own particular interests (whether these interests be those of a particular class or the state's own interests). The Chinese economist Yao Yang (b. 1964) was the first scholar to offer the idea of a "neutral government," and he once warmly praised the Chinese government as a neutral government whose "goals were the pursuit of the long-range interests of the society."[57] More recently, he has affirmed that China is indeed ruled by a neutral government, one that is separate from interest groups and that does not lean toward particular interests.

[55] Wang Hui, "Zhongguo jueqi de jingyan jiqi mianlin de tiaozhan" (The experience of China's rise and its remaining challenges).

[56] Xieerdeng Wolin (Sheldon Wolin), *Zhengzhi yu gouxiang: Xifang zhengzhi sixiang de yanxu yu quangxin* (Politics and vision: Continuity and innovation in Western political thought), Xin Hengfu, trans. (Shanghai: Shanghai renmin chubanshe, 2009), p. 292.

[57] Yao Yang, "Shifou cunzai yige Zhongguo moshi?" (Does there exist a China model?), available online at www.aisixiang.com/data/18839.html.

The problem is that when this neutral government plunders its citizens it does not "ask about their identity."[58]

Wang Hui's theory of the "Party-State that represents the universal interests" received a detailed endorsement from a constitutional-legal standpoint in the arguments of legal scholar Chen Duanhong (b. 1966). Basing himself on the theories of Rousseau, Emanuel Joseph Sieyès (1748–1836), one of the chief political theorists of the French revolution, and Schmitt, Chen distinguishes between two types of powers: the power to draft the constitution and the power to ratify the constitution. The power to draft the constitution is a people's greatest right and political resolution, it is higher than the constitution and is the original will behind the constitution; the power to ratify the constitution is a power granted by the constitution. "The power to draft the constitution is the origin of all rights and powers, and naturally exists through reliance on the existence of the community. It is indivisible and non-transferable. The right to ratify the constitution is derivative and divisible and relies solely on the constitution, it is constrained by the constitution and absolutely cannot encroach on the constitution."[59] Chen Duanhong is a radical. He upholds the sovereignty of the people's thought, believing that this is the highest sovereignty. The power to draft the constitution should be in the hands of the people, and the people have to be in the arena.[60] But in modern politics, the people cannot always be in the arena, in which case they can only entrust representatives to carry out popular sovereignty. In Chen Duanhong's view, the people's representatives are the CCP and the People's Congress, and the People's Congress is under the leadership of the Party. "The CCP was not created by the constitution, but was created by the Chinese people over the course of history. The Central Committee is the permanent representative structure of the people's right to draft the constitution. It is the representative of constitutional rights from the perspective of sovereignty."[61] Thus the theory

---

[58] Yao Yang, "Beijing gongshi de zhongjie" (The end of the Beijing consensus), no longer available online at the site cited by the author. It appears that this is in fact a Chinese translation of Yao's original English-language article, "The End of the Beijing Consensus: Can China's Model of Authoritarian Growth Survive?" *Foreign Affairs*, February 2, 2010, available online (paywalled) at www.foreignaffairs.com/articles/china/2010-02-02/end-beijing-consensus.

[59] Chen Duanhong, *Zhixianquan yu genbenfa* (Constitution-making authority and the basic law) (Beijing: Zhongguo zhifa chubanshe, 2010), p. 133.

[60] See ibid., ch. 2, "Renmin bide chuchang: Lu Suo guanmin maodun de zhexue shitu yu minzhi xuanquan lilun" (The people must be present: The philosophical design of Rousseau's theory of the contradiction between the people and the officials and the theory of the constitutional power of the people).

[61] Ibid., p. 24.

of radical popular sovereignty is transformed into a conservative theory of Party-State sovereignty. The Party-State represents the indivisible, non-transferable, highest sovereignty, transcending the constitution, and Rousseau's insistence that the people must be in the arena becomes the Party-State which is always in the arena.

In today's world of legal studies and political science, more than a few scholars believe in "the unity of the Party-State and the people." Indeed this has become a fashionable current, and the group includes some PhDs who have returned from studying abroad. They use German constitutional theories blindly imported into China, and discuss the legitimacy of China's static political structure in academic, technical terms, arguing that whatever exists is legitimate, and whatever is historical is appropriate. What they oppose are liberal constitutional principles, and in the name of popularly established constitutional powers they take the state's highest powers and bestow them on a super-state power that commands the constitution and the government. European continental theories of constitutional powers from Sieyès to Schmitt are extremely dangerous, because once the sovereign, in the name of the people, has the highest decision-making power, transcending that of the constitution, then authority and power are one, and the untamed horse that is power will no longer be constrained by the reins, and might well run far, far away. From a theoretical perspective, it seems that the will of the people is greater than that of its representatives, but just as Hardt and Negri, the authors of *Empire*, put it: the masses are heterogeneous, the plural expression of individual wills, but the people are always one, with a single will.[62] A unified popular will can only be represented, and the highest decision-making power of the popular will finally becomes the decision-making power of the highest sovereignty.

In comparing the French and American revolutions, Hannah Arendt (1906–75) pointed out that the fatal flaw in the French revolution was the belief that power and authority came from the same source – the people. And the success of the American revolution can be attributed to their understanding that power belonged to the people and authority to the constitution.[63] The republican government of ancient Rome followed Cicero's (106–43 BC) famous saying that power belonged to the people, while authority belonged to the senate. This ancient tradition

---

[62] See Maikeer Hate (Michael Hardt) and Andongniao Naigeli (Antonio Negri), *Diguo* (Empire), Yang Jianguo and Fan Yiting, trans. (Nanjing: Jiangsu renmin chubanshe, 2003), p. 107.

[63] Hannah Alunte (Hannah Arendt), *Lun geming* (On revolution), Chen Zhouwang, trans. (Nanjing: Yilin chubanshe, 2007), p. 149.

of dividing power and authority has developed down to the present day, and has evolved to become the Anglo-American constitutional system in which the power belongs to the people and authority to the constitution. Whether it is the people or the representative government exercising power on their behalf, they all must remain within the norms set by the constitution, and be restrained by the constitution. Chen Duanhong, following Sieyès's theory, divided drafting powers from powers conferred by the constitution. He acknowledged that powers derived from the constitution obey the constitution, but argues that those with the power to draft the constitution had a power with priority over the constitution, which transcended the constitution. The question is whether the will of the sovereign with the power to draft the constitution (regardless of whether it is an abstract people or a concrete "great eternal lawmaker") is a wholly subjective, exceptional power of decision, or is rather under the constraint of the highest law. The so-called highest law is what Arendt called the highest legal principle, above the constitution. In the Anglo-American constitutional system, natural law is the highest law, above the constitution, and later the principles of freedom and justice such as discussed by the American political philosopher John Rawls (1921–2002), which embody a more basic public rationality than the constitution. The authority respected by constitutional powers is the original spirit of the constitution, not the specific legal articles of the constitution: the highest law-making principles, with freedom at their core. Similarly, when the people possessing the power to draft the constitution choose their own style of common political life, they cannot stray from the highest law-making principles, which are the basic principles of the foundation of the state and the soul of the state. An important reason why England could have its Glorious Revolution in 1688, and why America could establish the United States out of a situation of widely diverging interests, was that a basic consensus existed concerning the fundamental principles of nation-building, a commonly recognized highest law-making principle behind the constitution. For this reason they achieved long-term authority and stability. The power to draft the constitution and the powers that issue from the constitution are mutually constraining. In daily politics, the government to which the people bequeath the power to rule must exercise its power under the authority of the constitution. Different powers are mutually balanced according to the standards of a unified constitutional authority, and also limited by shared constitutional principles. In the exceptional period of the drafting of the constitution, while the people have drafting powers that are higher than the constitution, these powers are still not decided willfully; the people's will to decide is not value-neutral, but is based on the value of the people's own highest interests in establishing the constitution, which is the ultimate support for the foundation of the constitution. This is the highest law-making principle, the supreme law, higher than the constitution. The supreme law is also the supreme authority, and constrains as well the people's powers to draft the constitution. The binary division of power and authority can effectively prevent the situation brought about by the unity of power and authority in which "he who has power has authority," or "there is no authority higher than power." Whether this power is in the hands of people with the right to draft the constitution, or in the hands of a government exercising the power granted by the constitution, in the absence of an agreement concerning the supreme law-making principles, this power is a frightening power.

To avoid the corruption of power, in addition to the theoretical constraints imposed by the highest law-making principles, an institutional balance of power is most important: the bad must be used against the bad, power used to constrain power. As the American political theorist Robert Dahl (1915–2014) pointed out: "In the absence of externally imposed constraints and limitations, any established individual or individual group will use tyranny against other individuals or groups. Once all rights and powers (whether executive, administrative, or judicial) are concentrated in the hands of the same few people, this means the elimination of outside constraints."[64] Yet, what Chinese statists most oppose is precisely constraints on state power. In his criticism of constitutional government, Wang Shaoguang says: "'Liberalism' and 'constitutional democracy' put 'freedom' and 'constitutional rule' above the 'people,' which is the equivalent of confining the 'people' to a 'bird cage.' To put it another way, 'liberal democracy' and 'constitutional democracy' are 'birdcage democracy.'"[65] In his view, as long as the rulers respond to the demands of the ruled, and represent the interests of the people, then this is genuine democracy and the power of the rulers should be unconstrained. Still, putting aside the fact that the democracy he is talking about is a form of "responsive authority" with the rulers as the subject, even in a democratic system where all the citizens elect the rulers, in the absence of effective supervision and a balance of power, the power of this democratically elected president will likely always produce "democratic tyranny." Wang Shaoguang once borrowed an idea from Michael Mann (b. 1942), the sociologist and student of social power, and divided state power into foundational power and arbitrary power, arguing that

[64] Luobote Daer (Robert Dahl), *Minzhu lilun de qianyan* (Preface to democratic theory), Gu Xin, trans. (Shanghai: Dongfang chubanshe, 2009), p. 29.
[65] Wang Shaoguang, *Minzhu silun* (Four theses on democracy), pp. 37–38.

centralized power based on democracy can strengthen the foundational power, by avoiding the use of arbitrary power.[66] But whether it is a Russian, Putin-style strongman democracy or the populist democracy of ex-president Chen Shuibian (b. 1950) in Taiwan, they all prove that when freedom as the highest value is missing, and when there is no balance of constitutional power or effective division of power, then even in a democratic system, arbitrary power will increase more quickly than foundational power.

Constitutional government has a double function: first, it grants legitimacy to state power, making a unified state will out of dispersed political forces. This is the function of "out of many, one." In addition, there is also the function of the division of power, or "out of one, many." The state will can be unified through constitutional government, but constitutional government is not strictly necessary, and can be achieved via dictatorship or authority. While dictatorship or authority can effectively make one out of many, it cannot prevent a unified state power from transforming itself into a lawless tyranny. The strong suit of constitutional government is that it can also unify the state will, but it is unified via authority and not power, the authority being the constitutional law. All state power must comport itself within the authority granted by the constitution. The nineteenth-century English idealist political thinker Thomas Hill Green (1836–82) argued that sovereignty possesses the dual aspects of will and power.[67] This suggests that the state will must be unified, but that the power of the state must be divided. Why must power be divided? Why must there be a constitution standing above democracy? In the *Federalist Papers* we find this excellent passage: "If men were angels, no government would be necessary. If angels were to govern men, neither external nor internal controls on government would be necessary."[68] Those who exercise power are ordinary people, not gods, and once an ordinary person is given unlimited, unconstrained power, then he can do great good, but can also do great evil. In the early period of nation-building in America, Madison understood man's dark side and the fallibility of his rationality, and as a result he invented the "birdcage"

---

[66] Wang Shaoguang, *Qumei yu chaoyue* (Disenchantment and transcendence), pp. 125–26.
[67] See Jin Yuelin, "T. H. Gelin [T. H. Green] de zhengzhi xueshuo" (T. H. Green's political theories), in Jin Yuelin, *Dao, ziran yu ren: Jin Yuelin yingwen lunzhu quanyi* (The way, nature and man: The complete translation of Jin Yuelin's English-language texts), Liu Peiyun, ed. (Shanghai: Shanghai sanlian shudian, 2006), pp. 296–97.
[68] Hanmierdun, Jieyi, Maidisen (Hamilton, Jay, Madison), *Lianbang dangren wenji* (The Federalist Papers), Cheng Fengjia et al., trans. (Beijing: Shangwu yinshuguan, 2004), p. 264. Translation taken from www.constitution.org/fed/federa51.htm.

of the constitution, balancing power with power, opposing interest to interest, balancing ambition against ambition.

A constitutional government without division of powers is not a real constitutional government. The "constitutional tradition" left by the Soviet Union is an anti-constitutional "constitutional regime," a dictatorial "constitutional government" without division of powers. All this kind of "constitutional regime" does is grant legitimacy to "dictatorship." And since this is the case, because of the external form constitutional rule has taken on, those who come later will not have to resort to revolution (whether violent or peaceful), will not have to draft a constitution from scratch, but can take the moderate path of the transformation of a constitutional regime, putting new wine in old wineskins. In an existing framework of constitutional rule, after many revisions of the constitution, provided that state will remains unified, one can gradually impose an internal balance of power on state power, and from the "constitutional rule" of a dictatorship implement reforms to arrive at a constitutional rule with division of powers, establishing a limited government, which is what constitutional rule is all about. Arendt noted that the American experience of nation-building illustrates that "division of power does not result in incompetence, but rather produces stable power."[69] There is no incommensurability between an efficient government and a constrained government. A limited government can also be a strong government with excellent administrative capacity.

After the death of the emperor and the disappearance of the heavenly mandate, the only legitimacy available in modern politics is that emanating from the people. The people have replaced the emperor and possess an undoubted secular sacredness. Schmittism, populist democracy, responsive authority – the common point they share is to cleverly borrow the name of the people, falsely borrow the form of democracy, and give the ultimate decision-making power of the nation and the state to a sovereign. This is like the nomination of the pope, or the embodiment of the imperial will. It transcends the constitution and law and possesses unlimited power to draft the constitution and exercise exceptional decision-making power. Any restriction on the sovereign is illegal and constitutes a challenge to the general will, a reversal of the absolute authority of the representative of the people's interests. Although statists in contemporary China have different academic and political backgrounds, they are all worshippers at the altar of the absolute authority of the state.

---

[69] Hannuo Alunte (Hannah Arendt), *Lun geming* (On revolution), p. 252.

The Divinization of State Rationality

The crucial point about the statist current to emerge in China over the past decades is its worship of state rationality. Over the course of recent European history, two traditions of rationality have emerged: Enlightenment rationality and state rationality. Enlightenment rationality's moral values are embodied in the freedom and liberation of the individual. But according to the German historian Frederic Meinecke's (1862–1954) analysis of state rationality, beginning with Machiavelli, the state has been seen as an organic body, like a person possessing its own existential and developmental logic, able to employ any means in the pursuit of these goals.[70] Once the state takes on the highest sovereign form, without external moral norms, then its inner power, like an evil spirit, can reproduce itself and expand outward.

What Chinese statism is searching for is just this sort of state rationality that has thrown off higher moral values. Jiang Shigong says:

> At a basic level, the nature of politics is the domination of the weak by the strong. As Weber put it, a mature politician must have an iron political will and the political ability to seek power, and this is precisely what we mean when we talk about "political power" or about who rules the country. Politicians do not follow any sort of grand moral theory, but rather assume the responsibility and historical mission for all humanity and for history. This is what Weber meant by the ethic of responsibility.[71]

Here, Jiang Shigong displays a superficial understanding of Weber. In fact, in Weber's view, a politician's first principle is power, and not justice; he does not require external norms of religion or morality, because the state has its own rationality.[72] Weber viewed state rationality as the ultimate value determining all political action. State rationality and historical responsibility characterized Weber's political attitudes throughout his life. Germany had a responsibility to the future of civilization, and was destined to become a master race. This was an ethic of responsibility assumed to achieve a certain end, and there were no particular ethical values contained within it. Yet Weber felt a great tension between the ethic of responsibility and the ethic of conviction, a tension which we absolutely cannot find in the Chinese statists. The ethic of conviction

---

[70] See Meinike (Friedrich Meinecke), *Majiyaweili zhuyi* (Machiavellism), Shi Yinhong, trans. (Beijing: Shangwu jinshuguan, 2008).

[71] Jiang Shigong, "Wukelan xianzheng weiji yu zhengzhi jueduan" (Ukraine's constitutional crisis and political decisions).

[72] See Su Guoxun, *Lixinghua jiqi xianzhi: Weibo sixiang yinlun* (Rationality and its limits: Excerpts from Weber's thought) (Shanghai: Shanghai renmin chubanshe, 1988), pp. 32–42.

adheres to a kind of values absolutism, in that people's behavior is responsible only to their motivation, while the motivation comes from a spirit of transcendent value. As long as this accords with belief, all of the responsibility can be shifted to God. But in an ethically pluralistic, secular era, people have been abandoned to an absolutely free world, and which values are reliable, or which values are more important than others, have become important questions. As a pessimistic liberal, Weber wanted to preserve the freedom of choice of the individual, but at the same time he believed in the relativism of values, and consequently all questions become those of individual choice and decisive willpower. What are the critical standards for judging different political choices? Here Weber puts the ethic of conviction aside, and upholds the ethic of responsibility, insisting that the individual has the responsibility to assume the "consequences" of his choice. But this didn't really solve the problem, and instead made it more complicated. What is the critical value of "consequences"? Weber did not provide a clear answer, saying only that the ethic of responsibility similarly requires the support of the ethic of conviction, and that a genuine, decisive person would make choices on the basis of his convictions, even in the absence of the "correct" endorsement of his behavior by a reliable God, and all consequences would have to be assumed by the individual. For this reason, not only did Weber's ethic of responsibility not solve the conflict in values, but instead made it more acute. For Weber, politics is not only an area where different interests compete for domination, instead the whole world is full of battles over values. On the question of ultimate values, Weber is a hesitant nihilist. In his view, the universal bureaucratic system can produce only a shrunken, subservient personality who is indecisive and shirks responsibility. The result of a harsh system demanding account-ability is a widespread inability to assume responsibility, or in other words, people are only responsible to higher authorities, but not for their own behavior or the beliefs that inform them, because bureaucrats have no beliefs. Weber saw the iron cage that the modern universal bur-eaucratic system erected around the personality, and hence placed his hope in a competitive democratic system, yet he was not taken by the inner values of democracy, and instead saw democracy as a systematized space for the conflict of interests and beliefs, out of which could emerge a sacralized political leader who would make political decisions and assume the burden of responsibility for the state. As for which values hold ultimate significance, there was no God to guarantee the choice, so the only choice was to rely on the leader's decisions. Despite these decisions and the assumption of secular responsibility, every few years voters would hold an election and make their own decisions in choosing

a different, competitive leader based on the results of their experience.
Weber's lifelong struggle with values was tragic to this point. He was a
sober realist, and firmly believed, like Nietzsche (1844–1900), in the historical meaning of "God is dead," which left the people with no ultimate
support to rely on; what freedom had brought them were heavy choices
that were difficult to bear. Yet the people also assumed responsibility for
the value choices for which God was originally responsible, and charged
themselves with an ethic of responsibility, taking on the cross of history –
not for God, but for themselves. If an ethic of conviction is concerned
only with responsibility for an objective, then as long as the objective is
good, all means can be employed, regardless of how evil they may be. But
from the standpoint of an ethic of responsibility, the means must also
stand up to an independent ethical test; worldly existence is precisely
this conflict of values, and the moral tension is omnipresent. Weber fully
grasped the paradox between an ethics of responsibility and an ethic of
conviction, and his genuine tragedy was that in a value-relative, polytheistic age, the individual torn between assuming an ethic of responsibility and clinging to his faith does not hesitate to employ the demonic
strength of state rationality to achieve his sacred ends.

China's statists lack the deep tension and tragedy we find in Weber's
thought. They are shallow worshippers of state rationality, a bunch of
ethical nihilists if viewed from the perspective of religious ethics.[73] The
emergence of statism in China in fact is intimately related to nihilism.[74]
Contemporary China's deepest crisis is a crisis of the soul; society as
a whole lacks a basic consensus on values and an ethical foundation.
Once traditional Confucian values were rejected, the Chinese people
lost their focus of identity, after which the nation and the state became

[73] Translator's note: This long passage on Weber, beginning with "What Chinese statists
are searching for," is omitted in the version published online in China, to be replaced by
"is closely related to a values nihilism. Contemporary China's deepest crisis is a crisis
of the soul, and society as a whole lacks a basic consensus on values and an ethical
foundation. With the destruction of the traditional Confucian value system, the Chinese
people lost their object of identity, following which the nation-state became a secular
object of emotional catharsis. And the pressure of the imperialist powers provided the
external historical conditions for this identity with the nation-state. The Communist
revolution established a state ideology aiming for a communist utopia, which during the
Mao era functioned as a substitute for Confucian thought, becoming the universal value
system of the Chinese people. Yet because of the extreme and cruel revolutionary practice during the Cultural Revolution, these values were rejected, and during the period
of reform and opening, China once again experienced a serious crisis of values." The
author can no longer remember exactly why the change was made, but assures me that
it was not because of censorship.
[74] See Xu Jilin, "Zouxiang guojia jitai zhilu" (Toward the altar of the state), *Dushu* 8; 9
(2010), available online at www.aisixiang.com/data/36515.html.

secular objects for emotional catharsis. Imperialist oppression supplied the external historical conditions for this identity with the nation-state. The Enlightenment movement of the 1980s substituted a set of Enlightenment values, but in the 1990s these Enlightenment values were constantly doubted and criticized, thus in the absence of traditional Confucian values and the initial weakening in Enlightenment values, all sorts of nihilistic values emerged in the Chinese intellectual world. Statism availed itself of the opportunity and became an illusory object of identity. Statism is a depoliticized politics, a devaluized value system, a de-ideologized ideology. The state's objectives in terms of values came to be utterly insignificant; all that mattered was the strength of the state itself. But if a strong state is not built on the civilized foundation of freedom, democracy, and the rule of law, then it is a material power and what Weber called "institutional rationality." This kind of high-efficiency, rationalized state has a "high adaptivity," and for this reason Wang Shaoguang views a state's "high adaptivity" as "institutional self-consciousness" and "institutional confidence" opposed by Western democratic systems. He believes that China, as a country with a "highly adaptive system," "can take the form of positive development, what is unfree can become free, what is undemocratic can become democratic."[75] As long as the state is strong, then it seems as if freedom and democracy will appear one after the other, and state rationality itself will become the highest, indeed the only, value. The state will be the highest sovereign, its concrete representatives possessing the highest decision-making power, transcending the constitution or ethical values. Jiang Shigong follows Schmitt's theory, discussing the emergence of opposition groups, and arguing that when the state is faced with a state of exception, the sovereign has supreme decision-making power, surpassing the constitution: "The sovereign is not in the position of obedience to the constitution, but rather that of saving the constitution at critical moments. What the sovereign relies on is not the constitution, but rather a decisiveness that is above the constitution. Political decisions in times of crisis obey the will of God, not the constitution."[76] Although the state's final decisions follow from the will of God, for Schmitt and for the Chinese statists, this God has no values existence, but merely an existence in terms of will. In terms of the content of values, both German and Chinese Schmittists are thoroughgoing nihilists, and once God is dead, then outside of the will to power (the

---

[75] Wang Shaoguang, "Dakai zhengzhixue yanjiu de kongjian" (Open up a space for the study of political science), *Zhongguo shehui kexue yuanbao* 27, January 13, 2009.
[76] Jiang Shigong, "Wukelan xianzheng weiji yu zhengzhi jueduan" (Ukraine's constitutional crisis and political decisions).

state), there is nothing else. The will of the state is thus the will of God, and the will of God is bequeathed to the sovereign in the form of a power of decision that is indivisible and unshared. The question that statism is really concerned with is not which values are good – in their perspective, in a multi-value postmodern society, this is a false question to which there is no ultimate answer – but rather who decides questions of values, who is the sovereign of the highest will – the sovereign with the final decision-making power does not require reasons for his political choices, and transcends all religious or ethical values. As long as he is responsible to himself, then he has assumed the burden of state rationality. Before the supreme sovereign, belief is greater than reason, as is the case before God. God is secularized to become the subject of the state. There is no need for reflection or doubt, only sincere belief.

The state is a man-made god, even if it has replaced God; still, as Schmitt discovered, Leviathan is a synthetic fake, a "god that can die." In his book *Machiavellism*, Meinecke noted that the Hobbesian state has a capacity for self-disintegration, because its self-centeredness and profiteering, no matter how rational, cannot create a social bond out of self-interested, dispersed individuals.[77] A higher moral or intellectual value must be added to state rationality, hence Hegel's (1770–1831) argument over historicism's theory of ends, which makes the state the highest good. Hegel's world spirit must gradually unfold in history, and needs a power like the state as the embodiment of the master of human life. But the ends have themselves become the means, and the world spirit is merely the moral expression of state power. State rationality thus obtains a great moral dignity. This kind of moral self-legitimation of state rationality, compared to the Hobbesian secular state rationality, is even more destructive, and is also the historical source for the evolution of German historicism and its identity of nation and state toward populist fascism.

Today's Chinese statists have also realized that because it lacks sacrality, a Hobbesian secular state rationality cannot ensure long-term stability. Even if the current political order is Hobbesian, their true interest is not in Hobbes, but rather Schmitt, the Schmitt who sacralized state rationality. The state is not only utilitarian, but is also romantic: the state cannot only enrich the people and maintain stability, but has its own inner goodness, its own sacred values. The sacred nature of the state of course no longer has a sacred transcendent source in God or the mandate

---

[77] See Shimite (Carl Schmitt), *Huobusi guojia xueshuo zhong de Liweitan* (The Leviathan in the state theory of Thomas Hobbes), Ying Xing and Zhu Yanbin, trans. (Shanghai: Huadong shifan daxue chubanshe, 2008).

of heaven, but is rather the secular "people's interests" or "Chinese civilization." Because statist thought does not exist in isolation it must also
rely on other "isms" – if not populism then classicism. In contemporary
China, statism, populism, and classicism place the state at the heart of
things, forming a subtle strategic alliance.

Populist statism deifies "the people's interests" and the "popular will."
It views these as the most important bases for legitimacy in modern political life. In the Confucian political tradition, paternalism was itself seen
as being in accord with morality, and for this reason, as long as there
is a state that proclaims itself to be responsive to the popular will and
representing the people's livelihood, it obtains a moral reason for existence. Questions like "how to realize the 'people's interest'?" or "what is
the 'popular will'?" are not really very important. What is important is
the unity of the people and the state and the molding of a sacred state.
Because the state represents the basic interests of the people it sacralizes
itself.

Classicist statism views the renewed rise of Chinese civilization as the
values basis for state existence, and a strong state becomes the vehicle
and the hope for the revival of civilization. In his criticism of Hegel's
theory of the relation between world spirit and the state, Meinecke points
out that the reason Hegel accords such an exalted position to the state
is that "he needed it to realize his vast vision, world spirit in history, and
the fact that world spirit realized itself gradually through history. So he
needed something like the power of the state within history which would
act as the vehicle for the goals of rationality at a particular and obvious
level, and at the same time could also be a vehicle ruling over the life of
all humanity."[78] Similarly, statism also projects the great blueprint of the
revival of Chinese civilization onto the body of a strong state, a state that
will be the means to bring about this cultural revival as well as its vehicle,
upending the question of means and ends, and what they call Chinese
civilization is only the value expression of state rationality, and the state
thereby obtains a moral sacrality.

Contemporary Chinese statists implant Schmittism directly into the
reality of the state, like the main character in the 2010 Christopher Nolan
(b. 1970) film, *Inception*, who implanted his thoughts in the dreams of
his counterpart. They are moving from political anthropology to political
theology, because they are working on two presuppositions about human
nature: one is a theory of self-preservation drawing on Machiavelli and
Hobbes, where each individual seeks to maximize his individual interest,

---

[78] Meinike (Friedrich Meinecke), *Majiyaweili zhuyi* (Machiavellism), p. 510.

and the Leviathan state is the best guarantee for the maintenance of public order and the achievement of individual happiness. The other is the German romantic theory of human nature, in which man has the power of self-creation and self-will, yet the achievement of the self of this organism relies on a state that is fully expressive of national personality. In the context of the statist base in human nature, the first is secular materialism, and the second is a kind of mystical idealism, and the two have come together in a wholly paradoxical manner to form a comprehensive "China model": a strong state exists, which can satisfy the people's need both for safety and a livelihood, at the same time serving as the perfect embodiment of the will of the entire people, which is different from the free creation of the "national personality" in the West. In this way, statism moves from a Hobbesian political anthropology toward a Schmittian political theology, and with the marriage of populism and classicism, statism is increasingly sacralized, and via a romanticized "interests of the people" and "Chinese civilization" will become the secular sources of a sacred state.

The histories of the rise of Germany and Japan illustrate that if state rationality lacks the constraints of religious, humanistic, or Enlightenment values, and if its inner power is allowed to expand, then state rationality can move from a Hobbesian utilitarianism toward a conservative romanticism, and be transformed into a values nihilism lacking in morality. This can finally give birth to a statist freak opposed to humanism and human nature, and the stronger the state, the more state rationality takes itself for granted, and the greater the danger of falling over the cliff.

O state, how many sins have been committed in your name!

3 Universal Civilization, or Chinese Values? A Critique of Historicist Thought since 2000

Translator's Introduction

This essay should be read in tandem with Chapter 2, as the historicist ideas examined by Xu Jilin in this text are closely related to the statist ideas explored in the earlier chapter. The related "choice" between universal civilization and Chinese values is similarly taken up in other chapters. The question is of course central to the crisis of modern Chinese identity triggered by China's fall from the apex of power in East Asian following the Opium War in the nineteenth century and continuing down to the present day: are we unique because we are Chinese, inheritors of a glorious, distinctive tradition, or are we Chinese as part of a shared world civilization?

In this text, published in 2010, Xu examines these questions through the lens of historicism, the body of ideas, German in origin, which emerged in reaction to Napoleon's imposition of Enlightenment ideas on the countries he conquered during the Napoleonic wars. For Xu – and for others, Xu does not claim to have invented these ideas – civilization, part of the Enlightenment, sought to be universal. The values of "liberté, égalité, and fraternité" should reign everywhere because they were "good" values that produced a "good" society. The German reaction, which eventually became a central source of historicism, insisted instead that culture – meaning local culture – was more important than civilization. Each people, defined by the community of the nation, which defined the boundaries of "local" culture, had a connection to its heritage, its soul, expressed through language, literature, and music. For the historicist, "our" values are important and "good" because they are "ours." No objective standard of "good" is possible.

Much of Xu's essay is given over to this history as it evolved in Europe in the eighteenth and nineteenth centuries, which may strike the Western reader as strange: why is a Chinese intellectual recounting this European history? Like most Chinese intellectuals, Xu is committed to the Confucian notion of jiaohua – transformation through education – and thus believes that there is a self-evident value in telling people where ideas come from. Here he is recounting the global origins of the civilizational values he thinks are good. But Xu moves from Europe to China, illustrating, for example, how the postmodern vision, adopted by modern New Left Chinese intellectuals like Zhang Xudong and Wang Hui, who insist that "modernity" is but one particular "culture" "universalized" by the power of capitalism and imperialism, is little different from the vision of German romanticism of the early eighteenth century that he has described. From this perspective, the widespread trend among Chinese scholars to "indigenize" Western scholarship, to "sinicize" the social sciences and create new historical paradigms to describe China's unique trajectory looks to be anything but "new," despite its faddishness. Instead of being "unique," it is a fairly "universal" reaction on the part of late-developers who find themselves at a disadvantage in comparison to stronger "universal civilizations."

Part of Xu's argument aims to pull the rug out from under those for whom China's "uniqueness" is important. Xu's argument is dual. First, claims to uniqueness (or exceptionalism) are a dime a dozen, and in practice can only be upheld through exaggerated "us/them" claims that needlessly create differences and enemies everywhere. Second, in China's case, claims to uniqueness fly in the face of the openness and universality of China's traditional culture, which proponents of China's uniqueness profess to defend. In other words, Xu is arguing that if China was and is unique, it is because of its universality. China's civilization, like that of all great civilizations, contained both local "culture" and universal "civilization," and the way forward for contemporary China must began with a recognition of this historical fact. Xu closes with an embrace of multiple universalisms which calls on China to join to world as a true equal – one who recognizes the equality of the other.

"The river flows east for ten years, and then west for ten years."[1] It would be difficult to find a more accurate way to describe the changes in the Chinese intellectual world. Ten years ago at the turn of the century, a great debate between the Liberals and the New Left on the themes of modernity, freedom, democracy, and justice had just concluded. These two groups, formed out of the divisions of the Enlightenment movement of the 1980s, had engaged in fierce, earth-shaking battles. In the twenty-first century, the internal divisions within Chinese intellectuals are set. Dialogue has become monologue, sarcasm has replaced debate. The decade of the 2000s that just ended was the decade of China's rise; after the 2008 Beijing Olympics and the global financial crisis, China's rise has become a fact acknowledged by the entire world. But what future direction will the risen China take? As a world superpower, what kind of civilizational values will China display to the world?

Against this new historical backdrop, contentious Chinese intellectuals developed a new intellectual focus, the subject being the proper values underlying China's development: should China continue the thirty-year policy of reform and development, uphold humanity's universal values and enter into mainstream global civilization? Or should she seek out unique Chinese values, and provide the world with a different example of modernity? Although this debate between "universal values" and

---

[1] Originally published as "Pushi wenming, haishi Zhongguo jiazhi: 2000 nian laide lishi zhuyi sichao pipan," *Kaifang* 5 (2010). Also available online at www.21ccom.net/articles/sxwh/shsc/article_2010060410790.html. Translator's note: This quotation is taken from *The Scholars*, a famous eighteenth-century novel by Wu Jingzi that pokes fun at scholarly life in China. In the original, the water flowed in each direction for thirty years rather than ten.

"Chinese uniqueness" was sometimes obscure and did not directly play out in the public arena, evidence of the battle could be seen in practically any discussion of China's problems. Behind all the discussions of "Chinese values," the "China model," "Chinese agency," etc., that have been popular in intellectual circles, we find a common theoretical premise, a historicism that is anti-Enlightenment and opposed to universal reason. This historicism of the early new century is vast and mighty, a magnificent spectacle, and has become a notable current of thought in China's contemporary intellectual world.

From the Universal Rationality of the 1980s to the Historicization of the Enlightenment in the 1990s

Particular and universal are always in opposition. Like the relationship of master and slave in Hegel (1770–1831), it is a dialectical existence that takes the other as its precondition. In the past 2,000 years of its traditional history, China stood consistently as a world civilization and a superpower, and in East Asia represented world civilization. This China-centrism was upended in the mid-nineteenth century, following European civilization's conquest of the world, at which point China began to be marginalized, becoming a particular case within universal world history. The struggle of several generations of Chinese from the late Qing forward was to bring about a wealthy and powerful China, a modern universal country like the West. But the founder of New China, Mao Zedong (1893–1976), was strongly opposed to Western universal civilization, and he led an experiment in another kind of modernity that not only overturned European and American capitalist civilization, but also turned its back on the orthodox socialism of the Soviet Union. Mao sought to use China's particular historical and cultural traditions to achieve his goal of national wealth and power and national equality in a Maoist modernity, through the routinization of popular movements powered by a near-religious revolutionary spirit. Mao's achievement, which the New Left scholar Wang Hui (b. 1959) has dubbed an "anti-modern modernity," rejected Western modernity, yet still held universal ambitions that China would chart a uniquely Chinese path by achieving the communist ideals of saving the world's people. These utopian ideas, with implications for the universe, nature, humanity, nation-states and universal laws, could not reach fruition because of the cruelty of their application and their betrayal of basic secular humanism. After the end of the Cultural Revolution, under Deng Xiaoping's (1904–97) leadership, China quickly returned to the path of secularism, opened her doors, and for the second time entered global universal civilization.

From the perspective of intellectual history, the 1980s started in 1978 with the policy of reform and opening, and continued through the early 1990s when the global Cold War concluded. The 1980s were characterized by a second Enlightenment movement, following that of the May Fourth and New Culture movements in the late 1910s and 1920s. From the transcendent world of communism we returned to the universal rationality of philosophy and anthropology. From China's unique path, we returned to universal history with the West at its center. Although in the 1980s we called for the "revival of the Chinese people," the real point of departure was neither the people, nor the country, but rather "humanity," an abstract "humanity" that transcended the particular limitations of concrete races, peoples, or countries. Mao Zedong's Cultural Revolution was understood as a feudal despotism having betrayed universal human nature, and consequently, what the Enlightenment sought was a universal modernity in accord with basic human nature. The legitimacy of modernity comes from the common principles of humanity, not from the interests of a particular people or country or from a single historical and cultural tradition. In the 1980s, the world's measuring-stick served as the standards for the Chinese people, and the world's reality was China's future. A people's values should be weighed in the scales of world opinion. There was of course patriotism in the 1980s, but a kind of cosmopolitan consciousness could be sensed beneath it. If China wanted to carry out a national revival, the most important thing to do was to join world universal history. In comparison, China's particular historical and cultural traditions became negative capital, something to be abandoned in the process of becoming part of universal world history. What Chinese patriots worried about in the 1980s was not "the loss of China," but rather "being cut off from the world," their common concern was how to go from closed off to wide open, from "yellow earth" to "blue civilization."[2] For these reasons, there existed in Enlightenment thought in the 1980s a deeply rooted, unthinking secondary narrative: China versus the world, tradition versus modernity, history versus norms, particular versus universal ... In fact these were all different expressions of the same secondary narrative: "China" symbolized closed-in and backward, a particular tradition that hindered the achievement of modernity; the "world" meant progress and the future, universal values and norms.

---

[2] Translator's note: The references to "yellow earth" and "blue civilization" come from *River Elegy*, a controversial six-part television documentary shown in China in 1988. One of the main arguments of the documentary was that China must abandon its closed, inward-looking focus on the "yellow earth" of China and join the freer, more open civilization of the West, symbolized by the "blue" of the oceans.

This "world" was a model that could be copied, which was precisely Western modernity. With the end of the Cold War in the early 1990s, the Western model seemed unchallengeable. Li Shenzhi (1923–2003), the establishment intellectual turned liberal critic after 1989, remarked excitedly: "The comparisons and choices made in the two or three hundred years since the world experienced the industrial revolution, and particularly the century-long Chinese experiment, the greatest in the history of the world, all provide ample proof that liberalism is the best system, and possesses the most universal values."[3] The curtains closed on the end of the 1980s with the optimistic cry that "history is over."

Compared to the "long" decade of the 1980s, the 1990s were "short." It was short because from every perspective it was a transitional period, bearing transitional characteristics like divisions, combinations, ambiguities, and recurrences. Once the Enlightenment ideas of the 1980s took on discursive leadership – which was also the origin of the subsequent division – there occurred a huge split in the Enlightenment camp whose core value had been universal reason: liberalism came to be opposed to the extreme left, humanistic spirit to market secularism, universalism to nationalism ... These antagonistic binaries that had originally been contained within the same group rapidly crawled out from under the banner of the Enlightenment and set up their own camps, thus setting the stage for the fierce intellectual battles of the 1990s.[4] And every battle undermined the intellectual and practical foundation required by Enlightenment thought for its very existence.

The challenge to the universal Enlightenment narrative in the 1990s came first from the emergence of anti-Westernism. In the new Enlightenment of the 1980s, the West was the world model for modernity, the symbol of the final destination of the universal history of the entire world. But by the middle of the 1990s, with the division of the Enlightenment camp, there occurred a split in the symbol of the West, and in the eyes of the newly arisen extreme left and the extreme nationalists, the Western model became an object to be transcended. Literary scholars such as Zhang Yiwu (b. 1962) and Chen Xiaoming (b. 1959) used the newly imported postcolonial theories of Edward Said

---

[3] Li Shenzhi, "Hongyang Beida de ziyou zhuyi chuantong" (Carry forward Beijing University's liberal tradition), in Liu Junning, ed., *Beida chuantong yu jindai Zhongguo* (The Beijing University tradition and modern China) (Beijing: Zhongguo renshi chubanshe 1998), pp. 4–5.

[4] See Xu Jilin, Luo Gang et al., *Qimeng de ziwo wajie: 1990 yilai Zhongguo sixiang wenhuajie zhongda lunzheng yanjiu* (The self-disintegration of the Enlightenment: Studies of important intellectual and cultural debates in China since the 1990s) (Changchun: Jilin chuban jituan gongsi, 2007), chs. 1–8.

(1935–2003) to re-examine Chinese Enlightenment discourse since the May Fourth movement, and pronounced them to be a "Western orientalism" colonialized in China suggesting that Chinese had come to negate their identity by adopting a Western perspective. They proclaimed that modernity in China was over, and that it should be replaced with a "Chineseness" informed by native consciousness. New Left intellectuals like Cui Zhiyuan (b. 1963) and Gan Yang (b. 1952), who, like many of their cohort, had studied abroad, advocated a "second thought liberation" on the basis of Western "analytical Marxism," "critical legal studies," and "neo-evolutionism." This would allow China to liberate herself from "Western superstition," and would locate a Chinese path that transcended capitalism and socialism via a number of institutional innovations such as "new collectivism." In 1996, anti-Western thought produced the derivative volume, *The China that Can Say No*,[5] venting, in a concentrated fashion, the hateful views of the extreme nationalists toward the West.[6]

As the Western sun slipped below the horizon, the Chinese moon rose in the shadows of the trees. If the atmosphere of the 1980s was one of saying goodbye to the East and moving toward the West, then in the 1990s, as China truly became part of globalization and comprehensively embraced the West, at the same time the West no longer represented ideal universal values, but instead was transformed into a monster that oppressed China. De-Westernization, discovering history in China, efforts to nativize intellectual discourse – these became the new trends in the intellectual world. Even liberals began to rethink binary narratives of the 1980s like "tradition and modernity" and "China and the West," whereupon appeared two revised narratives of modernity: cultural nationalism and cultural liberalism.

As a corrective to the intense anti-traditionalism of the 1980s, cultural nationalist thought, emerging in the early 1990s, is, in a narrow sense, a kind of cultural conservatism, but more broadly describes widespread efforts to nativize scholarship. The cultural conservatism of the 1990s, through a re-evaluation of figures in modern Chinese intellectual history such as Du Yaquan (1873–1933) and other scholars associated with the neo-conservative Xueheng group active in the 1920s and 1930s and a reappraisal the of the activities of China's New Confucians during the

---

[5] Translator's note: Xu calls this volume "derivative" because it mimicked an earlier Japanese volume, Shintaro Ishihara and Akio Morito, *The Japan that Can Say "No"* (New York: Simon & Schuster, 1992), original Japanese version 1991.
[6] On currents of anti-Western thought in 1990s China, see Xu Jilin, "Zai juda er kongdong de fuhao beihou" (Behind the great and empty signals), in Xu Jilin, *Ling yizhong qimeng* (Another kind of Enlightenment) (Guangzhou: Huacheng chubanshe, 2000), ch. 6.

Republican period, newly affirmed the historical value of the theory of reconciling China and the West, in hopes of bringing about a linkage between humanity's universal civilization and the Confucian tradition. Much like Republican-period figures identified as New Confucians, such as the cultural nationalist politician Zhang Junmai (1887–1969), the philosopher and rural reformer Liang Shuming (1893–1988), and academic New Confucians like Xiong Shili (1885–1968) and Mou Zongsan (1909–95), cultural conservatives in the 1990s divided doctrine and institutions into two categories. In terms of institutions, they affirmed basic Enlightenment goals, accepting the legitimacy of the values of democracy and science. The core of their reflection was: how to navigate the passage from the old "inner sage" (Confucian doctrine) to the new "outer king"[7] (democracy and science)? How can traditional Confucian thought respond to and transform modern values? From a broader perspective, what cultural conservatism was seeking was the nativization of Western intellectual discourse: how to draw lessons from China's "local knowledge" to transform the genealogy of foreign social science knowledge into native discourse with Chinese characteristics. No matter whether it was cultural conservatism or the nativization of knowledge, the basic standpoint remained universalism, and they admitted the universal legitimacy of modern values in China, hoping only that after arriving in China it would have special indigenous resources. The moderate cultural nationalism of the 1990s was not like the historicism to be discussed below; its proponents did not prove their own existence through opposition between China and the West. Instead they hoped, by reconciling Eastern and Western civilizations, to bring about a modern universal civilization with Chinese characteristics.

While cultural nationalists sought to link up with modern values, liberals were also looking to nativize themselves. In the 1990s, the political scientist Liu Junning (b. 1961) was an extreme advocate of British-style conservative liberalism. His concern was where liberal Western values might find native resources in China, especially given that liberalism is somewhat lacking in transcendental values. In his view, if liberalism lacked the transcendental values to sustain an indigenous transformation, "then the people will not identify with universal values and their institutional

---

[7] Translator's note: The distinction between "inner sage" (learned person) and "outer king" (person who accomplishes great things in the world) is fundamental to Chinese Confucian cultivation, and insists on the connection between perfectioning the self as a first step toward public service. In an ideal world, one would lead naturally to the other, but in fact, the poles often became choices when positions were not available or when the emperor did not embody Confucian morality. For further discussion, see Joël Thoraval, *Spécificités de la philosophie chinoise* (Paris: Cerf, 2003), pp. 16–18.

forms at the level of belief." He attempted to integrate the Daoist sage Laozi's traditionally Chinese "Way of Heaven" with liberalism, thus imbuing secular universal values with transcendent indigenous sources, developing a kind of "Heavenly Way liberalism."[8] This kind of indigenous transformation of liberalism is similar in essence if different in approach to the cultural conservatism discussed above. The difference is that liberalism takes universal values as its core, and looks for corresponding sources within the Chinese tradition, but these resources have only an instrumental value. By contrast, cultural conservatism upholds the Confucian tradition as an irreplaceable internal value, and seeks to prove that it is not in conflict with modern democracy and science.

Reforms in the 1980s were not really thoroughgoing, and the Enlightenment was a Kantian abstract concept, a kind of rational metaphysics, the notion that things would happen of themselves. In order to become part of the "world," we imagined a "de-sinicization," which would take us through all the barriers tradition had set against modernity. When in the 1990s reforms entered a period of hardship and attack, Enlightenment thinkers for the same reason abandoned their metaphysical studies and returned to the human world, to China's concrete historical context and actual conditions, after which these thinkers had no choice but to "re-sinicize," embracing the study of native Chinese questions instead of abstract value norms. From another perspective, the universal philosophies built by the Enlightenment thinkers were fiercely resisted and attacked in the 1990s by various proponents of postmodern thought, which threatened the very foundation of universal values, and what was left was the spiritual remains of relativism and nihilism. To fill the vacuum created by the decline and fall of universal values, nativist narratives such as "Chinese values," the "Chinese model," and "Chinese agency" began to appear, and after the brief transition of the 1990s, historicist thought majestically entered the scene in the twenty-first century.

The Challenge to Universality: The Rise of Historicism

Historicist thought was a response to the Enlightenment movement. According to the classic work of German historian Friedrich Meinecke (1862–1954), historicism in Europe emerged as an independent stream of thought in the transition between the eighteenth and nineteenth centuries in Germany, even if its roots are as ancient as those of rationalism.

[8] See Liu Junning, "Tiandao yu ziyou" (The way of heaven and freedom), available online at www.comment-cn.net/culture/chinaculture.

Historicism has two core concepts: character and development.[9] From the natural legitimacy of ancient Greece, through the Protestant ethics of the Middle Ages, to secularized Enlightenment rationality – all of these held that historical values were proven objectively and everywhere in nature, in the will of God and in human nature. But historicism believes that there are no objective laws, transcendent will, or universal human nature behind history – history exists only in a particular form, and the nation is the collective expression of this form. In this world there exists no universally valid set of values or universal order transcending history or culture. Instead, all human values belong to a particular historical world, to a culture, a civilization, or a national spirit. The legitimacy of values is determined solely by concrete historical and cultural traditions, and can be judged only from the perspective of people and nations. As the American historian Georg G. Iggers (b. 1926) put it, the point of historicism is to "refute the rationality of the Enlightenment movement and notions of humanism," and "to affirm that man has no basic nature, but only history."[10]

Although China was not the birthplace of the spirit of historicism, the violent force of the Enlightenment movement provoked a reaction to universal reason, as in other non-Western countries, where there appeared various forms of historicism channeling the popular expression of opposition to the universal spirit. Although the cultural conservatism of the 1990s took seriously the historical and cultural traditions of a nation, it did not oppose the universal goals of the Enlightenment, and instead sought to integrate Confucian culture and Enlightenment ideals, as well as locating China's particular path within the universal values of the Enlightenment. But at the beginning of the twenty-first century, historicism placed the Chinese tradition in direct opposition to universal values, and the object of their resistance was not merely the "current West" detested by anti-Westerners, but rather the "ideal West," in other words the universal values represented by the Enlightenment.

As the American political scientist James Schmidt (b. 1932) has pointed out: "The Enlightenment movement is a historical fact in Europe, but the question 'What is Enlightenment?' is without a doubt a thoroughly German question."[11] "What is Enlightenment?" means that the universal

---

[9] See Meinike (Friedrich Meinecke), *Lishi zhuyi de xingqi* (Historicism: The rise of a new historical outlook), Lu Yuehong, trans. (Nanjing: Yilin chubanshe, 2009).

[10] Geaoerge Yigeersi (Georg Iggers), *Deguo de lishiguan* (The German conception of history), Peng Gang and Gu Hang, trans. (Nanjing: Yilin chubanshe, 2006), p. 3.

[11] Zhanmusi Shimite (James Schmidt), *Qimeng yundong yu xiandaixing: 18 shiji yu 20 shiji de duihua* (What is Enlightenment: Eighteenth-century answers and twentieth-century questions), Xu Xiangdong and Lu Huaping, trans. (Shanghai: Shanghai renmin chubanshe, 2005), preface, p. 1.

concern of late-developing countries is their hope to overcome their particular character through Enlightenment, and become universal countries like England and France. What universal countries seek after is not the authentic character of their people, but rather a universal human nature that transcends the nation. Kant's classic answer to the question at the time was to "have the courage to use your own reason." When the question of "What is Enlightenment?" was raised again in China in the twenty-first century, it had already passed through the filter of 1990s postmodern thought, and had evolved from a Kantian-style model definition to a Foucauldian interrogation which asked: "How did history construct Enlightenment discourse?" "How did modernity evolve from European particularity into a universal myth?"

The critique of Enlightenment values began with the deconstruction of the notion of the universality of Western values. Zhang Xudong (b. 1965), a Chinese-born scholar who teaches at NYU, employs the Hegelian dialectic to overturn the received understanding of universality and particularity: "Universality is merely a particular expression of particularity, a transitional expression of particularity ... to put it in terms of Hegelian dialectics, universality is the self-understanding of particularity, but is not its objective truth."[12] So-called universal civilization is a kind of self-proclaimed particular civilization, a transitional, inflated kind of self-consciousness of a particular civilization, and after we return universal civilization to its concrete European context, it is only a particular expression of Western civilization, a man-made historical myth during the period that Western civilization expanded throughout the world. "Beginning with private property, subjectivity, the rule of law, civil society, public space, constitutional rule, step-by-step arriving at international law, the notion of universality finally expands to world history, and ultimately uses the concepts of world history and universality to defend its own particular path and its own particular interests."[13]

This is culture resisting civilization. When English and French thought were transmitted to Germany in the early nineteenth century, the German intellectual elite used German culture to resist Anglo-French civilization. In modern German, "civilization" (*Zivilisation*) means common values and essence belonging to all of humanity, while "culture" (*Kultur*) stresses differences between peoples or ethnic characteristics. The expressions of

---

[12] Zhang Xudong, *Quanqiuhua shidai de wenhua rentong: Xifang pubian zhuyi huayu de lishi pipan* (Cultural identity in the age of globalization: A historical critique of Western universalist discourse) (Beijing: Beijing daxue chubanshe, 2005), p. 14.

[13] Zhang Xudong, "Quanqiuhua shidai de Zhongguo wenhua fansi: Women xianzai zenyang zuo Zhongguo ren?" (Chinese culture reflexion in the age of globalization: How should we be Chinese now?), *Zhonghua dushubao*, July 17, 2002.

civilization are comprehensive, and can include materials, techniques and systems, as well as religion and philosophy, but culture is necessarily spiritual, and does not talk about the existential value of "humanity" in the abstract, but rather about certain values created by particular peoples or ethnic groups.[14] As Iggers said: "The cultural war was between German *Kultur* and Anglo-Saxon *Zivilisation* – an ideology via which the German elite sought to consolidate their ruling power over the German people. There is a stark difference between the German 'idea of 1914' and the French 'idea of 1789.'"[15] The "idea of 1914," Germany's rationale for World War I, grounded in national strength and power, was German historicist culture resisting Anglo-French civilization. From his classicist position, the German-American political philosopher Leo Strauss (1889–1973) saw German historicists as value nihilists, who were lovers of particular national cultures, which they used to denounce the universal civilization of humanity. Strauss's civilization includes not only modern European civilization, but more broadly refers to ancient Greek civilization, whose legitimacy was based in nature. Civilization is a human culture of how people cultivated people, and has an objective foundation in nature; civilization is something that is discovered, not something that is created What German nihilists denounce is not modernity, but rather civilization itself.[16] Civilization has eternal principles that belong to all humanity and can be applied throughout the world. Culture is historicist, and belongs only to particular peoples or ethnic groups, and changes as times evolve. The great battle between culture and civilization is a contention between particularity and universality, the object being to resist universal civilization from ancient times down to the present, and to protect the essential nature of national culture.

From the point of view of Chinese historicists, Western universal modernity posited a Hegelian-style view of historical goals, an inevitable fate that awaited all non-Western nations in the contemporary world, which was to evolve from tradition to modernity, so as to achieve the same homogenized status as universalized Western countries. As the New Left

---

[14] See Nuobeite Ailiyasi (Norbert Elias), *Wenming de jincheng: Wenming de shehui qiyuan he shehui xinli qiyuan de yanjiu* (The civilizing process: Sociogenetic and psychogenetic investigations), Wang Peili, trans. (Beijing: Shenghuo, Dushu, Xinzhi Sanlian shudian, 1998), vol. 1, pp. 61–63.

[15] Geaoerge Yigeersi (Georg Iggers), *Deguo de lishiguan* (The German conception of history), p. 3.

[16] Lieao Shitelaosi (Leo Strauss), "Deyizhi xuwu zhuyi" (German nihilism), in *Sugeladi wenti yu xiandaixing: Shitelaosi jiangyan yu lunwenji* (The question of Socrates and modernity: Strauss's lectures and essays), Peng Lei, Ding Yun et al., trans. (Beijing: Huaxia chubanshe, 2008), pp. 116–18. This appears to be a collection edited by the Chinese, and not a direct translation of an existing book by Strauss.

scholar Wang Hui said: "'Modern,' as a time concept, divides things up so as to exclude other periods from the modern, and in this sense, 'modern' is an exclusivist concept. It excludes other things living in the same time and space, and builds a hegemonic hierarchical structure."[17] The Hegelian-style view of the ends of history, through the chronological ordering of traditional and modern, backward and advanced, collapses all of history into a developmental process with a unified point of destination. All nations in their development will eventually reach a common "sacred moment," which is when they arrive at Western modernity. This modernity that takes the West as its sole model excludes other developmental possibilities and becomes a unitary hegemonic hierarchical structure, so that even if what you seek is a unique Chinese path toward modernity, there is still no way to avoid the overwhelming presence of Western universal civilization. Koyasu Nobukuni (b. 1933), the well-known Japanese scholar of Confucianism, meant much the same thing when he criticized modern Japan's "unique path" as merely "a reflection on modernity from within modern thought." Although one may wish to transcend modernity, finally one winds up falling back into the laws of Western universalism.

How to fight back against the fate of a unitary civilization? Historicism begins by resisting Western universalism and proceeds toward a resistance to all universalisms in the world. Since there are no eternal objective values, and everything changes with the evolution of history, then the only true value is the true character of the nation, the comprehensive national spirit. And since so-called universal modernity is an empty, man-made myth, non-Western nations are right to "think modernity from outside modernity," to follow their own path outside Western modernity. This is plural modernity. Wang Hui argues that "plural modernity on the one hand admits that modernity has a certain inevitability and value, yet on the other insists that in different traditions and societies, different models of modernity have appeared, and one cannot simply dismiss them as traditional modes because of their differences with Western modernity."[18] In the early twenty-first century, the notion of modernity as a unitary civilization experienced a huge change as it was "de-chronologized"; henceforth, there was not one modern sun, but many. The paths toward modernity of different nations and peoples all shared similar values and senses of autonomy, and no value standards existed at a higher level. The Chinese argument for plural modernity clearly was

---

[17] Wang Hui, "'Zhongguo zhizao' yu linglei de xiandaixing" ("Made in China" and another kind of modernity), *Zhuangshi zazhi* 181 (2008).
[18] Ibid.

inspired by the thoughts of Japanese and Korean scholars on the nature of East Asian modernity; scholars such as Sun Ge (b. 1955), a professor of literature who focuses on Chinese relations with East Asia, Wang Hui, and Daniel Bell (b. 1964), a Canadian scholar who defends China's New Confucians, are all familiar with these scholars of East Asian history, and have shifted their research on modernity from Europe and North America to East Asia, and through their work on East Asian and Chinese history and culture. Their work suggests that East Asian modernity does not trace its origins to Western influence, but instead has its own historical origins, out of which developed the East Asian model of modernity, which constitutes a challenge to Western universalism.[19] In this way, the case for universal modernity has been historicized and spacialized.

Enlightenment rationality believes that human nature has an objective existence, and that ultimate moral values and universal principles exist in the world. Yet historicism scorns these universal principles, believing in the creative power of national will to transcend objective limitations. As Meinecke pointed out, the creation of historicism involved an arduous struggle with natural-law concepts in which historicists broke the shackles of natural-law concepts and beliefs concerning the supremacy of humanity and the homogeneity of human nature, and added ideas concerning the fluidity of life.[20] If there is no universal human nature, and no universal principles higher than national will, then each people can rely solely on its own history, culture, and traditions to fully develop its own character and will, and freely create its own national principles. Unlike the civilization of humanity, national culture possesses no objective existence waiting to be discovered within human nature, but instead is the product of choice and the creation of free will. The internal nature of national culture is plural and different, not unified and universal.

This historicism, which worships personality and will, can locate a corresponding tradition of voluntarism in the history of Chinese thought. From the Ming dynasty's Neoconfucian Wang Yangming's (1472–1529)

---

[19] On East Asian modernity, see Sun Ge, *Zhuti lunshu de kongjian: Yazhou lunshu zhi liangnan* (A space to discuss agency: Two difficulties in talking about Asia) (Nanchang: Jiangxi jiaoyu chubanshe, 2002); Wang Hui, "Yazhou xiangxiang de puxi" (Imagined genealogies of Asia), in *Xiandai Zhongguo sixiang de xingqi* (The rise of modern Chinese thought) (Beijing: Sanlian shudian, 2004), vol. 2; Danier Baier (Daniel Bell), *Minzhu xiansheng zai Zhongguo: Dongfang yu Xifang de renquan yu minzhu duihua* (East Meets West: Human rights and democracy in East Asia), Kong Xinfeng and Zhang Yanliang, trans. (Taibei: Zuoan wenhua chuban gongsi, 2009); Danier Baier (Daniel Bell), *Chaoyue minzhu yu ziyou* (Beyond liberal democracy), Li Wanquan, trans. (Shanghai: Sanlian shudian, 2009).

[20] See Meinike (Friedrich Meinecke), *Lishi zhuyi de xingqi* (Historicism: The rise of a new historical outlook), translator's introduction, p. 5.

thought and its emphasis on the "liberation of the conscience," to the
Qing dynasty's Gong Zizhen (1792–1841) and his insistence that "my qi
creates heaven and earth" asserting the power of the self to influence in
universe; from Liang Qichao's (1873–1929) "individualism" to Zhang
Junmai's (1887–1969) "creative national will" – and including Mao
Zedong's destructive and creative "anti-modern modernity" – we can
discover a clear historical genealogy of Chinese historicist thought. Wang
Hui argues that:

Modernity is not a naturally existing, prefabricated thing, but is something that
we create, not a fixed template. And if modernity is something that is created,
that means that we can interrogate the direction modernity takes and the
conditions under which it is created. For this reason, when people describe
different modernities, the idea is to create different values and different modern
orientations.[21]

On the one hand this is a call by China's New Left for a "second thought
liberation," an unrestrained adulation of creativity in thought and
practice; on the other, modern historicists also employ a great deal of
Western theory and approaches as endorsements for their own "Chinese
values" and "Chinese model." The combination of a Lu Xun-like
"appropriatism"[22] with an infatuation with unique creativity can produce
very amusing contrasts. There were similar situations in Japan in the past.
The well-known Japanese political theorist Masao Maruyama (1914–96)
criticized this in his *Japanese Thought*:

On the one hand, the Japanese 'academy' spends its days peddling imported
'products' [i.e., Western ideas and theories], and on the other hand, society has
also created an opposing phenomenon – the worship of "originality." They call
occasional thoughts and piecemeal fragments "originality," according such things
an extreme adulation, which is continually reproduced through the promotion of
the critics and the popular media.[23]

As Iggers pointed out, historicist beliefs are grounded in the will, not
rationality, and the moral order constructed out of the spontaneity of the

---

[21] Wang Hui, "'Zhongguo zhizao' yu linglei de xiandaixing" ("Made in China" and another
kind of modernity).
[22] Translator's note. "Appropriatism" (*nalai zhuyi*) was a term coined by the writer Lu
Xun in 1934 in opposition to the "give-away-ism" (*songqu zhuyi*) which Lu thought
characterized China's dealings with the world, and especially Japan. The notion is to
make careful choices in appropriating from the outside world, to be active and engaged.
See the discussion in Gloria Davies, *Worrying about China: The Language of Critical
Chinese Inquiry* (Cambridge, MA: Harvard University Press, 2009), ch. 1.
[23] Wanshan Zhennan (Masao Maruyama), *Riben de sixiang* (Japanese thought), Qu
Jiangying and Liu Qiubin, trans. (Beijing: Shenghuo, Dushu, Xinzhi Sanlian shudian,
2009), p. 6.

personality and the will paves the way for the relativization of all values.[24] When Chinese historicism launched its challenge to universalism, no longer believing that modernity was grounded in humanity's universal values, or that there were absolute rights and wrongs in human nature, they also from a certain angle illustrated the crisis of values in contemporary China. The direct expression of this crisis is the disappearance of universality, leaving nothing but a vacuum of values, a "vast expanse of empty earth."[25] To paraphrase Mao Zedong, on this blank sheet of white paper, one can draw all kinds of new and beautiful images, and create any number of Chinese brands of modernity. Leo Strauss once noted that for historicists, "the only way to break with existing standards is by creating other standards that are purely subjective. They have no basis outside of individual free choice ... The summit of historicism is nihilism."[26] Itô Toramaru (1927–2003), the Japanese scholar of Chinese literature, once described the Lu Xun spirit as "active nihilism": having seen through the delusion of modern society's values, unlike secular nihilists, he neither simply drifted with the tide nor simple-mindedly defied convention.[27] He was neither a stoic nor a cynic. "Active nihilism" employs Lu Xun's "passerby spirit" and begins in emptiness, but combatively takes action to create a new world.[28] Similarly, when faced with globalized universal civilization, the response of contemporary Chinese historicists was: "No! I believe in nothing!" All they believe in is themselves, their transcendent will to create their own values. And the organism creating these values is not only the active individual, but also the active nation, the national body that is currently creating the miracle of China's rise.

When universal narratives come into question, the true values are found only in the life and the body of the nation, which is precisely China's situation. But then, the question is: "What is China?" Behind the national narratives contained in terms such as "Chinese values," the "China

---

[24] Geaoerge Yigeersi (Georg Iggers), *Deguo de lishiguan* (The German conception of history), p. 25.

[25] Translator's note: A quotation from the famous early Qing novel, *The Dream of the Red Chamber*, by Cao Xueqin, describing the end of the family chronicled in the book, the notion being that everything, no matter how elegant and refined, eventually returns to dust.

[26] Lieao Shitelaosi (Leo Strauss), *Ziran quanli yu lishi (Natural right and history)*, Peng Gang, trans. (Beijing: Shenghuo, Dushu, Xinzhi Sanlian shudian, 2003), p. 19.

[27] Yiteng Huwan (Itô Toramaru), *Lu Xun yu zhongmolun: jindai xianshi zhuyi de chengli* (Lu Xun and theories of the end: The establishment of modern realism), Li Dongmu, trans. (Beijing: Shenghuo, Dushu, Xinzhi Sanlian shudian, 2008), p. 117.

[28] Translator's note: *The Passerby* is a play by Lu Xun, found in his collection *Wild Grasses*. The passerby is himself the central character, who continues to march forward, even if he does not know why, nor where he is going, symbolizing a dogged commitment to continue in the face of difficulties.

model," and "Chinese agency," lies a binary unrecognized until now: a totalized China and a totalized West. In this type of binary construction, China and the West are both abstract symbols of "the other." When a totalized China, as a symbol, is defined by the West, a homogenous West is similarly defined by China. Behind the symbols is an illusory ideology, which takes all of the difficulties of modernity commonly encountered by different civilizations in the process of modernization and simplistically reduces them to conflicts between Eastern and Western civilizations. After a century and a half of openness to the world, in reality there no longer exists a transparent "China" that can easily be distinguished from the West. The West's various civilizations and traditions, from the rationality of the capitalist system, liberal ideas and values, and even Marxist socialist theory, have all come to be deeply embedded in contemporary Chinese reality, and have been internalized as parts of China's own modern discourse and historical practice. Contemporary China is already the half-breed offspring of foreign and indigenous cultures. To obtain a national community unsullied by the West, some extreme nationalists intentionally inflate the binary antagonisms between China and the West, in the hopes of using this resistance to purge the West and to forge a pure, pristine China. A young scholar of philosophy said it thus:

In the past thirty years, Chinese philosophy has accomplished a certain transformation of its agency: from a subject sustained by resistance to a subject engaged in a dialogue. Yet there is a great danger contained in this transformation: in the earnest search to be understood, China has lost its agency at a basic level. Thus I feel even in the dialogue, there must be a consciousness of resistance.[29]

The political best-seller *China is Not Happy*, cooked up by Ma Erdu, the original author of *China Can Say No*, also takes resistance to the West as the primary method of producing "us." With the success of this book there appeared a series of "China" bestsellers – *China Need Not Copy Anyone*, *How Did China Do It?*, *China Has Stood Up* – the whole thing coming together as a splendid "China chorus."

Yet the "China" in this chorus is ambiguous to the point that the existence of this "us" as a national community ultimately relies on the Western "other." Sadder still, in the dialogue with the "other," Chinese subjectivity is lost, and it is only through resistance to the enemy that we can realize our identity as "us." The Chinese legal scholar Jiang Shigong (b. 1967) straightforwardly divides the world into the enemy

---

[29] "Jin sanshinian xueshu zhuangkuang yu 'Zhongguo sixiang' de weilai" (The academic situation of the past thirty years and the future of "Chinese thought"), *Wenhui dushu zhoubao*, December 26, 2008.

and us on the basis of attitudes toward China: "The whole world must either be our friends and support China's peaceful rise, or must be enemies and constrain or dismember China."[30] This kind of identity politics built on dividing the outside world into "enemy and friend" requires as a prerequisite high internal levels of uniformity and coercion. When we resist the "other," there is an enemy, but the "us" that is the subject is unclear, and we only arrive at a temporary self by relying on the "other." Even if there are certain values in antagonism with the West, it all remains an indistinct, unreflexive national uniformity. Naoki Sakai (b. 1947), a Japan-born professor of Asian Studies at Cornell University, once criticized the Japanese critical intellectual Yoshimi Takeuchi's (1910–77) resistance to the West in the following terms: "To oppose the Western invasion, the non-West must unify as national subjects. The heterogeneity existing outside of the West can be organized as a stubborn form of resistance to the West. A nation can use heterogeneity to oppose the West, but within that country, uniformity must be given pride of place."[31] But this homogeneity is a false, weak uniformity, and this "China" is mysterious and formulaic. At a time when universal values are relentlessly historicized and contextualized, the China as conceived by the historicists possesses in fact merely an empty sense of sovereignty. Beyond political sovereignty and economic sovereignty, does China have any cultural sovereignty, any academic sovereignty? The national and state consciousness of sovereignty constructed after the modern period is sustained almost completely by a "Chinese agency," whose value content has been largely hollowed out. As a civilization and empire, traditional China's subjectivity was sustained by Confucian civilization; aside from sovereignty, what sustains today's China's "subjectivity?" When there are diplomatic, political, or cultural conflicts with the West, China has difficulty coming up with a narrative of values to explain herself, falling back on a crude statement that "this is China's sovereignty and China's internal governance" to stave off criticism from outside. A "subjectivity" that discusses only sovereignty and ignores civilization deeply marks China's own crisis of identity: a great civilization with 5,000 years of history, after a century and a half of struggle has morphed into a "purely sovereign" nation without civilizational content.

[30] Jiang Shigong, "Wukelan xianzheng weiji yu zhenzhi jueduan" (Ukraine's constitutional crisis and political decisions), *21 shiji jingji baodao*, December 15, 2004.
[31] Jiujing Zhishu (Naoki Sakai), "Xiandaixing jiqi pipan: Pubian zhuyi yu teshu zhuyi de wenti" (Modernity and its criticism: The question of universalism and particularism), available online at www.douban.com/group/topic/70645645/.

Fighting for Universality in the Context of China's Rise

The year 2008 was very important for both China and the West. Beijing successfully staged the Twenty-Ninth Summer Olympics with an unprecedentedly stunning opening ceremony and a gold-medal harvest that surpassed that of the United States. And as the world marveled at China's rise, a financial crisis exploded in the United States and went on to roil the entire planet. While countries everywhere experienced negative growth, things remained rosy in China, where, buoyed by strong government investments, GDP achieved its 2009 growth target of 8 percent. China rapidly strode onto the world's center stage, and according to some Western analysts, if trends continue, will displace the United States by 2050 to become the world's superpower.[32] If, prior to 2008, the scenario was that "the world discovers China," after 2008 it changed to that of "China rises in the world." This huge and rapid change also produced a subtle psychological change in China's intellectuals, who were already oriented toward historicism. Not long before they had been timidly discussing the particular experience of China's modernity; now their tone grew more arrogant, and the "Chinese experience" previously described by Deng Xiaoping as a pragmatic matter of crossing the river by feeling the stones, now was elevated to a systemic "China model." This model not only corresponded to China's particular national character, but also evolved into something big enough to stand toe to toe with the West as an alternative modernity and the newest model that could be emulated by non-Western countries. In the past, "Chinese exceptionalism" served to resist the attacks of universal values. Now, the exceptional became universal, and the "China model" set sail for the international stage to seize the discursive power of global civilization.

The description offered by Pan Wei (b. 1960), a well-known professor of international relations, was most apt: "The Cold War was the first time in history that a battle of life or death between great civilizations was fought on ideological terms. The history of the Cold War proves that success or failure in terms of a battle of political systems is the key to the rise and fall of civilization."[33] In other words, the reason that the USSR lost in the Cold War conflict between the USA and the USSR was not because of military preparedness, but instead a loss of discursive authority. First,

---

[32] See Mading Yake (Martin Jacques), *Dang Zhongguo tongzhi shijie: Zhongguo de jueqi he Xifang shijie de shuailuo* (When China rules the world: The rise of the Middle Kingdom and end of the Western world), Zhang Li and Liu Qu, trans. (Beijing: Zhongxin chubanshe, 2010).

[33] Pan Wei, "Ganyu Xifang zhankai zhengzhe guannian douzheng" (Dare to engage the West in struggles over political concepts), *Huanqiu shibao*, January 28, 2008.

the Soviet intelligentsia was conquered by the West, and subsequently the ruling groups were also conquered, leading in the end to collapse and surrender at the level of ideas, and the whole nation fell into the despair of failure. Pan Wei anxiously observed: "If China collapses in the future, if the China model fails, this may well begin with the question of political discursive power; we might fail because people told us over and over again that we were going to."[34] He cited Huang Ping (b. 1958), a Chinese sociologist who works on the United States, to the effect that: "Our country has solved the problem of being beaten and being starved; now the problem is that of being cursed." Because discursive initiative is in the hands of the West, everything China does is wrong. Pan Wei suggests that China should wage discursive warfare against the West in the field of ideology: "First, we must tear down so-called 'universal' values, decrying the 'emperor's new clothes,' exposing the absurdity of this panacea. Second, we must truthfully sum up China's manner of existence, and export it as a 'Chinese path' or a 'China model,' a narrative or a theoretical explanation that will convince the intellectual world." In the past few years, many explanations of the China miracle and the China model have appeared. Joshua Cooper Ramo (b. 1968), an American journalist and business consultant, proposed the so-called "Beijing consensus," arguing that China's developmental model differs from the neoliberal "Washington consensus," and possesses its own characteristics that can be promoted throughout the globe. The Beijing consensus consists of building on one's own experience; instead of blindly following the West, other countries should continually innovate and experiment as they pragmatically "cross the river by feeling the stones," seeking out economic development that is sustainable and expandable; domestically, the government is permitted to guide the market, while internationally it remains determined to protect its financial sovereignty.[35] Pan Wei's version of the China model is a social model where the officials and the people are integrated in an organic harmony, a political model "with its base in the people" where one party represents the masses and exercises political power, and an economic model where state enterprises direct the "citizens."[36] The New Left economist Yao Yang (b. 1964) argues that the China model has four chief characteristics: centralized government,

---

[34] Ibid.
[35] See Qiaoshuya Kupo Leimo (Joshua Cooper Ramos), "Beijing gongshi" (The Beijing consensus), in Huang Ping and Cui Zhiyuan, eds., *Zhongguo yu quanqiuhua: Huashengdun gongshi haishi Beijing gongshi?* (China and globalization: Washington consensus or Beijing consensus?) (Shanghai: Shehui kexue wenxian chubanshe, 2005).
[36] Pan Wei, "Zhongguo moshi, Renmin Gonghehuo de chengguo" (The Chinese model: Sixty years of success of the People's Republic), *Lüye zazhi* 4 (2009).

decentralized finances, a new democratic path, and a pragmatic party.[37] Zhang Weiwei (b. 1957), a specialist in international relations and most prolific defender of the China model, identifies eight experiences behind China's success, including a focus on popular livelihood, the notion of government as a necessary virtue, the conviction that good governance is more important than democracy, and that legitimacy must be based in performance, among others.[38]

All of these varied "China models" exhibit a full-blown statist commitment to wealth and power as ultimate goals. In recent years, certain developments in the intellectual world have been worthy of attention: nationalism has evolved from moderate cultural conservatism to extreme political conservatism, and an anti-modern Straussianism has worked hand in hand with an embrace of Carl Schmitt's ideas exalting the rationality of the state. The extreme left wing has moved collectively to the right, toward an identification with the statism of the current ruling order. The emergence of statism is intimately linked to historicist thought, and philosophical historicism has evolved into political statism, as there exist surreptitious local connections between the two.

Historicism rejects the universal reason of the Enlightenment, and does not acknowledge the existence in the world of universal human nature or eternal principles. Everything is determined by time and place, historical and cultural changes vary throughout the world, and for this reason individualism is one of historicism's core principles. But historicism's individual is not the atomized individual found in liberalism, and is instead the ego of a larger whole, a "true ego" such as defined by this larger whole. In his study of Fichte's[39] notions of individualism, Isaiah Berlin (1909–97) pointed out that Fichte's ego was not the same as Kant's moral autonomy, and instead his isolated self morphed into the true subject, the ego existing merely as an organized part of the larger model, the collective ego of a nation or a state. "The self-determination of the individual has now become the realization of the collective ego, and the nation has become a community forged via a unified will."[40] The historicist individual is not merely an individual but more importantly an individual who lives for the collective – the

---

[37] Yao Yang, "Shifou cunzai yige Zhongguo moshi?" (Does there exist a China model?), available online at www.21ccom.net/newsinfo.asp?id=6112&cid=10342300.

[38] Zhang Weiwei, "Zhongguo chenggong beihou de bage linian" (Eight concepts behind China's success), available online at http://theory.people.com.cn/GB/10158261.html.

[39] Translator's note: Johann Gottlieb Fichte (1762–1814) is seen as the founder of German idealism, intimately linked to historicism.

[40] See Yisaiya Bolin (Isaiah Berlin), *Ziyou ziqi beipan* (Freedom and its betrayal), Zhao Guoxin, trans. (Nanjing: Yilin chubanshe, 2005), pp. 68–71.

nation. Compared to the abstract individuality and universal reason at the center of Enlightenment rationality, historicism is more concerned with the individuality of different nations and states. Nations and states possess a double character: in the context of humanity at large, they have a unique individuality; while in the context of their own citizens, they are a community possessing a common culture and a common will. Since the state is a unique, free individual, it can obey the principles proper to that state's rationality, having no need to respect the universal values of humanity. From another angle, as the highest moral unit, representing the citizens' true, complete public interests, the state possesses a moral mission that all citizens must obey as part of their "true ego." In this manner, historicism begins by praising individuality, but finally winds up in a mysterious posture of organic obedience to the state; it begins with resistance to the universal rationality of the Enlightenment, and ends by pledging allegiance to the spirit of state power.

German historicism already traveled down this road in the early nineteenth century, and historicism in early twenty-first-century China is repeating Germany's errors. In the 1990s, the writer Mo Luo (b. 1961) was a reasonably influential Nietzschean individualist in the literary world, but in his recent and controversial *China Has Stood Up*, published in 2010, he has been "transformed" into a rabid anti-Western statist. He describes his intellectual "transformation" as follows: "In the past I shouted at power from the perspective of the little people; now I shout at strong Western nations from the perspective of a relatively low-level country."[41] When individuality is based on willpower and finds nothing to support its self-belief, because of an emptiness of values, then the individual turns to a larger "individuality" – an allegiance to a comprehensive nation and state. Moreover, all of this is done in the name of the weak opposing the strong, but in this instance the goal of opposition shifts from power at home to power abroad, and in the process strangely winds up identifying with the strong domestic power that was once the object of opposition. All of the narratives of the "China model" discussed above seek to locate a national "individuality" different from the West and consistent with China's history and current reality, through resisting the West and rejecting universal values: either a custodial authoritarian politics, with a Confucian exterior and a Legalist interior, discovered in post-Qin traditional history; or perhaps a path to wealth, power, and modernity derived from China's sixty-year experience of national

---

[41] Yang Shi, "Mo Luo qingsuan Mo Luo: Cong ziyou zhuyi xiang minzu zhuyi qiaoran diaotou" (Molou destroys Molou: His abrupt U-turn from liberalism to nationalism), *Zhongguo xinwen zhoukan* 9 (2010).

construction. Either would allow China to proudly proclaim to the out-side world: "Stop using universal values to talk about China! China has its own unique democracy, its own unique constitutional government, its own made-in-China modernity!"

Chinese historicism not only opposes Western values, it also refuses to acknowledge even those universal values endorsed by different civilizations. Chinese historicists insist that the values of various nations have no common measure, and that every country has its own unique modernity. As a result, modernity loses its universal, established values, and the only remaining contents to be affirmed are a nation's wealth and power as measured by its GDP and Max Weber's institutional rationality. What Mao Zedong's "anti-modern modernity" affirmed was a Legalist-style rich country–strong army type of modernity, and what it rejected was the institutional rationality of modernity. Deng Xiaoping's reformist line inherited Mao's understanding of modernity as wealth and power, insisting that development is a necessary path, but at the same time adopted a consensual strategy that transcended ideological divisions and emphasized an institutional rationality that accords with Western theories. Weber's institutional rationality means using instrumental rationality to organize all of society through cost-analysis accounting and impersonal bureaucratic management, or in other words, universal company-style management. This kind of institutional legitimization eschews values and politics in favor of rational reforms that aim to increase efficiency and control. This legitimacy can be integrated into any political system, including liberal constitutional regimes as well as modern authoritarian systems. When statists abandon modern universal values and throw out the ethical principles and chief institutional components of modernity, their remaining idea of modernity is only one of wealth and power and value-neutral institutional rationality. This kind of modernity without values and politics is merely a means to an end, a modernity without values.

Western modernity is a civilizational composite containing many contradictory elements. Wealth and power versus freedom and dem-ocracy, the will to power versus respect for the individual, capitalist rationality versus received tradition, statism versus internationalism ... A tension has always existed between these binaries born of internal struggle over the course of modern Western history. Wealth and power and Enlightenment can be said to represent different faces of Western modernity. In the early period of capitalist development, a modernity based on wealth and power with materialism and statism at is core suppressed Enlightenment values, and led to the spread of colonialism and the World Wars, among other evils. As Meinecke pointed out:

The emergence of the German national personality of the Hitler period was made possible by the incessant transmutation of the power of the soul since Goethe (1749–1832). We can understand this as a disruption in a spiritual equilibrium between reasonable and unreasonable power. On the one hand there was an exaggerated development of a calculating intelligence, and on the other an emotional desire for power, wealth, and safety. Consequently, the will that determines behavior was driven into dangerous territory. Anything that technically helped calculations and could be realized, as long as it brought wealth and power, was regarded as having been proven right – right even in a moral sense, as long as it could serve the interests of one's own nation.[42]

When a nation no longer possesses a spirit of universal values that governs its country's behavior, and seeks only to maximize its own interests, the ethical question "what is good?" is replaced by the positional question "what is ours?" and the demonic elements in the national soul can take on unlimited dimensions, and diverge from the path of modernity.

When Chinese statists reject the West and pursue China's unique path, they employ the most Western of methods to realize what they take to be Chinese ideals. They reject the precious universal values of Western civilization, and adopt the West's most savage emphasis on wealth and power. In 1941, Japan launched the Pacific War in the hopes of supplanting the West, a goal that Koyasu Nobukuni described as follows:

Can this Asia, an antagonist born out of the universal pretensions of "modern" Europe, escape "modern" principles? Is not the fact that this antagonist can climb onto the stage of world history precisely the result of the development of modern European world history? And is not what made Japan into the strongest antagonist precisely that Japan successfully accepted the basic necessities of the principles of European statehood?[43]

Naoki Sakai criticized Japan's ideology of "transcending modernity" in this way:

What they opposed was that in the Eurocentric world system, the Japanese supposition of unity had, coincidentally, been relegated to a position outside of the center. And what they hoped to bring about was a situation where the world would change so that the Japanese occupied the center and a position of agency so that they could use Japanese notions of universal standards to decide on other particularities. In order to achieve this goal, they were willing to praise any Western thing that conformed to the structure of the modern nation-state, even if

---

[42] Meinike (Friedrich Meinecke), *Deguo de haojie* (The German catastrophe), He Zhaowu, trans. (Beijing: Shenghuo, Dushu, Xinzhi Sanlian shudian, 1991), p. 87.

[43] Zian Xuanbang (Koyasu Nobukimi), *Dongyalun: Riben xiandai sixiang pipan* (The theory of East Asia: Critique of modern Japanese thought), Zhao Jinghua, trans. (Chuanchun: Jilin chubanshe, 2011), p. 236

in so doing they were far distant from any anti-Western determination and were simply following the will to arrive at modernity."[44]

Here, the path to modernity naturally refers to a modernity of wealth and power without values and ethics, and which for this reason could create a high-level unified national will uniting the nation and the people. Contemporary Chinese statism is also like this. Even as they reject the Enlightenment values created by Western civilization, they at the same time embrace the most frightening modernity of wealth and power. On the face of it they are confronting the West, but in fact as they fight their battles they become spiritual slaves of the West, spiritual slaves most lacking in civilized values.

Behind the modernity of wealth and power lies a deep nihilism of values. The values of different modernities have nothing in common, spiritual values and political civilizations are all unique, there is no "universal" worth discussing; the only universals are material power and institutional legitimacy, where comparisons are possible through quantitative calculations and practical efficiencies. It's a winner-take-all fight. Once God is dead, the spirits of various ethical virtues fall into a perpetual battle, and there is no longer any ultimate value ruling over them. As Iggers criticized German historicism: "History is no longer a meaningful process, and instead becomes a field of value conflict where no resolution is possible ... Weber left us a dangerous legacy, because while he scrutinized the original intent of all values, he avoided scrutiny of the most worshiped idol of the entire tradition, which was the idol of the state."[45] Mo Luo once opposed this, but his bones are now shrouded in the shadow of nihilism: "Feelings of existential emptiness and spiritual falsehood paralyzed me. Feelings of loss and sadness kept me from breathing ... When I confronted the loneliness of my soul, I came to doubt at a basic level the importance of concepts like 'humanity,' 'life,' 'truth,' 'justice,' 'value,' etc."[46] When the vast emptiness oppressed him with its crushing loneliness, he buried himself in the bosom of statism, and found his salvation in the illusion of patriotism: "When the state becomes the basic organizing principle in human society, then standards of and distinctions between the statesman and the criminal, the sage and the devil, are unrelated to individual morality. All one cares about it

---

[44] Jiujing Zhishu (Naoki Sakai), "Xiandaixing jiqi pipan: Pubian zhuyi yu teshu zhuyi de wenti" (Modernity and its criticism: The question of universalism and particularism), available online at www.douban.com/group/topic/70645645/.

[45] Geaoerge Yigeersi (Georg Iggers), *Deguo de lishiguan* (The German conception of history), pp. 223–24.

[46] Mo Luo, "Xiezuo de xiandu" (The limits of writing), in Mo Luo, *Chiruzhe shouji* (Notes of one who is ashamed) (Hohot: Neimenggu jiaoyu chubanshe, 1998), p. 466.

is which nation's interests are being served, which nation's life is being harmed. In simple terms, this standard is actually what we call 'patriotism.'"[47] Among the ruins of ethical values, there is nothing aside from national will, and the national interest becomes the only embraceable value. In such a manner, historicism slips gradually from relativism into nihilism, and finally into the bottomless abyss of statism.

While one group of historicists seeking wealth and power slips into statism, another group of humanistic historicists transcends the modernity of wealth and power and seeks to rebuild Chinese civilization so as to seize back universal discursive authority from the West. The first to do this consciously was Gan Yang. As early as 2003, Gan Yang proposed that China should evolve from a nationalist country to a civilized country. His idea of a "civilized country" was not one that had accepted universal civilization," but rather a "de-Westernized" Chinese civilization. Taking Turkey as his example, he argued that if a country follows the West, destroying its own national cultural tradition, then this is a "self-castrating form of modernization" which finally can produce only a "self-dividing country." Gan Yang argues: "I believe that China will opt for the path of 'modernization but not Westernization.' China is not an ordinary little country. China's long history of civilization means that it is a great country with 'civilizational desires,' a great country with its own 'civilizational interests.' For this reason China will not be satisfied to be a third-rate country like Turkey, nor will it be satisfied to be a vassal of the West."[48] In the cultural conservatism of the 1990s, the goal of reviving Chinese civilization was solely to protect the particularity of national culture. By contrast, in the 2000s, against the backdrop of China's rise, those working to revive Chinese civilization nourished a strong "civilizational desire" to seize universalism from the West. Zhang Xudong says: "If today we raise the question of 'Chinese values' in a globalized perspective, the point is to place these 'Chinese values' within the framework of 'universal civilization' and continue the reflection there."[49] In his view, there is no tension between Chinese values and universal values, because the West has no patent on universal values, and "Chinese values" are necessarily an organized part of "mainstream world values." The meaning that should be accorded to "Chinese values" is that neither in theoretical nor philosophical terms do we acknowledge that

[47] Mo Luo, *Zhongguo zhanqilai* (China stands up) (Wuhan: Changjiang wenyi chubanshe, 2010), ch. 7.
[48] Gan Yang, "Cong 'minzu guojia' zouxiang wenming guojia" (From a "nationalist country" to a civilized country), *21 shiji jingji baodao*, December 29, 2003.
[49] Zhang Xudong, "Zhongguo jiazhi de shijie lishi shiming" (The world-historical mission of Chinese values), *Wenhua zongheng zazhi* 1 (2010).

Chinese practice must accept any *a priori* existing frame of reference. The realization of Chinese values is a historical experience with universal significance, a revolutionary collective act of "destroying the old world and building the new,"[50] in the words of the famed Cultural Revolution poster.

In that case, how should we carry out the revolutionary experiment of "Chinese values," and return to the mainstream of world universal civilization? If the extreme left-wing historicists emphasize the fight between China and the West, and strive to use the agency of Chinese values to bring down the hegemonic power of Western civilization, then the classicists pay more attention to the battle between ancient times and the present day, hoping to use Chinese and Western classical values to criticize and transcend a modernity that descends ever further into crisis. In their view, the core of the struggle between China and the West is the struggle between ancient times and the present. Contemporary China already identifies completely with Western modernity, and if we want to save modernity from the dead-end road on which it finds itself, the important thing is to respect nature and the way of heaven, to return to the classical traditions of ancient Greece and pre-Qin China. The Chinese and Western classicism emerging in the 2000s is completely different from the cultural conservatism of the 1990s. Although the latter was in pursuit of the particularity of Chinese culture, it did not entertain doubts about the legitimacy of universal values. By contrast, the classicists of the 2000s no longer acknowledge the legitimate basis of modern civilization, and their goal is to remake modern society by returning to the classics, thus creating a classical anti-modern "modernity." A group of young Chinese classicists puts it like this: "The Chinese intellectual tradition, with its core in the rites and music of the Xia–Shang–Zhou Three Dynasties period (roughly 2100–210 BC), and which has evolved for several thousand years without disappearing, continues at an important level to provide the basic vision of how we pursue the good life. From a historical perspective, China's modernity is not a separate civilization outside of China's classical civilization."[51] And this path to civilization with Chinese characteristics "is not the original 'Chinese path' associated with 'Chinese characteristics,' but is a universal path discovered by China."[52] What the 1990s cultural conservatives were

[50] Ibid.
[51] Zhongguo sixiang bianweihui (Committee on Chinese Thought), "Zhongguo sixiang congshu yu jikan zongxu" (General preface to the Chinese thought collection and periodical), *Wenhui dushu zhoubao*, December 26, 2008.
[52] Chen Yun, "Tianxia sixiang yu xiandaixing de Zhongguo zhi lu: Zhongguo wenti, Zhongguo sixiang, Zhongguo daolu lungang" (*Tianxia* thought and the path forward for

hoping for was merely a particular Chinese modernity that would be sanctioned by universal civilization; what the classicists of the 2000s are seeking is a new civilization that coincidentally will be "discovered in China" and that will have universal value for the entire world. Western domination of the East is yesterday's news. The "Chinese century" in which the East will dominate the West is fast approaching.

In dealing with questions relating to Chinese and Western civilizations, Chinese historicists have adopted a position with double standards: on the one hand they criticize the West as being a particular civilization with false pretensions to universality, and on the other they view their own civilization as having universal merits from the outset. This pragmatic double standard is without a doubt a subconscious "clash of civilizations" designed to "distinguish myself from the enemy," as Schmitt counseled. Is civilization universal or particular? The answer clearly cannot be based on a method of "distinguishing myself from the enemy." All high-level civilizations throughout the world possess a double nature. From the perspective of historical genealogy, they all are linked to particular social and cultural traditions, which serve as the historical conditions for their production and development, and in this sense all civilizations are particular. But from the perspective of the comparative contents of civilizations, no matter if it's Christianity, Islam, Hinduism, or the humanistic Confucian civilization, none insists on a particular national personality, and all address humanity's questions from a universal perspective grounded in God, the universe, nature, or society. And all high-level civilizations possess internal universal values. From the time of the emergence of the axial civilizations, all high-level civilizations that have developed in particular cultural contexts have sought to break through the particularities of regionalism, to arrive at a universal nature in the world that transcends their own people and nation. Because different civilizations contain common universal concerns, they can engage in deep dialogues and carry out a "blending of horizons" among and between civilizations.

"Reaching the Same Goal by Different Routes"; "Parting Company"; "Many Expressions of the Same Principle"

There are two extreme tendencies in contemporary Chinese thought. One is the fundamentalist proposition that "there is one civilization," which believes that the paths to modernity followed by the various

modern China: Chinese problems, Chinese thought, and an outline of the Chinese way), *Sixiang yu wenhua* 8 (2008).

countries and peoples of the world are "different routes to the same end."
The 10,000 rivers flow together regardless of whether they pass through
yellow soil, red soil, or black soil – they all eventually converge at the
"blue civilization" of the West. In this view, China's future has only one
path, the path toward universal modernity represented by the West. In
complete disaccord with this is the historicist theory of the "relativity
of civilizations." Those who hold this view argue that given differences
in the paths to modernity followed by different peoples and countries,
and given differences in national character and culture, all possess their
own values and cultures possess no common standards. There is no
universal civilization experienced by peoples of different cultures, and
the model for globalized modernity is not "different routes to the same
end" but rather "parting ways." You take your thoroughfare, I'll take
my single-plank bridge, and we have little in common to discuss. The
New Confucian Wu Zengding (b. 1971) believes that "Each civilization
is destined to be misunderstood, nor can it accept the highest ideals of
other civilizations. Between civilizations there are no so-called universal
values, because any 'universal value' is universally valid only within that
culture and once it leaves its natural frontiers, it is destined to become a
dignified excuse for the pursuit of expansion or conquest."[53] Whether it
is the "different routes to the same end" of the "theory of a single civilization," or the "parting of the ways" of the "theory of civilizational relativism," both arguments require further discussion.

   Orthodox liberalism sees the West as the universal model of civilization. This Hegelian argument for the unitary development of civilization led to the Russo-French political thinker and statesman Alexandre
Kojève's (1902–68) criticism of the unattractive "homogenous universal state," in which the plural culture and the richness of different
peoples would be thoroughly destroyed by a homogenous unitary civilization. Universal civilization truly does exist, but there are two different
understandings of it. In his *The Clash of Civilizations and Remaking the
World Order*, Huntington clearly distinguished between two narratives
of universal civilization: one is the analytical framework of the ideology
of the Cold War or the binary "tradition versus modernity," in which
universal civilization is explained as a civilization with the West as the
model and which non-Western countries all had to emulate. The other
is a framework containing multiple civilizations, where universal civilization refers to public values commonly recognized by various civilized

---

[53] Wu Zengding, "Quanqiuhua shidai de Zhongguo wenming" (Chinese civilization in the
age of globalization), available online at www.chinareform.org.cn/open/view/201010/
t20101010_45827.htm.

entities and communities of culture, as well as certain social and cultural institutions that are commonly acknowledged and reproduced.[54] Prior to the mid-1990s, while the intellectual world was still fumbling its way between Cold War thought and models of modernity, Eurocentrism truly dominated the innocent souls of the Chinese. In the past decade and more, following the rise of "rethinking modernity," the notion of universal civilization has experienced an internal transformation. The West is like the East, and is nothing more than one among many particular civilizations. What we call universal civilization is a composite built out of common features of different particular civilizations, the basic values permitting humanity to achieve peaceful coexistence and healthy development. Universal civilization is not a fixed, unchanging state, but instead evolves with the times and with the addition of more civilizations, which means that its contents are in a perpetual process of reconstruction. Universal civilization is dynamic and historical, and not marginal or ambiguous, not something that can be willfully interpreted or developed. In the face of the decline of transcendent notions like God or the mandate of heaven, universal civilization continues to bear the deep imprint of the Enlightenment, and civilization serves as an institutional guarantee for people existing as people, a protection of the freedom and equality necessary to the respect of human nature. This has already been written into a series of basic clauses in the charter of the United Nations, and many countries have signaled their agreement. These are already the core values of humanity.

Having arrived in the twenty-first century, there are all kinds of globalized modernities. If we look carefully, we find that there are differences in similarities and similarities in differences. If we judge according to the American sociologist Talcott Parsons's (1902–79) three iron laws, which define the characteristics of universal modernity as individualism, democracy, and the market economy, then truly there is no way to explain this. This illustrates that understanding modernity in essentialist terms already faces an insurmountable internal obstacle. To overcome this difficulty and untie the internal knot of tension between universal and plural modernities, Wittgenstein's (1889–1951) theory of "family resemblances" might provide us with a new path. In his study of the meaning of words, Wittgenstein discovered that these meanings were not fixed, but only took on certain meanings in concrete historical settings. At the same time, the same words in different contexts remained

[54] See Saimouer Hengtingdun (Samuel Huntington), *Wenming de chongtu yu shijie zhixu de chongjian* (The clash of civilizations and the remaking of world order), Zhou Qi, trans. (Beijing: Xinhua chubanshe, 1998), pp. 43–45.

linked in terms of meaning, which he called "family resemblances." In other words, members of the same lexical family share similar features without sharing the same exact content. In the context of our attempt to understand the universal values of modernity, Wittgenstein's theory of "family resemblances" is very useful, particularly when these values take on clear definition in uncertain historical contexts. This reminds us that modernity is not a rigid nature or a fixed, unchanging goal; it is not Parsons's three iron rules. Modernity means a set of values that includes freedom, rights, democracy, equality, universal brotherhood, wealth and power, happiness, etc. These are all modern values. According to Isaiah Berlin's theory, these values are rarely internally harmonious, and there are often conflicts among them. Thus one has to choose between different modern values. Different nations and different peoples accord different priorities to different values. The reason that there are different modernities in today's world is because of different understandings and management of value priorities. For example, England and the United States pay more attention to freedom and the rule of law, France values democracy, and East Asia privileges development, wealth, and power. Different modernities imply differences in value priorities. Yet if we regard them all as modernities, then they possess most of the set of values associated with modernity, and they share the marks of "family resemblance." Different modernities have both similarities and differences; modernities possess different levels of quality – there are good and bad. When a country's modernity overstresses a particular value, for example national wealth and power, then the citizens lack basic guarantees of their rights; in other cases democratic institutions are there but not the corresponding legal order, which encourages corruption and bribery; in still others society is egalitarian, but everyone is struggling in universal poverty ... We can qualify all of these as not being good examples of modernity. Only this kind of understanding enables us to get out of the morass of the "theory of a single civilization" and at the same time to not fall into "values relativism."

In a move that is the opposite of the orthodox liberals who employ "universal values" to replace "Chinese values," China's historicists have constructed an artificial antagonism between "universal values" and "Chinese values." It is as if universal values are all Western values, and China's "good stuff" must confront the Western "good stuff." In fact, Western modernity has a complicated dual nature, and contains both Enlightenment values of universal civilization as well as values that justify the wild expansion of the state. Humanity's universal values naturally are not the monopoly of the West, but are instead the result of the participation of all high-level civilizations, even if we surely cannot say that they are unrelated to the West. The crux of the question is *which* Western civilization is adopted: is it the universal values of freedom and democracy, or the reckless pursuit of state expansion? What is surprising is that China's historicists seem to be unlike left-wing Japanese scholars such as Koyasu Nobukuni and Naoki Sakai. When the Chinese historicists criticize Western military interventions, their aim is not to criticize the Machiavellian pursuit of wealth and power – in fact, they are rather enthralled by that. Instead, the targets of their criticism are the Enlightenment values of freedom and democracy. Thus an attack on Western modernity becomes a negative choice: they abandon the civilizational values that constrain humanity from pursuit of naked self-interest, and keep only the most frightening Machiavellism.

What China's historicists care about is only the distinction between "us" and "the other," how to define "Chinese" values so that they will be "good" values, believing that as long as a value is "Chinese" then it's "good." This kind of closed-minded "theory of distinguishing self from enemy" cannot build an effective values legitimacy, because there is no way to deduce, either logically or in terms of history, that "our" values are necessarily the same as "good" or "desirable" values. If China's goal were not to cling to a nationalist state structure, but instead to rebuild a great civilized country with greater influence on world affairs, then her every word and act, all that she says and does must begin from universal values, and in a globalized dialogue provide her own unique understanding of universal civilization. This understanding will not be culturalist, and cannot use such common defenses as "this is Chinese particular national character," or "this is China's sovereignty, and no one has the right to say otherwise." Instead, China must use the standards of universal civilization to convince the world of China's rationality. As a great country that influences the world, what China should build is not a particular culture adapted to one country and one people, but instead a civilization of universal values for all humanity. Values that are "good" for China, particularly core values that relate to basic human nature, must similarly be universally "good" for all humanity. Universal civilization is not only "good" for "us," it also has value for "the other." The universality of Chinese culture can only be constructed from the perspective of all humanity, and its point of departure cannot be China's particular values and interests. Historically speaking, Chinese civilization was understood as *tianxia*, a kind of universalism examined in greater length in Chapter 6, and in this globalized age, how *tianxia* can be transformed into a universalism that accords with universal civilization is a goal that a great civilized country should embrace.

Universal civilization is a civilization that takes "cultural pluralism" as its base. It is different from the "theory of single civilization" with its "different routes to the same end," and from "cultural relativism" and its "parting of the ways." The basic idea of "cultural pluralism" is "many expressions of the same principle." It admits that while there are basic differences between cultures, they can still understand one another, and on certain important core values – such as notions of freedom, equality, universal brotherhood, justice, harmony, etc. – might even arrive at a consensus on the basic values that different nations and cultures might embrace in contemporary society. It is only in the prioritization of these values, which are given most importance, that different peoples and countries can have their own understandings and choices. "Cultural pluralism" can coexist with universal civilization, and advocate replacing cultural resistance with cultural dialogue, thus achieving a value consensus within universal culture through all sorts of civilizational dialogues and exchanges. Chinese culture is truly unique, in the same way that Western culture is unique, but Chinese culture is after all a great axial civilization, and within its particularity exists a rich universality, a universal civilization that can be shared with the other cultures of humanity. "Chinese exceptionalism" looks like political correctness, and as it brings civilization down to the level of culture, greatly diminishes Chinese civilization, and is truly not China's foundation.

In the intellectual history of Europe, early historicism made its own particular theoretical contribution, serving as a corrective to the universal reason of the Enlightenment, which erred in overlooking the cultural particularity of other national cultures, and thus planted the roots for the establishment of multiple national cultures within the universal ideals of humanity. It was after Fichte that historicism began its conservative turn, and gradually joined hands with national power, becoming hysterical. Ideological currents with influence in history have many branches, and they follow their own logic. Historicism has a complex internal genealogy, its tradition in Europe is as ancient as that of the Enlightenment, and we can find traces in Italy, England, and France. Why did it change after arriving in Germany? After the destruction of the Nazis, Meinecke, the expert on German historicism, painfully reflected on this, and argued that nineteenth- and twentieth-century German historicism had abandoned the humanistic tradition of the Enlightenment movement and figures like Goethe (1749–1832), Kant, and Herder,[55] and instead linked up with Prussian conservative

---

[55] Translator's note: Johann Gottfried Herder (1744–1803) was a German philosopher whose work greatly contributed to the development of German historicism.

nationalism, which finally destroyed the good name of German culture.[56] This sad episode in Germany's past should ring an alarm bell for China's historicists: you can cling to a historicist standpoint regarding "Chinese values" and the "China model," but the question is with whom, in the plurality of Chinese civilization, your historicism is going to ally? With what tradition will you merge? With the humanistic Confucian tradition? Or the Legalists and their emphasis on wealth and power? Or the political tradition with a Confucian exterior and a Legalist interior? From its origins, Chinese civilization was never a homogenous whole, and from early times has weathered the impact of ideological fragments waiting to be revived. Let's see what kind of tradition your historicism fancies, with what historical tradition it might have chemistry.

In fact, early European historicism was part of Enlightenment thought, and not in conflict with humanistic values. In his discussion of the Italian political philosopher and Enlightenment figure Giambattista Vico (1744–1803) and the German intellectual Herder, both of whom were representative figures in early European historicism, Isaiah Berlin points out that they were not cultural relativists who were misunderstood at the time, but were instead genuine cultural pluralists. Cultural relativists believe that the values of different cultures have no comparative common measure, which means there is no absolute right or wrong. Any "good" is relative, limited, and "good" only in relation to a particular nation; there is no universal "good" for the whole of humanity. By contrast, cultural pluralists acknowledge humanity's universal values, but note that in different historical and cultural contexts, universal values take on different cultural forms and concrete expressions. Separated from a basis in national culture, universal values become rootless. If one takes cultural relativism a step further, we arrive at a Nietzschean nihilism. But cultural pluralism can coexist with Enlightenment universal values. Berlin argues that different cultural values are equal – equally true, equally ultimate, equally objective; values do not exist in a graded hierarchy. With regard to human nature, no matter how complicated, good, or bad the person may be, he or she must possess common characteristics shared with humanity at large. Different cultures similarly possess common values. Despite the differences between national cultures, their cores are mutually overlapping; these core values and ultimate ends are wide open and commonly pursued by humanity. We can and must transcend our own particular cultural, national, and class values, break through the closed

---

[56] See Meinike (Friedrich Meinecke), *Deguo de haojie* (The German catastrophe).

box in which cultural relativism hopes to confine us and enter into the culture of "the other." Only if we fully develop our power of imagination, can we always understand the soul of "the other," his life goals, and thus realize the commonality and plurality of human culture.[57]

Universal values or Chinese values? Maybe this is a false question. The proper answer is: rebuild Chinese values on the basis of the concerns of universal civilization.

---

[57] See Yisaiya Bolin (Isaiah Berlin), *Niuqu de renxing zhi cai* (The crooked timber of humanity), Yue Xiukun, trans. (Nanjing: Yilin chubanshe, 2009), pp. 78–89.

4   After the "Great Disembedding": Family-State, *Tianxia*, and Self

Translator's Introduction

In this article, published in 2015, Xu Jilin uses Charles Taylor's Modern Social Imaginaries, *a retelling of the history of Western modernity which ends in a discussion of multiple modernities, to offer a similar retelling of the narrative of modern China. Although the text was originally published in the scholarly Journal of Fudan University in Shanghai, it is in fact not a particularly "academic" text, but rather seeks to shape public opinion in China by engaging other intellectuals and by educating the Chinese reading public on matters of history, politics, and society.*

By using Taylor's 2003 volume as a foil and a model, Xu suggests that China's history is part of world history, or at least that there are similarities in the patterns of development followed by important world civilizations. In part, this is a none-too-subtle criticism of the many Chinese thinkers who argue for the utter uniqueness of China's historical experience. At the same time, Xu takes pains to highlight the particularities of China's past, contrasting traditional China's "social imaginary" with that of the West. The long discussion of the relationship in China between the "family–state," tianxia, and the self is meant to educate Xu's readers in the intricacies of self and social definition under Confucianism, and he takes pains to illustrate both the strengths and the weaknesses of the traditional order.

Xu further highlights the speed and incompleteness of China's "disembedding" from its traditional social order compared to that of the West, arguing that China's social revolution is still ongoing. Among other things, the state has taken on too much power, at the expense of community and self – a theme that recurs repeatedly in this volume. Finally, Xu address the need for a "re-embedding" of self and society. In contrast to liberals who insist on China's pressing need for free markets and the rule of law, Xu counsels attention to rebuilding communities, and suggests that China's historical traditions might contain useful elements in that process.

Throughout this essay Xu demonstrates his novel appropriation of liberal thought. His basic concerns draw from the liberal tradition; hence the protracted use of Taylor. Yet the conversation he builds is both international and deeply Chinese. He cites the noted pre-war Confucian philosopher Liang Shuming and the contemporary Taiwanese professor of philosophy (and specialist on liberal thought), Shi Yuankan, as both wrestle with the challenge of modern liberal ideas in a Chinese context. Most fundamentally, however, this essay shows Xu Jilin thinking through liberal ideas by using core Chinese concepts: jiaguo *(family-state)* and tianxia. *His liberal solution, the call to re-embed self and society in contemporary China, is expressed through these particularly Chinese conceptions of "state and society" and "nature" that may well constitute a novel contribution to international liberal thought.*

In his 2003 book *Modern Social Imaginaries*, the Canadian political philosopher Charles Taylor (b. 1931) argues that in the process of the transformation from traditional to modern society, there occurred an axial revolution in the form of a "great disembedding." Both the real and imagined worlds of traditional society were embedded in a series of frameworks including the cosmos, nature, and society. In the European Middle Ages, this was a sacred world ruled by God; in traditional China it was a continuum of the family-state and *tianxia*. Individual behavior and the meaning of life could only be understood and properly valued from within these frameworks. But after the seventeenth-century scientific and religious revolutions in Europe there occurred the "disenchantment" discussed by Max Weber (1864–1920). The individual, law, and the nation-state gradually slipped away from the sacred cosmic world and achieved an independent autonomy. This was the "great disembedding." In China the "great disembedding" occurred in the late nineteenth and early twentieth centuries, in the transition from China's final dynasty and the establishment of her first republic, when the self escaped from the communal framework defined by the family-state and *tianxia*, becoming an independent individual.

China's "great disembedding" was a revolution fighting to throw off the family-state and *tianxia*. The late nineteenth-century reformer Tan Sitong (1865–98) called it "breaking the bonds." But did the Chinese people obtain freedom after the great disembedding? Or did they become slaves to the Leviathan of the modern state? Or perhaps nihilistic individuals living in a vacuum? Will a "re-embedding" be required for individual life to once again have meaning, the individual being reinserted into a family-state/*tianxia* framework invested with a new significance? As we construct a new family-state/*tianxia* order today, how should we reconstruct a modern self? And what is the connection between the realization of the self and the construction of the family-state/*tianxia* order? These are the questions to be discussed in this essay.

The Family-State/*Tianxia* Continuum and the Self at its Core

The subject and starting point for China's family-state/*tianxia*, the continuum providing the framework of meaning in traditional China, was humankind. The Confucian philosopher Mencius (372–289 BC) said: "The root of *tianxia* lies in the state; the root of the state lies in the family; the root of the family lies in the person."[1] Thus what I call the family-state/*tianxia* is a social continuum with the self at its core. But the self of traditional society possessed neither authenticity nor autonomy as understood in modern times; the significance of the self was not self-evident, and was instead embedded in the hierarchical organic relationships of the family-state/*tianxia*. The self extended into the outside world, but achieved personal identity within the continuum of self, family, state, and *tianxia*.

Why say that the family-state/*tianxia* is a continuous community? In the ancient Roman tradition, state and family were two clearly distinguished domains, which is very clear when we look at the line dividing public law and private law. But in traditional Chinese society and politics, contract-based law was not at the heart of regulation, and instead an ethical system of ritual and music served as the basic social framework. The system of ritual and music linking state and family together came from the Western Zhou (1046–771 BC) feudal system. The son of heaven enfeoffed the princes to establish kingdoms, and the princes allotted land and people to the nobility to establish families, forming a pyramidal feudal hierarchical system. By family-state/*tianxia*, we mean this patriarchal-feudal system linking the nobles, the princes, and the son of heaven (the ruler). The son of heaven represented *tianxia* (the equivalent of the modern state), the princes represented the kingdoms (the equivalent of modern localities), and the nobles represented fiefs (the equivalent of modern villages). Within the family-state/*tianxia*, the enfeoffments and the loyalties created a community combining blood, culture, and politics, so that those involved were both relatives and rulers or servants, like a big family. At the same time the enfeoffed princes and nobles had absolute sovereignty over their fiefs, and were not subject to the control of the son of heaven. For this reason, the kingdoms and villages of the princes were independent, not subordinate to one another, and each had its own particularities. The patriarchal network englobing scholars, senior officials, dukes, princes, and the Zhou son of heaven was sustained by a dense and complex system of Zhou rituals.

During the transition between the Spring and Autumn (771–476 BC) and the Warring States (475–221 BC) periods, the Western Zhou feudal-ritual system collapsed, but the notion of family-state was preserved and developed in the great unity of the imperial bureaucratic system

---

[1] Originally published as "'Da tuoqian' zhi hou: Jiaguo tianxia yu ziwo rentong," *Fudan xuebao* 5 (2015). Also available online at www.aisixiang.com/data/93838.html. Robert Eno, "Mencius: An Online Teaching Translation," www.indiana.edu/~p374/Mengzi.pdf, p. 74. Translation slightly modified to suit the purposes of this text.

established by the Qin (221–206 BC) and Han (206 BC–220 CE) dynasties. During the reign of Emperor Han Wudi (r. 141–86 BC), the Legalist administrative system was combined with the system of Confucian music and ritual, and the "three bonds" ideology that insisted on the fundamental hierarchical bonds between ruler and subject, father and child, and husband and wife, championed by the Confucian scholar Dong Zhongshu (179–104 BC), became the core ideology of the Chinese empire for 2,000 years. The patriarchal lineage ethics empowering father over son and husband over wife was highly integrated into the family-state bond between ruler and subject so that the political relationships of the monarchy were an expanded version of lineage ethical relationships, and ethics and politics were highly integrated. In Chinese law and politics, there were no purely public relationships, and everything was personalized and relativized: relations between ruler and subject, official and people, and between the people, all were relative, situational relationships governed by personalized ethical norms; what was lacking were rigid norms governing politics and contracts. Consequently, many personalistic principles based on patriarchal lineage practices came to be deeply embedded in state law and politics. Law was approached via ritual and regulated by ritual, and politics was highly ethicized and privatized, creating China's particular ritual-legal system and personalized political tradition, which has continued to develop to this day.

Within the family-state/*tianxia* continuum, the state is relative and extremely ambiguous. In ancient China, the modern word for state, *guo*, meant the territories bequeathed by the son of heaven to the princes in the Western Zhou; in the Spring and Autumn and Warring States periods *guo* became multiple kingdoms competing for hegemony; after the Qin unification in 221 BC, *guo* became the monarchy based on dynastic power, and the historical dynastic regime took the form of a unified empire, as under the Han, Tang (618–907), Song (960–1279), Ming (1368–1644), and Qing dynasties (1644–1911). Of course, China was not always ruled by unified dynasties. There were confrontations between north and south, conflicts between the central plains and the many kingdoms on the periphery, as in the Wei (220–65), Jin (265–420), Northern and Southern dynasties (420–589), Five Dynasties (907–60), Ten Kingdoms (907–79), Northern and Southern Song (960–1127 and 1127–1279), and the Liao, Xia, Jin dynasties (907–1125, 1115–1234, and 1038–1233). But traditional Chinese people had a hard time imagining an abstract community that was greater than the dynasty but less than *tianxia*. If we have to locate such a concept in ancient times, "*sheji*," a deity of the soil and harvest in ancient Chinese religion, where ancient emperors supposedly sacrificed, may be the best we can do, but its meaning is far from the richness of the modern notion of nation, as it suggests a primitive lineage community. For this reason, the twentieth-century Chinese Confucian thinker Liang Shuming (1893–1988) said that traditional Chinese people only had a notion of dynastic regime, but no concept of nation-state: "In the minds of the Chinese people, what is close to them is family, and what is far from them is *tianxia*. The rest they more or less ignore."[2] As for the sense of *guo* within the notion of family-state/*tianxia*, in precise terms, it meant the concrete dynastic regime. This dynastic regime with the sovereign at its core is only one central link in the family-state/*tianxia* continuum; from below it is governed by the norms of patriarchal lineage ethics; from above it is constrained by universal *tianxia* values. Politics in a monarchical nation thus lacks autonomy. In a ritualized political system governed by ethics, public and private are often relative and ambiguous, and for lineages, the dynastic regime seemed to mean "public" – one meaning of public being the government and government officials. But "*gong*," the word for public, has yet another meaning: absolute, transcendent ethical values, which the government represents but which belong ultimately to *tianxia*. For this reason, from the point of view of *tianxia*, the dynasty is private, and as the seventeenth-century Confucian thinker Gu Yanwu (1613–82) noted, the loss of the country is but the loss of a dynastic family, while the loss of *tianxia* is the loss of shared meaning, whose end result is mutual destruction [lit., cannibalism].[3]

The relationship between family-state and *tianxia* is like that between the soul and the body. *Tianxia* represents the highest values of truth, beauty, and goodness, but for these values to be realized in the human world, they must inhabit the institutional bodies of the patriarchal lineage and the dynastic state. These values are constructed by the Confucian teachings that combine ethics and politics into one, and by regulations and popular customs. The values of *tianxia* are not far from the people, and indeed are found in the people's legal-political order and in daily life. Separated from the body of the family-state, the heavenly way becomes a lost soul. From another perspective, the legitimacy of the patriarchal order and the state is not self-evident and can be proven only via transcendent *tianxia* consciousness, or the higher mandate of heaven, the heavenly way, or the heavenly principle. The reason that Chinese people

---

[2] Liang Shuming, "Zhongguo wenhua yaoyi" (The importance of Chinese culture), in Liang Shuming, *Liang Shuming quanji (The complete writings of Liang Shuming)* (Jinan: Shandong renmin chubanshe, 1990), vol. 3, p. 163.

[3] Gu Yanwu, *Rizhilu* (Record of daily knowledge), juan 17, "zhengshi." Available online at https://zh.wikisource.org/zh/%E6%97%A5%E7%9F%A5%E9%8C%84/%E5%8D%B 717#%E6%AD%A3%E5%A7%8B.

regard the family-state as sacred, as having real, unshakable authority, is because it is the embodiment in human form of the transcendent values of *tianxia*. Respect for the family-state order is respect for the way of heaven. At the same time, if a family head or a ruler's behavior does not conform to the great way of heaven, if it betrays the words of the sage, then the individual has no more moral duty of loyalty and filiality toward him, and should there emerge a tyrant who goes against heaven, then in the extreme ideology of Mencius, the people can follow the heavenly mandate and rise up in revolt, replacing the monarch with another one who is worthy.

In the continuum of family-state and *tianxia*, beginning with the self, the family-state is but an intermediary, and the most important elements remain the two poles of the self and *tianxia*. In traditional China, *tianxia* had two closely related meanings: one was the universal value order of the cosmos, similar to the Western will of God, or the will of heaven, referring to the highest values of the cosmos or of nature, the greatest good for human society and for the self. Another meaning of *tianxia* was ritual rule leading from small prosperity to great harmony, wherein human society conforms to the universal order of the heavenly way and develops economically and socially as a result. The first *tianxia*, as the vehicle of values for the mandate of heaven, need not employ the mediation of the family-state; the self can communicate directly with this *tianxia*. Mencius talked about his theory of "heaven and the people," which later was promoted by Neoconfucians of the Song (960–1279) and Ming (1368–1644) dynasties and especially by the school of Wang Yangming (1472–1529), who argued that because the individual's inner mind possesses primordial innate knowledge, it can directly connect with heavenly principle. Innate knowledge is heavenly principle and heavenly principle is innate knowledge. The self has a direct connection with the Way and does not require the assistance of the family-state. The latter kind of *tianxia* is the cultural and ethical order of the real world, and if the individual wants to connect with this *tianxia*, he must "align his family and order the state" so as to "bring peace to *tianxia*," in the words of the well-known Confucian classic, *The Great Learning*, and here the family-state serves as an essential link between the self and *tianxia*. Unlike in an otherworldly Buddhism or a Christianity turned toward heaven, the realization of the innate knowledge of the Confucian individual requires moral practice in the public affairs of the lineage and the dynastic regime. The realization of innate knowledge is not only a matter of grasping heavenly principle, but more importantly has to do with putting heavenly principle into practice.

Thus in the continuum containing family-state and *tianxia*, the traditional Chinese self had a dual nature. One self could not take leave of the family-state's concrete ethical order and directly communicate with *tianxia*; the individual was always attached to a certain ethical and political order, and if separated from the order of the family-state, the self no longer existed. The other self was an independent "heavenly person," who could circumvent the family-state's reigning order and contact transcendent heavenly principle directly through his innate knowledge, as already noted. Of course the Daoists, who viewed the family-state as a burden, believed all the more that the self could combine with the heavenly way through a free aesthetic search, thus entering into a good and beautiful natural order. The dual nature of the self in Chinese culture led to the creation of two antagonistic extremes within the Chinese personality: they are strict familialists, conservatives who are loyal to their lords and love their country, yet at the same time they are free and undisciplined naturalists. In the same body we find a complex personality combining authoritarianism and anarchism, and these extremes are often unstable. The obedient subject who usually respects ritual and law can, in times of chaos, become a "heavenly person" or even a rebel who rejects all authority and acts without restraint.

In sum, the traditional Chinese self was embedded in dual natural and social orders. In the one he was a heavenly person, belonging to a universal order with the heavenly way at its center, and the ultimate values of this self were to be achieved in the transcendent heavenly way of this cosmic order. The other self was a member of a family or a subject of the dynasty, so this self always existed within a certain patriarchal or monarchical order. The self carried out its moral duties within a formal ritual-legal system and a tradition of popular customs whence it obtained its concrete status identity. This sense of status was relative and situational, yet within fixed relationships was also clear and absolute. Between the family-state and *tianxia* there existed both a high-level continuum as well as an unbridgeable rupture, and the self was embedded in this crevice between the continuum and the rupture. Chinese culture placed great emphasis on heaven, earth, and man as the three basic components of the cosmos, and in the larger complex of family-state and *tianxia*, man is the self, the family-state is the earth, and *tianxia* is the heaven. In the real world, man (the self) bases himself on the earth (the family-state) to communicate with heaven (*tianxia*). The so-called individual is always a self within a particular historical-cultural context, and always exists within the family-state/*tianxia* community, from which he obtains his self. But in the spiritual world, because the self possesses innate knowledge, it can also transcend the family-state and link up directly with the heavenly way; in this case the self emerges with the status of a "heavenly being," and receives sacred meaning directly from the transcendent heavenly way, and is transformed into the will of the sage. And this will, within the real order of the family-state, might become the very order itself.

It was precisely these subtly divergent orientations within traditional Chinese culture that in the modern context evolved to become a Chinese-style revolution, or "great disembedding."

The Rupture in the Modern Family-State/*Tianxia* Continuum

The "great disembedding" revolution that occurred in modern times refers to the removal of individuals from various networks of cosmic, natural, and social relationships, and their becoming a true, independent individual. According to Charles Taylor, in Europe this process was a "long march" lasting for as long as five centuries, and included two aspects: one was "humanity's humanistic turn," in which mankind as a whole came to be "disembedded" from the cosmic order, becoming a "human subject" on the same level as the natural world; the second was "the individualistic turn," in which the individual's "inner self" was discovered and granted unique value, allowing individuals to be "disembedded" from organic communities and to achieve self-understanding in an individualistic sense. Individual self-understanding no longer relied on any outside framework of meaning, and had its own authenticity, becoming a "free-floating independent individual," a concept that has been constructed in modern times, becoming an important modern social imaginary.[4]

In China, the "great disembedding" revolution began in the transition between the late Qing and early Republican periods, has been underway for more than a century, and continues today. The most important precondition for the emergence of a true self in China was the self-rupture and disintegration of the family-state/*tianxia* continuum.

Within the family-state/*tianxia* continuum, the state was originally an ambiguous intermediary, and did not occupy a central position. But the state rose abruptly in the modern period, and this rise played a central role in the dissolution of the family-state/*tianxia*. The modern state is not the traditional dynastic regime, but is rather a nation-state community with political autonomy. Its political legitimacy no longer derives from a transcendent mandate of heaven, but instead is based on the will of the

---

[4] See Liu Qing, "Meiyou huanjue de geren zizhuxing" (Individual autonomy without illusions), *Shucheng* 10 (2011).

people and historical agency. From another perspective, state law has been separated from the ritual order and patriarchal relationships, and has an autonomous nature. For this reason, the rise of the nation-state is a hugely important historical event that recast the relationship between the individual and the family-state/*tianxia*, and overturned the family-state/*tianxia* order itself.

First came the breakup of family and state. Intellectuals linked to "China's Enlightenment" in early twentieth-century China universally considered that traditional China knew only the family and not the nation-state, that it lacked the modern sense of nation-state consciousness. To build a European-style nation-state, the first necessity was to "de-familialize." By criticizing familialism, the state would be separated from patriarchal ethics and obtain its independence. In 1904 the *Jiangsu* magazine published a piece entitled "Theory of the Family Revolution," which was very clear:

What is the family revolution? It is removing the yoke of the family and engaging in political activities; it is eliminating family love so as to seek political happiness; it is doing away with the closed family education so as to open up political knowledge; it is breaking down the closed world of the family so allow for sacrifice to politics. It is getting rid of family slaves and establishing politically legal persons, it is sweeping away the evil consequences of the family and reaping the harvest of the great name of politics.[5]

During the iconoclastic New Culture movement of the late 1910s and 1920s, the family was universally seen as the hotbed of despotism, so that the construction of a democratic republic would require the destruction of the patriarchal family, and the Confucian ideology of the three bonds became the first target to be attacked. Under the assault of this movement, state and family were torn asunder, and the public space of politics was separated from the private space of society. However, this was only at a conceptual level, and in political practice, the remnants of family-state integration remained very strong, and ruling the country through claims to morality remained a primary belief of generations of rulers. Imagining the state via the family, Confucian personalistic principles continued to rule the political realm, and the moralization and privatization of politics became a basic characteristic distinguishing Chinese politics from Western rule of law.

Next came the breakup of state and *tianxia*. Once the nation-state became an autonomous body, it escaped the constraints of the

---

[5] Jiating lixianzhe (The family constitutionalist), "Jiating geming shuo" (Theory of the family revolution), *Jiangsu* 7 (January 1904).

transcendent world and its sacred values, and established its own standards of value. Beginning from the late Qing, under the pressure of national and racial decline and interstate competition, the nation-state's own goals came to be wealth and power. With the help of Social Darwinism's momentum, statism crushed the traditional *tianxia* value system, and national wealth and power replaced virtue and the people's livelihood as the central measures of national revival. Traditional belief in *tianxia* was a civilizational view based on virtue and moral rule, but in late Qing/early Republican times, the subject of civilization experienced a change, and China's moral civilization based on *tianxia* was transformed into a modern civilization of freedom and democracy with the West as its subject. Thereupon the traditional relationship between the state and *tianxia* was transformed into a conflict of values between wealth and power on the one hand and civilization on the other. The nation-state's rational goal was the creation of national wealth and power, and the modern universal values replacing *tianxia* were justice, equality, and freedom, which led to an irreparable rupture in the relationship between wealth and power and civilization. The process of national revival in the century and a half since the late Qing is one in which wealth and power have basically eclipsed civilization, and the rationality of the nation-state has ridden roughshod over universal values. The decline of *tianxia* and the rise of the nation-state meant the loss of equilibrium in the family-state/*tianxia* continuum, and the destroyed family-state no longer possessed the transcendent values of *tianxia*. All that remained were secular utilitarian goals.

The destruction of the family-state/*tianxia* continuum was a liberation for the individual. Familialism was seen not only as a hotbed of political despotism, but also as the greatest obstacle to individual liberation and autonomy. The youth of the period hastened to abandon the villages, and thronged into the free and open cities, and if there was no reason to be nostalgic for the village, it was because of the suffocating patriarchal family and the rituals that constrained individuality and were linked to the family. The cities were highly mobile societies of strangers. Freed from the traditional social and cultural communities, everyone became a free and independent atomized individual.

Yet this modern individual, despite being "disembedded" from the "bonds" of the family-state, entered into yet another status network: that of citizenship, intimately linked to the nation-state. The citizen and the nation-state were born at the same time. When the traditional self escaped from his status as a member of a family or local community, the defin-ition of his status exited the private territories defined by the Confucian relations of ruler–subject, father–son, husband–wife, teacher–student, and friend–friend, and under the ever strengthening legal power of the nation-state, each individual gained an equal, identical status, that of citizen. With the modern loss of social intermediaries, individuals found themselves face to face with the state, and the new relationship between individual and nation-state, constructed on legal and political grounds, no longer possessed its original, warm-hearted, personalized, ethical flavor, but was instead a non-individualized, impersonal relationship of legal power. Because of the influence of German and Japanese nationalist thought in the late Qing, there was a pervasive "integration of citizen and state" in the understanding of the relationship between the individual and the nation-state. But the honeymoon between citizen and nation-state was soon over, as during the May Fourth period citizens and the state divided and fell into conflict. From this point forward, liberalism, which emphasized individual rights, and statism, which leaned toward state authority, parted ways. Liang Shuming, who proposed a communitarian commitment to rural reconstruction, hoped to find a way out of the binary conflict between individual and state, and once again embed them in ties of kinship and locality, rebuilding private ethics between people outside of public, legal relationships.

The May Fourth movement was a very particular period, when the traditional self was transformed into the modern true and free individual, and the original *tianxia* of the sacred heavenly way was transformed into the modern world based on humanism. The new individual and the new world had no need to call on the mediation of the family-state; they could communicate directly not only in the spiritual-psychological realm, but also in the secular world. The well-known May Fourth thought leader Fu Sinian (1896–1950) famously said: "I only admit the existence of humanity at a high level. At a lower level, 'I' am real. All of the intervening groups between 'me' and humanity, like the family, local communities, the state, etc., are idols. For the sake of humanity we should cultivate a 'true self'."[6] Intermediaries are real, but idols are illusory. In the eyes of contemporary intellectuals, the family, local communities, and the state were all man-made idols that needed to be destroyed. In the vast universe, only humanity and the individual were real. The world of humanity had universal reason and values, and individual value and significance could only be understood in the framework of universal values and the long river of human history. These were the "little me" and the

[6] Fu Sinian, "'Xinchao' zhi huigu yu qianzhan" (Review and future perspectives for "New Wave"), in Fu Sinian, *Fu Sinian quanji* (The complete writings of Fu Sinian) (Changsha: Hunan jiaoyu chubanshe), vol. 1, p. 297.

"big me" that the prominent May Fourth figure Hu Shi (1891–1962) spoke of:

> My "little me" has no independent existence, but has direct or indirect relations with a vast number of little selves; it has mutually influential relations with society and the world; it has a karmic relationship with past social worlds and the future ... My present "little self," in relation to the limitless past of my indestructible "big self," must assume great responsibility. And to the limitless future of my indestructible "big self," as well.[7]

In the late Qing and early Republican periods, anarchism and internationalist thought were both popular for a time, their influence extending to some of those in revolutionary parties, and an entire generation spanning the Enlightenment group and the cultural conservatives. This too is closely linked to the disintegration of the family-state order, as the direct communication between self and *tianxia* expanded from the spiritual dimension to the dimension of social practice, forming an important historical tradition in modern China.

Rebuilding a New Family-State/*Tianxia* Order

The rupture of the family-state/*tianxia* continuum had an enormous impact on Chinese political life, ethical life, and daily life. We can note two negative impacts: first, with the loss of the constraints imposed by society and *tianxia*, state authority took on immense proportions; and second, following its "disembedding" from the community of the family-state, the modern self became an atomized, rootless individual, and lost its existential meaning.

While the traditional family-state *tianxia* as a whole will not be reproduced in modern society, and indeed broad trends have favored the dismantling of such unities, the mutual disassociation of family-state and *tianxia* nonetheless rolled out the red carpet for state rationality to attain its greatest power. The family-state and *tianxia* need to reconnect on the basis of a new understanding and in a new structure, making clear the boundaries between them and the same time providing mutual checks and balances.

Let's start with family and state. According to the theory of Habermas (b. 1929), modern society is divided into a systems world and a lifeworld. The systems world is organized around the axes of

---

[7] Hu Shi, "Buxiu: wode zongjiao" (Immortality: My religion), in Hu Shi, *Hu Shi wenji (Hu Shi's writings)* (Beijing: Beijing daxue chubanshe, 1998), vol. 2, pp. 529–32.

market and power, while the lifeworld is a non-instrumental world of free exchanges of human feelings. Obviously the state (politics) belongs to the systems world, while the family (society) belongs to the lifeworld. The values of these two worlds differ: the systems world uses rights and contracts to govern the market, and the rule of law and democracy to constrain power. The lifeworld is composed of private exchanges, employing human ethics and morality to regulate human relationships. Habermas particularly emphasizes that both of these worlds are legitimate, as long as they remain within their own spheres. The problem is that in today's society, the systems world is colonizing the lifeworld. Principles of market and power have expanded into the lifeworld so that natural interactions between people have taken on an impersonal, unfeeling, amoral texture, and if it's not hierarchical power that dominates, it is the money of market exchange. State power in particular has increased, becoming omnipresent; in the lifeworld, power principles have replaced ethical values in much of daily life. In China, the reverse situation also exists, in the sense that the lifeworld has also colonized the systems world. Ethical principles of the Confucian lifeworld have invaded political space, employing personal connections in a sphere that should be governed by contracts among equals, and injecting human relations into what should be a serious context of rule of law.

The family and the state are different worlds, and the family and state should be divided, but this does not mean that family and state are completely different categories and that political life should be completely de-ethicized. Is the modern nation-state merely a political-legal community, or, like the family, is it also a cultural-ethical community? This relates to the dual nature of the nation-state: the state is the political-legal system, a de-ethicized, de-culturized political-legal community; the nation contains a country's particular historical, religious, linguistic, and customary traditions and is consequently a richly ethical and cultural national community. The first (state) community is completely different from the family, but the second (national) community is inseparable from the family, existing in a complex, tangled, internal relationship. The community of a nation-state is not simply a legal community, an "orderly republic," as imagined by rights liberals; instead it is an "ethical republic" possessing its own general will and civil morality. Both the general will and civil morality are built on the basis of a richly organic national cultural tradition and common political culture. Today we should dispense with two extreme views of the state. One of these views sees the state and family as completely separate, and the state as a tool completely devoid of internal values; the other lumps state and family together, thus naturalizing and familializing the state, arguing that the state, like the family, possesses absolute natural authority. "L'État, c'est moi," insists on this view, arguing that the state is nothing other than the "family *tianxia*." We should immediately note that while the state may look like the family, it is not. The nation-state is not a tool, nor is it a new sacred soul; it belongs to all of the citizens, as a community with inner values and shared destiny. Whether you love or hate the state, it exists, and moreover has been internalized to become part of the fate of every individual. For this reason, all citizens have a responsibility to work hard to realize their own ideal national state community, and participate in national construction and institution building, allowing their country to truly become worthy of the love of each citizen, who will see it as a psychological and physical home to be proud of.

Now let's discuss state and *tianxia*. In the modern age, transcendent *tianxia* values have been desacralized, and state rationality has become the highest principle. But within a disenchanted modern society there exist two different kinds of rationality: in addition to state rationality there is also secularized, universal Enlightenment rationality which has replaced the transcendent will (of God or the mandate of heaven). This Enlightenment rationality represents the new *tianxia* values of our modern, globalized age, which in the form of individual freedom and equality constitute a new universal civilization and a strong constraint on state rationality. But state rationality always nourishes an inner desire to trammel all religious and humanistic constraints. With power as its sole goal, the state becomes a supra-moral Leviathan. State legitimacy is no longer based on a transcendent religion or a moral metaphysics, but on a supposed unity between state and citizen. Once the state achieves a high level of sovereignty, and is freed from external moral norms, then its internal power reproduces itself like an evil demon, and expands outward. At the outset, state rationality and Enlightenment rationality were both internal requirements of modernity, each possessing its own internal values, and were not in a relation of means and ends. Yet the histories of the rise of Germany and Japan illustrate that if state rationality lacks the restraints of religious, humanistic or Enlightenment values, and allows its internal power to expand, then state rationality moves from Hobbesian instrumentalism toward conservative romanticism, becoming a values-nihilism lacking in morality, and finally giving birth to a freak nationalism that is anti-humanism and anti-human nature. The greater state capacity becomes, the more state rationality believes its own discourse, and the greater is the probability that it will fall into a terrible crisis.

Re-embedding: Self in the New Family-State/ *Tianxia* Order

The individual in modern society is a product of the "great disembedding," who left the family-state/*tianxia* community to become an atomized individual with a true self. A "disembedded" individual is an unencumbered self, about which the Chinese political philosopher Shi Yuankang (b. 1943) offers this incisive commentary:

> Modern man sees the self as an entity existing independently in the world. The being described in Descartes's famous saying "I think therefore I am" is precisely this sort of self. What constitutes the self are not the values that are chosen, but rather the fact that the individual has the capacity to choose. The self is constructed out of the capacity to choose, and its relationship to goals is merely a relationship of possession and the goals do not constitute part of the self. Even if the self accepts certain values, there remains a gulf between the values and the self.[8]

In the view of Canadian political scientist C. B. Macpherson (1911–87), the modern individual is a "possessive individualist." In a possessive market society, the nature of the individual is understood as owning himself. He is neither a moral subject nor a member of an organized social group. He is just himself, and proves himself through self-possession and through possession of his property.[9] Society is organized by just such owners. In the past, a person's self-understanding and identity were connected to the community of the family-state/*tianxia*, but in modern secular times, the self has become a concept drawn from economics or political science, an agent of wealth and power, and a person's basic nature is connected to ownership and control. Secular society is a market society based on power and money, and organized by possessive "economic rationalists." The atomized individual of the secular age has no group and no history, and is an economic actor full of material desires and pursuits. Individuals stand alone and face the whole world, a market world based on interests, lacking in warmth and meaning. The relationship between the individual and this market world is merely one of material desires and utilitarianism, an impersonal relationship composed of exchange, possession, and control.

---

[8] Shi Yuankang, "Shequn yu geti: shequn zhuyi yu ziyou zhuyi de lunbian" (Group and individual: Debates between collectivism and liberalism), in Shi Yuankang, *Cong Zhongguo wenhua dao xiandaixing: dianfan zhuanyi (From Chinese culture to modernity: The transformation of norms)* (Taibei: Dongda tushu gongsi, 1998), pp. 96–98.

[9] Laisinuofu (Michael Lessnoff), *Ershi shiji de zhengzhi zhexuejia (Political philosophers of the twentieth century)* (Shanghai: Shangwu yinshujia, 2001) (pp. 93–142 are devoted to a discussion of Macpherson).

This does not mean that in modern society there is no family-state, group, or nation outside of the atomized individual. It is rather that for the individual everything is instrumental, whether it's the traditional family, local or religious groups, or a modern social organization – all of these are outside of the self, not part of the self. These exterior groups are only means the individual can employ to realize the self, but the relationship between the individual and the groups is one of owner and owned. The individual has his true self, and can at any time discard these exterior possessions, or perhaps choose another group with greater instrumental value. The relationship of the individual to the nation-state is also like this. For the citizen, the nation-state is a tool to be used to achieve individual rights or a public good, to avoid a Hobbesian "all against all" rule of the jungle. The nation-state is merely a "necessary evil" to preserve peace and order. But the state has no internal value or meaning for the individual; the legal and political systems are tools to bring about individual rights, and for the individual, the national cultural community has only an occasional existence subject to future possible choices. As a result, the individual "disembedded" from the family-state/*tianxia* becomes a naked, lonely, unattached, unsupported self. Yet all these mutually divided selves, who mutually objectify and instrumentalize one another, have no choice but to rely on the "necessary evil" of a government to build a common world, even if this government has only an instrumental existence.

Is this the modern self, the modern society that we are hoping for? In this kind of society built out of atomized individuals and instrumental family-states, can the individual find a true self?

Although Charles Taylor argues that the modern individual is a true self, he nonetheless stresses that this true self can attain self-knowledge and identity only within certain social and cultural frameworks, and that exchange and dialogue with other selves is also indispensable to self-creation. Taylor says: "My discovery of my identity does not mean that I was independently created; instead the discovery involved other people, and was realized in half-private, half-secret internal dialogues. In a culture of authenticity, relationships are seen as key to self-discovery and self-affirmation."[10]

For contemporary Chinese who want to escape the emptiness of the atomized individual, they can find self only in a renewed family-state/*tianxia* order. The atomized individual is based in rights liberalism, but this kind of liberalism is incomplete, and requires the complement of a

---

[10] Chaerse Tailuo (Charles Taylor), *Xiandai xingzhi yinyou (The malaise of modernity)*, Cheng Lian, trans. (Beijing: Zhongyang bianyi chubanshe, 2001), pp. 54, 56.

communitarian self, which will lead to a renewed understanding of the relationship between individual and state that includes republicanism and cultural nationalism, and a strengthened internationalism that will allow the individual to achieve an authentic self within universal civilization.

Contemporary communitarianism shares with Confucianism an emphasis on the role of the community in building the inner values and significance of the self. Where communitarianism differs from Confucianism is that state order is a basic organizational system for Confucians, whereas for Western communitarians the role of state order is replaced by the liberal rule of law, which compensates for the insufficiencies of rights liberalism. But once we acknowledge the basic legal rights of citizen and state, then bringing in the community as an intermediary between the individual and the state and emphasizing the importance of communities like the traditional family, church, or any natural voluntary organization, constitute indispensable elements in the make-up of a healthy individual and are not simply instrumental factors. Communities are not merely spaces for the exchange of interests, but are nodes where many kinds of small communities exchange emotions. The self-understanding of an individual must always rely on the mediation of a particular cultural and historical tradition, and the social-cultural net-work supplied by a community is precisely the backdrop against which self can be realized.

The view of a contemporary republican state is different from that of liberalism. Republicanism believes that the state is not merely a tool designed to realize individual rights and interests and collective well-being, but instead has its own general will and common good. This general will and common good derive from the will of each citizen and their participation in the public arena, which also exists at a higher level than the individual will and interest. For the individual, the republican state is also constructed, and is not a tool; the inner self of the citizen can only be realized through participation in public political life, in the process of pursuing the ideal state and striving to realize the unity between the individual and the state. From this perspective, the state also has inner value for the citizen, as a political community worthy of love and the choice one has made to belong to it. In addition to being a legal and political community, the modern state is also a national cultural community. For the citizens of this state, the state's historical, religious, linguistic, and cultural traditions are primordial, and not subject to choice; these are also parts of the construction of self and self-attachment, allowing the citizens of different nations and states to distinguish themselves from one another, forming a distinctive "us," which yields a sense of national self-belonging. Self always exists in relation to a certain national historical tradition, the self is a self within a cultural stream.

The modern self has three natures: the first is universal human nature; the second is the self as part of a particular political and cultural stream; and the third is a particular self freely chosen on the basis of a compromise between universal human nature and particular culture. Communitarianism and republicanism separately emphasize society and politics as the institutional sources of exterior norms and constraints on self, creating the second kind of self; but the first kind of self is more often realized in the relationship between the individual and *tianxia*, where *tianxia* represents universal human nature and the universal civilization constructed on its basis. Whether the realization of the self is appropriate and legitimate in universal terms is not susceptible of validation on its own terms; nor is a particular cultural-political community a guarantor of legitimacy. Only in the context of universal human nature and universal values do we arrive at a common measure of universal significance, and this is how the self and *tianxia* can circumvent the mediation of the state and achieve direct communication in a modern manner. Even if self is already determined in the new family-state order of contemporary society, this does not mean that there is no longer any space for free choice. Self-realization is not only about identity, it is also constructed, and in the process of pursuing the self, we can also model a new family-state, rebuild communities, the state, and the world. The self and the family-state are variables that shape one another; they are active, dynamic elements mutually embedding one another.

After the "great disembedding," both the new family-state order and the modern self find themselves faced with a "re-embedding." The self must arrive at a new understanding within the new family-state/*tianxia* order, and the family-state/*tianxia* must be rebuilt in the process of the remodeling of the self. This is reciprocal "re-embedding," a dynamic process moving toward an ideal world. Who am I? Who are we? Where is the family-state? Where is *tianxia*? In the final analysis, these are all the same question.

5   What Body for Confucianism's Lonely Soul?

Translator's Introduction

This essay was originally published in 2014 in Southern Weekend *(Nanfang zhoumo), one of China's most popular weekly newspapers, known for its relatively liberal and independent stance. As such, compared with most of the other essays in the volume, the tone of this text is less formal and less academic (there are no footnotes in the original). Often, Xu attempts to write both for his colleagues and for the educated public. Here he appears to be writing for the public in general, although many references are still fairly learned. The text is closer to a long op-ed than to a scholarly article, in accord with Xu's vision of himself as a public intellectual.*

The subject of the essay is the role that Confucianism will play in China's future, a topic often addressed in contemporary China, if more frequently by New Confucians and other cultural conservatives than by liberals. Consequently, if Xu's quarrels are basically with the New Left in his essays on statism and historicism, here his "adversaries" are New Confucians like Jiang Qing,[1] who argues that Confucianism should become China's "national religion" and serve as the core of China's future politics via a tricameral arrangement that will include a meritocratic Confucian elite, a separate body of descendants of Confucius himself, and a third elected body. Xu is scornful of the New Confucians, in part because of what he sees as their nakedly political ambitions, but also because, as an intellectual and historian, he doubts the quality of their "Confucianism." Consequently, as he does elsewhere in this volume, Xu uses history as a means to frame the issues, get the "facts" straight, and render his judgement, which might be read as a sort of liberal appropriation of Confucianism.

It is perhaps striking that Xu takes for granted that Confucianism will necessarily play a role in China's future (and that a discussion of China's future does not include the words "socialism," "communism," "revolution," "Mao," or "Deng"). The point is to decide – intellectually – which role Confucianism should play, which Xu frames as a series of choices. The first choice is for Confucianism to resume a political role much like it had under the dynasties, a choice that Xu implicitly associates with the propositions of China's contemporary New

---

[1] Originally published as "Rujia guhun, roushen hezai?" *Nanfang zhoumo*, September 4, 2014. Also available online at www.infzm.com/content/103951. A helpful English-language introduction to and discussion of Jiang's views can be found in Jiang Qing, *A Confucian Constitutional Order: How China's Ancient Past Can Shape its Political Future*, ed. Daniel A. Bell and Ruiping Fan (Princeton, NJ: Princeton University Press, 2012).

Confucians. For Xu, this is not possible, first because the New Confucians have oversold the supposed "benevolence" that was at the heart of Confucian rule. Following his fellow liberal Qin Hui,[2] Xu argues that traditional rule in China was in fact dominated by a Machiavellian Legalism masquerading as compassionate Confucianism. And even if Xu admits that there were many periods of strong, effective rule under the dynasties, the Legalist-Confucian order never solved the riddle of good government: "the legitimacy of rule, effective limits to power, and orderly succession."

A second choice would be for Confucianism to become the religion of the Chinese people. Not the state religion, which would be part of the first choice, but a genuine religion that addressed popular concerns concerning the meaning of life and death. Here, Xu finds Confucianism itself wanting. Traditionally, Xu insists, Confucianism was an elite affair; "cultivated gentlemen" adopted it as a life strategy and a personality type. Of course, some elements of Confucianism deeply penetrated and structured China's "little tradition," whose operating principles included filial piety, hierarchy, and kinship ties. Confucian rituals were omnipresent, but, in Xu's reading, did not respond to transcendent questions of life and death as did Buddhism, Daoism, Islam, and Christianity.

Xu's choice for the future of Confucianism is as a "civil religion," a term he borrows from the influential American sociologist Robert Bellah (although the idea goes back to Rousseau). Civil religion refers to the basic values that bind a community. These values may have been "religious" at some point, supported by scripture and preached in places of worship, but at some point have become secularized and inform both daily social interactions and political practice. A recurring theme in Xu Jilin's work – and in contemporary Chinese culture at large – is the moral vacuum in which China finds itself. Maoism debunked and discarded Confucianism, but the revolutionary culture created in the People's Republic was itself discredited by the excesses of the Cultural Revolution and by the materialism of the reform period. For Xu, Confucianism can and should fill this vacuum, both because as a central part of China's past it continues to resonate with many of China's people, and because it can easily coexist with liberal political institutions. Thus the future China that Xu images is one in which social cohesion is provided by a re-embrace of Confucianism, and democratic politics provided by liberalism.

For 2,000 years, Confucianism served as traditional China's common culture and official ideology, but a hundred years ago, under Western attack, Confucian culture disintegrated, losing its institutional and social basis. Despite the efforts of several generations of New Confucian scholars to turn back the tide and carry forward the lost tradition, Confucian principles are still but a lonely soul,[3] drifting about in the sky of a small number of elites, unable to reconstitute its body on mother earth.

---

[2] Qin Hui is profiled online in Australian National University's "The China Story." See www.thechinastory.org/key-intellectual/qin-hui-%E7%A7%A6%E6%99%96/. See also, Qin Hui, "Dividing the Big Family Assets," in Wang Chaohua, ed., *One China, Many Paths* (London: Verso, 2003), pp. 128–59.

[3] Translator's note: Xu here modifies the well-known historian Yu Ying-shih's reference to Confucianism as a "wandering soul," first employed in a talk given in Singapore in 1988.

Traditional Confucianism was impressive because it had two institutional bodies. The first was the Han dynasty appointment of the Masters of the Five Classics and the examination system established under the Song. Thanks to these institutional innovations, Confucianism became the official ideology established by the monarchy, and Confucian scholars also became the sole source of officials serving the empire. The second body was the custom of social organization via patriarchal lineages, rituals, and popular religion. Confucianism was premodern culture's "little tradition," and was deeply embedded among the people, becoming the source of daily ethics conduct, if at an unconscious level. Yet these two bodies were both shattered by the arrival of modern society, and the institutions completely disappeared. After a century of tribulation, Confucianism seems to have hopes of revival in the twenty-first century, but most of the current excitement is confined to the academy, where a small number of elites argue for its vigorous return, in the hopes of reversing the desolate state of institutional Confucianism. But the soul of Confucianism continues to float; if the skin is not saved, where will the hair grow?[4]

How can one transform a Confucianism which for a century has had its soul divorced from its body, so that it can find an institutional attachment? Compared to the older generation of academic New Confucians like Mou Zongsan (1909–95), Tang Junyi (1909–78), and Tu Wei-ming (b. 1940), who emphasized Confucian doctrine, there is today a new generation of Confucians who have begun to understand the importance of institutional Confucianism. This, plus the encouragement of the authorities, together with the spiritual hunger of society at large, has provided an unprecedented opportunity to the institutional Confucians for the revival of Confucianism. So the question is: which body will the soul of Confucianism inhabit? Will it look up, and manifest the Way through winning the rulers? Or will it look down, and manifest the Way by enlightening the people?

Confucianism as Official Ideology: A Dead-End Idea

Unlike Protestantism or Buddhism, Confucianism is not only a philosophy of life, but also has a strong political nature. Indeed, its greatest accomplishments lay in government, in realizing the goal of ruling the

---

For a published version of Yu's lecture, see Yu Ying-shih, *Zhongguo wenhua yu xiandai bianqian (Chinese culture and modern change)* (Taibei: Sanmin, 1992), pp. 95–102. John Makeham pursues a similar strategy in his *Lost Soul: "Confucianism" in Contemporary Chinese Academic Discourse* (Cambridge, MA: Harvard University Asia Center, 2008).

[4] Translator's note: A Chinese four-character expression (*chengyu*), which means "how to restore something once its original foundation has disappeared?"

country and bringing peace to the world. Despite the Confucians' heavy political burden, they had fatal weak spots: compared to Protestants, Confucians lacked economic power, as well as an independent organization that would have allowed them to stand up to monarchical power. Compared to the citizens of ancient Greece, they also lacked systemic channels permitting political participation. Although Confucian scholars supposedly swore by Confucius's injunction to "set their will on the Way," and sincerely believed that this Way was superior to the king's power, in fact, in political practice, the Way could only be achieved through power. The ideal of carrying out the Way required flattering the ruler and using his power.

Because of this unbreakable linkage between Way and power, from ancient times down to the present day, all ambitious Confucians seeking to serve society learned to take the path upward toward power, and constantly sought out enlightened rulers in the hopes of transforming their personal studies into ruling ideology. Confucians need enlightened rulers, and enlightened rulers need Confucians. The lesson that Han Wudi (r. 141–87 BC) and subsequent emperors drew from the fact that the Qin dynasty fell after the reign of the first emperor was that relying solely on legalists and draconian laws to rule the country was insufficient. Violence and intimidation can subdue the people, but will not win their hearts. Confucianism preaches benevolent paternalistic government, which rules in the people's interests. Adding Confucian principles to Legalism brought long-term legitimacy to imperial rule. As a result, most of China's emperors, from Han Wudi through the great Qing emperors, ruled through a combination of a Confucian exterior and a Legalist interior, occasionally seasoned with elements drawn from Huang-Lao Daoism[5] and the *realpolitik* of the hegemon.

The alliance between the monarchy and the Confucians was limited, mutually exploitive and fragile. The monarchy was superstitious and Machiavellian. As the physical embodiment of power, even the emperor most familiar with the Confucian classics knew that the blood flowing through his veins was the blood of Legalism, and believed that the "laws and methods of governing" were all-encompassing. As for Confucians, benevolent rule was the goal and the monarchy a means to that end. But even the best Confucians were only tools for the dynasty; the heart of the emperor remained Legalist. Look at the late Qing Foreign Affairs movement of the late nineteenth century, the 1898 Hundred Days' reform

---

[5] Translator's note: Huang-Lao Daoism (the Daoism of the Yellow Emperor and of Laozi) was an influential body of thought in the early Han period, combining Daoist, Confucian, and Legalist traditions.

and the New Policies of the early twentieth century, all of which sought to reform China through partial Westernization; while scholars and the Qing court both claimed to be "protecting the country," in fact both had ulterior motives. What the scholars sought to protect by strengthening China was *tianxia*, the civilizational order dear to Confucians, while the Qing court sought to strengthen China so as to protect the empire, the physical territory dominated by the Manchu nobility. To save *tianxia*, the Confucians were willing to change dynasties; to keep their empire, the Qing were willing to sacrifice *tianxia*.

Since the alliance between the monarchy and the Confucians was based on mutual exploitation, and since their ultimate goals were not the same, a split was inevitable. For the Confucian scholar, serving a ruler was like serving a tiger: if he managed to give his all to a ruler for a certain time, then the pain and effort of his life was worthwhile. In the Former Han period, the fiercely ambitious Han Wudi "discarded the hundred schools and accorded his sole respect to Confucian methods," and the great Confucian scholar Dong Zhongshu (179–114 BC), who gave the empire the Yin Yang and Five Elements theories[6] in a new "Confucian" intellectual synthesis, received imperial favor. But what the emperor wanted was the legitimacy that Dong's theory conferred on the empire, and he hated Dong's notion of the "concordance between heaven and man" which placed the "heavenly mandate" above imperial power. In 135 BC, the Gao temple in Liaodong where Han Wudi sacrificed to his ancestors burned to the ground, and in thoroughly scholarly manner, Dong Zhongshu argued that this was an expression of heaven's anger with the ruler. Dong composed a memorial entitled "Disasters Resulting from Unusual Phenomena" but someone secretly informed the court before he could submit it. Han Wudi was furious, and decided to have Dong Zhongshu beheaded. Later he relented out of respect for Dong's abilities, and granted a pardon, but Dong lost his position, and he never again intervened in the affairs of government. He spent his sunset years studying and writing.

The link between Confucianism and Legalism suggests that the monarchy and the Confucians ruled *tianxia* together, but in fact in terms of power the bond was unequal and lacked institutional guarantees. Imperial power was active and dynamic, while the scholars were passive. The political space available to the Confucians depended completely on

---

[6] Translator's note: Yin Yang and Five Element theories are cosmological explanations for the origin and evolution of natural and social life that preceded Confucius (and the Zhou period in general) by centuries. Dong Zhongshu "integrated" them into his version of Confucian doctrine.

whether the ruler was enlightened, on the extent to which he was open to their proposals. Over the centuries, China knew good times and bad in cycles of good governance and disorder. This was not caused by the system but rather by the nature of the rulers and ministers who governed the state. Of course there were the enlightened reigns of the Wen (r. 180–157 BC) and Jing (r. 157–141 BC) emperors under the Han, the peak of Tang prosperity during the Kaiyuan period of the Tang (713–41), but as twentieth century Chinese historian Qian Mu (1895–1990) said, even if Han Wudi or Tang Taizong (r. 598–649) were able rulers, they still did not establish a good system. Under an enlightened ruler, everything flourishes, but if he is followed by a poor ruler, the people are lost as government disappears. What was lacking was precisely long-range institution building.

The twentieth-century New Confucian Mou Zongsan had an important insight: premodern Chinese politics paid attention to ruling, but not to government. Confucianism provided abstract theories concerning paternalistic rule in the people's name, and Legalism provided mature tools to control society and ride herd on a bureaucracy. But Confucian doctrine was too empty, and Legalism too focused on the nuts and bolts of ruling, and neither was able to achieve a government transcending the ruler and according the greatest power to the legislature, which would be a hardy constitutional order.

Of course, traditional Confucian politics was not without value. Over the course of several thousand years of historical practice of alliances with and struggles against imperial power, Confucians accumulated a rich store of political wisdom: the marriage of moral and political authority, the collaboration of Confucians and rulers to rule *tianxia*, the practice of listening to criticism from below, the examination system and the censorate – such political wisdom and institutional practice derived from the popular will and took heavenly principles as their highest value. With Confucian scholars serving as a nexus of social power, over a comparatively long period they limited imperial absolutism, so that in certain dynasties and periods Chinese politics maintained an enlightened, rational order, enabling the ancient Chinese empire to maintain more than 2,000 years of enlightened rule over a vast territory, a huge population, and a varied culture.

Yet Confucian politics had internal limitations that it could not overcome. It had abstract doctrine and was skilled in the craft of ruling, yet it lacked basic laws in matters of government administration, so that at its best it still had to rely on the individual moral character of virtuous rulers and officials, and could not at a basic level resolve the three core questions of modern politics: the legitimacy of rule, effective limits to power, and orderly succession. From this perspective, the value of restoring Confucian politics in a modern society is not immediately obvious. Whether Confucianism can have value in the future is entirely dependent on how Confucianism is attached to the system. If we return to a system with a Confucian exterior and a Legalist heart, consistent with the ancient Qin–Han system, an old system which was never entirely functional for 2,000 years, how can we expect it to flourish in the twenty-first century?

The true hope of political Confucianism is to be carefully grafted onto a modern system containing the rule of law and democracy, after which the wisdom of the elite would transcend private interests and cancel out the populist politics of one man–one vote, and the public-minded notion of "the world belongs to all" (*tianxia weigong*) would redirect struggles between interest groups toward common concerns. Confucian politics itself is neither good nor bad in the abstract; everything depends on who it partners up with. If it can, as the former generation of New Confucians like Mou Zongsan and Tang Junyi suggested, relocate its place within a legal, democratic framework, then it might generate its own transformation.

Confucianism as Religion: An Unrealizable Dream

The road up toward official ideology is a dead end. But Confucianism still has another option, which is to take the road down to the people and transform itself into a Confucian religion, becoming a religion of the soul, like Protestantism, Islam, Buddhism, and Daoism.

In the past few years, the process of secularization in China has hollowed out people's souls. In response to spiritual emptiness, a vacuum of values and loss of meaning, Protestantism, Catholicism, Buddhism, Daoism, Islam, and many kinds of popular religion have developed very quickly, accompanying the spiritual crisis provoked by secularization, and the religious revival has reached a point of no return. Where is Confucianism in all of this? Can Confucianism transform itself to become like Buddhism, Daoism, Christianity, and Islam, a genuine religion with a place among the people?

Turning Confucianism into the Confucian religion has been tried in the past. The late Ming left-wing Confucians, Wang Yangming (1472–1529), and the Taizhou school transformed the Zhu Xi (1130–1200) orthodox Neoconfucian tradition and set its sights on the people, giving lectures to the masses. They believed that everyone possessed innate knowledge and that everyone could become a sage. They preached among the common people of all walks of life and attracted a good many followers, and were not far from establishing a religion. Of course, the greatest effort to turn Confucianism into a religion was undertaken in the early Republican period by Kang Youwei (1858–1927) and Chen Huanzhang (1881–1933) and their organization, the Confucian Religion Society. Kang Youwei was merely the spiritual leader; the real organizer was Chen Huanzhang, the philosophy Ph.D. from Columbia University. Chen not only set up the Confucian religion in a way that imitated Protestantism, he also added modern content and rituals. Still, his efforts ended in failure. The most important reason for the failure was that although Kang and Chen circulated among the people, their hearts were in the imperial court. They couldn't bear the indifference of the people, and sought to use state power to make Confucianism into a state religion. Those involved in the Confucian Religion Society were old and young fogeys from the Qing court as well as frustrated, unemployed politicians and traditional gentry. They were backward-looking and greedy, and unconcerned about saving souls – their ambitions were political. The Confucian Religion Society was not even up to the standards of the Wang Yangming movement of the late Ming, and was quite distant from society and out of touch with the common people. They borrowed Christian forms, but had none of the Christian spirit; they did not resist political power, or diligently sow their seeds among the people, and displayed none of the true religious spirit of changing the world through saving people's souls.

In the past few years, the New Confucian group led by Jiang Qing (b. 1953) has set off on the same dead-end path as the Confucian Religion Society. They have set up popular academies and studies, but are not content with grassroots society and instead want to return to the halls of power and have Confucianism recognized as the national religion, with the traditional Four Books and Five Classics at the center of education, or perhaps even the subject matter for national exams. If Confucianism were to become the national religion, and the Four Books and Five Classics[7] the subject of the college entry exams, that would be the end of the Confucian religion, which would either turn into a ruling ideology or a stepping stone to self-promotion that scholars would honor and loathe at the same time.

According to my own observations, there is a great difference between popular Confucian religion on the mainland and in Taiwan. Taiwan's Confucian religion has a grassroots feel and a human touch. It is rooted in popular society and concerned with the suffering of the people. It is

---

[7] Translator's note: The Four Books and Five Classics were the core of the Confucian textual corpus, and the basis of the examination system by which government officials were selected from the Song dynasty forward.

devoted to the reconstruction of the spiritual order. On the mainland, while some of the followers of Confucian religion are among the people, most seem like grifters or officials. These two occupy different positions, but they share a personality type in that they both want to tell people what to do.

Huang Jinxing (b. 1950), a Taiwan-based scholar of Confucian religion and Confucian temples, has pointed out that the traditional Confucian temple was a sacred space closely linked to state power. Sacrifices at the Confucian temple were displays of state power, in a space that the people dared not enter, a closed space that evoked respect and fear. There was a Confucian whose pen-name was "man awakened from dreams," who even in his dreams wanted to eat a piece of cold pork in the Confucian temple, exclaiming that "it would be a shame to live a whole life without eating a piece of sacrificial meat."[8] Huang Jinxing pointed out that the common people respected Confucius but felt no intimacy toward him, and that Confucian religion "is at the base a national religion, not the religion of a private person. It is a public religion, not an individual religion." The basic nature of Confucian religion is too elitist, and its preoccupations are the great questions of governance, and in a society that lacks democracy, Confucianism has no other choice than to rely on state power to carry out its ideal of saving the world.

For the average person, the heavens are distant and the emperor far away. The average person's religious needs are for salvation, spiritual support, faith in destiny, and a sense of the meaning of life and death. Buddhism, Daoism, Christianity, and Islam all make such promises and hence can serve as something for the people to believe in. Confucianism has a religious character, but it is a scholar's religion that pays more attention to the here and now, human affairs, and rationality. Jiang Qing built his Yangming Study in Guizhou, and led followers there to read the sacred books, but they have no connection with local villagers, who don't identify with Jiang and his followers. The villagers also took the tiles specially made for Jiang's study and used them on a Buddhist Goddess of Mercy (Guanyin) temple in the village that needed them more. Clearly, today's Confucian revival remains the affair of a small number of elites running around in their own little circles. It has nothing to do with grassroots society.

This is not surprising. Confucianism is not a religion of revelation, and belief is not the most important thing. What Confucians hold dear

---

[8] Translator's note: Xu's tone is sarcastic here, suggesting that many Confucians dreamed only of becoming an object of sacrifice in the Confucian temple.

is individual cultivation, in which one achieves a certain enlightenment at the level of knowledge, and then through moral practice becomes a model gentleman or a sage. But the demands in terms of knowledge and moral character are too high, and can be the ideal of only a small number of scholars. Average people need "belief," or more precisely, they hope to obtain spiritual protection through simple religious rituals. It doesn't matter whether it is the protection of a transcendent god, or a simplistic religious ritual. These two are Confucianism's weak points. Were Confucianism to become a popular religion like Christianity or Buddhism, this would go against Confucianism's original nature, and abandon its historical tradition and social position. The Confucian tradition has been very well preserved in South Korea and Taiwan, yet to date we see no moves toward the creation of a Confucian religion at the level of individual religious meaning. Why would this happen on the mainland where the Confucian tradition has been cut off?

Confucianism as a Set of "Civil Teachings"; Investing Hope in the People

Historical Confucianism had a single soul, yet it had three bodies, or modes of existence: one was as the "national religion" of the rulers and officials, and another was as Neoconfucian philosophy. Both of these have fairly clear religious components. The third is as a religion of order building on ethical and moral concerns. Instead of calling this a religion, I prefer to adopt the contemporary New Confucian scholar Qiu Feng's (b. 1966) term "civil teachings."

These "civil teachings," as I understand them, refer not to the Western notions of religion that we might find in Confucianism, but instead Confucianism's own "human transformations." We can identify four dimensions: First, Confucianism is less concerned with belief and revelation than other religions, and instead seeks to carry out the Way through rational self-consciousness and moral practice. Second, Confucianism does not communicate with the spirits to ask for protection via prayer, worship, and other religious means, nor does it aspire to an eternal life in a transcendent realm. Instead it focuses on actual life as lived, and through civil transformation, employing the rituals of secular daily life, conveys Confucian doctrines to people's hearts, producing excellent customs. Third, Confucianism does not provide the meaning of life and ultimate values for individual spiritual order, but rather builds an ethical, moral order commonly shared by society as a whole, through the transformation of "benevolence" into "ritual." Fourth, Confucian ethical and moral values and its norms are internalized in other formal religions, in popular religions, in ancestor worship, and in sacrifices in daily life. This is what is meant by the expression "using the spirit world to inculcate virtue." Confucianism might be seen as a sort of "latent religion," quietly working among the people, who employ it without their conscious knowledge.

Looking at the three historical bodies of Confucianism in the context of modern society, the idea of hoping for a new honeymoon with state power as official ideology is a dead end. I would add that seeing it as a tool for self-cultivation is also the affair of a small number of elites, with little relationship to most citizens. In my opinion, Confucianism's most important function in China's future is to develop into a set of civil teachings with common ethics and morals at its core that would contribute to the reconstruction of a proper Chinese social order.

In that case, if Confucianism were seen as civil teachings leading to the establishment of an ethical, moral order, then what would its relationship be to other religions and to liberalism?

China is different from the West in that it is polytheistic. Confucianism, Daoism, and Buddhism were combined as the "three teachings," but Daoism and Buddhism were religions, while Confucianism was a sort of civil teaching, and all three had their own function and territory. Qiu Feng argues that China has "one civil teaching and many religions," which in a word sums up the true nature of the relationship between Confucianism and other religions. Because Confucianism was a civil teaching that sought only to create public order, it maintained an open, inclusive attitude to other religions that worked at the individual, spiritual level. Even though the Neoconfucianism of the Song and Ming periods incorporated Buddhism into Confucianism and developed its own cultivation system and sense of life direction, Confucianism remained nonetheless too rational and its teachings too elevated. It was a religion only for scholars, and ordinary people couldn't digest it. And even among scholars, Confucianism as a system of religious cultivation had its limits, because it talked about only the present world, not about the after-life. Given its over-emphasis on human concerns and its insufficiency in matters of gods and spirits, those Confucians who were concerned about cycles of rebirth or who had spiritual pursuits turned to Buddhism or Daoism or Christianity.

From the opposite perspective, Buddhists, Daoists, and Christians living in the Confucian world also followed secular Confucian ethics, honored their parents, sacrificed to their ancestors, and respected local customs, which produced Confucianized Christians, Buddhists, Muslims, and Daoist priests. As a set of civil teachings, Confucianism was supple and yielding, and worked its way into all religious traditions, whether native or foreign. On the one hand it nativized and Confucianized foreign religions; on the other, it absorbed elements from other religious traditions, further consolidating its position as a civil teaching that transcended other religions.

So is Confucianism, seen as a set of civil teachings, in conflict with liberalism, which also seeks to establish a good public order? Although Confucianism and liberalism are both secular theories, they nonetheless have their own points of emphasis and territories. Even if liberalism has its own ethical values, at base it is a set of political philosophies, and it pursues political philosophies that conform to personal ethical values. While Confucianism, seen as civil teachings, has its own political thoughts, it remains at base a set of ethical philosophies, and it pursues a ritual and political order in daily life. The Confucianism that truly conflicts with the political philosophy of liberalism is not the Confucianism of civil teachings, but rather political Confucianism, the doctrine of rulers and officials. Of course, this conflict is not absolute. As I said above, some of Confucianism's political wisdom can complement areas where liberal politics are insufficient.

Confucianism as civil teachings should not conflict with liberalism. Should the two come to blows it will be at their own expense and will profit their common enemy, Legalism. They should act like husband and wife on the weekend, sometimes together, sometimes apart, helping one another out. According to the theory of Habermas (b. 1929), modern society is divided into a systems world and a lifeworld. The systems world revolves around the market and power. Liberalism aims to be the master of the world of systems, using power and contracts to set norms for the market, and using law and democracy to constrain power. But outside of the world of systems there is another world that is not utilitarian, where people exchange feelings. In many countries, this world is governed by religion, but in China, this is the territory that Confucianism should govern.

Habermas particularly stresses that the systems world and the lifeworld each have their own values, which are valid as long as they do not transgress their boundaries. The problem is that in today's society, the systems world is colonizing the lifeworld, applying the principles of the market and of power, so that the natural relations among people are full of utilitarianism bereft of personality, feeling, and ethics. If it's not the domination of hierarchies of power, then it's the control of the money from market exchange. In China, we also have the inverse situation, wherein the lifeworld invades and colonizes the world of systems. As the ethical principles of the lifeworld, Confucianism invades market space or political territory, looking for connections in the egalitarian space of the market, talking about personal connections in the sober world of the legal order. In these cases, Confucianism transgresses its proper status, and the harm it does is not less than what occurs when systems colonize the lifeworld.

In today's twenty-first-century world, systems are increasingly globalized and universalized. This is what modern civilization is. But the lifeworld is different, its space is cultural, and different countries, different peoples, different groups quite rightly have their distinctive cultures and lifeworlds. Civilization is universal; culture is particular. The reason why Confucianism is important to China is that China lives not only in a universal civilization governed by systems, it also has a vibrant lifeworld with its own history, tradition, and cultural nature. "The end of history" is not frightening from the perspective of systems. It is frightening to imagine the end of the lifeworld, the "universally homogenized state" that worried the Russo-French philosopher and statesman Alexandre Kojève (1902–68). From this perspective, China needs Confucianism, a Confucianism of civil teachings that protects the lifeworld itself.

China's future cultural order should be three-dimensional. The first dimension is that of political culture, which has to do with the proper choice, the right choice, of our common political order. Here, liberalism will play a leading role, but the Confucian tradition and the socialist tradition will both contribute their wisdom. The second dimension is that of that of public ethics, with the way we envision human relationships. This is the proper territory of the civil teachings brand of Confucianism, which ethical liberalism and other religious traditions will serve as complements. The third dimension is that of the individual soul, and has to do with choices concerning morality, the meaning we attribute to life on earth, questions of life and death, or forgiveness and salvation. This will include Confucianism, Daoism, Buddhism, Christianity, and Islam in a plural space with many religions. China's particular tradition of religious pluralism will allow Chinese citizens to make their choices from within this space, or even combine them to make their own.

Which body will the lonely soul of Confucianism inhabit? As a doctrine for rulers and officials, history has shown that this is a dead end. As a form of cultivation, it's only a religion for the elite. The broadest perspective for Confucianism in China's future is as a civil teaching that will build a public ethical order. This civil teaching should not be propagated by state power, but should join together with civil society, and develop naturally and spontaneously at the popular level. From its origins with Confucius, Confucianism began in the countryside, and developed among the people. Only later did it enter into the imperial court and become official doctrine, and finally it followed the dissolution of imperial power and fell into desuetude, becoming a lonely soul for a full century. If Confucianism wants to reassume a full, vibrant life, its only choice is to return to its original point of departure, and take up its place once again with the people.

6   The New *Tianxia*: Rebuilding China's Internal and External Order

Translator's Introduction

Although the major themes of this 2015 essay are found in other texts in this volume, they are woven together here in an imaginative way to address a topic that Xu does not often address – Chinese foreign policy. He starts with a fairly familiar presentation of the traditional notion of tianxia *(literally "all under heaven"), which, in Xu's words, connoted both "an ideal civilizational order, and a world spatial imaginary with China's central plains at the core." In one sense, then, China was* tianxia, *the embodiment, when the system functioned at its best, of the set of principles that justified imperial Confucian rule. But* tianxia *was open, not closed; like the twentieth-century American dream,* tianxia *was understood, by the Chinese, as a kind of universalism to which other cultures could aspire. Xu illustrates his point less through discussion of China's traditional tribute system, and more through exploration of the historical relations between the Han people and the various non-Han "barbarian groups" on China's peripheries, his point being that the processes of assimilation, borrowing, and integration were multiple, complex, and non-problematic at an ideological level. In other words, prior to the arrival of the notion of the nation-state, "Chinese" and "barbarian" were not understood in racial terms but in civilizational terms. An open, universal* tianxia *welcomed Asia's "huddled masses" as long as they recognized* tianxia*'s brilliance.*

Xu then uses this history lesson to turn the tables on his familiar adversaries: in this instance, China's ultra-nationalists and those, like Zhang Weiwei or Pan Wei,[1] who use China's "uniqueness" to argue that China must ignore the West and return to its own civilization. He argues that their patriotism and national pride are based in a misreading of Chinese history: when China was great in the past, China was open, not closed, and if China wishes to be great again it must

---

[1] Originally published as "Xin tianxia zhuyi: chongjian Zhongguo de neiwai zhixu," in Xu Jilin and Liu Qing, eds., *Xin tianxia zhuyi*, no. 13 of *Zhishi fenzi luncong* (New *Tianxia*, Intellectuals series) (Shanghai: Shanghai renmin chubanshe, 2014), also available online at www.21ccom.net/articles/thought/zhongxi/20150825128247_all.html. Original translation by Mark McConaghy and Tang Xiaobing, edited by David Ownby for stylistic consistency. For English-language works by Zhang Weiwei, see, among others, *China Wave: Rise of a Civilizational State* (Hackensack, NJ: World Century Publishing Corporation, 2012); for Pan Wei, see *Western System versus Chinese System* (Singapore: East Asian Institute, National University of Singapore, 2010).

adopt the same posture because civilizations by definition must be universal. He argues further, building on themes developed in Chapter 2, that even the patriotism and national pride of those who preach a narrow-minded China Dream are the products of China's embrace of the nation-state and the nation-state's goals of wealth and power. In other words, the pride that China's rise has inspired is largely a pride born of playing the West's game well. China's own "game" is still forgotten.

Xu then attempts to imagine a world in which some version of tianxia *replaces China's contemporary state-driven posture. In the context of China's problematic relations with non-Han people on the peripheries – chiefly but not exclusively Tibetans and the Muslim peoples of Xinjiang – Xu suggests that the Qing dynasty politics of "multiculturalism," which recognized self-rule for minority groups within certain limits, functioned better than current policies, which are a mixture of forced integration and forced modernization. In the context of the geopolitics of East Asia, Xu imagines a world based on shared* tianxia *values rather than interest-based alliances or antagonisms. And in the world at large, Xu proposes the creation and propagation of a* tianxia *2.0, which will be "de-centered and non-hierarchical," and hence ready to contribute to the construction of "new universalisms" – i.e., to give substance to the postmodern order.*

The rise of China may well be the event that will have the greatest impact on the twenty-first century. Yet despite the expansion of China's power, the country's internal and external orders have grown increasingly tense. Domestically, national greatness has not generated a centripetal force attracting the various minority nationalities in the border regions to the center. Instead, ethnic and religious conflicts continually erupt in Tibet and Xinjiang, to the point that one now sees extreme separatism and terrorist activities. Internationally, the rise of China has made its neighbors nervous. Conflicts over islands in the South and East China Seas have brought the threat of war to East Asia, and the outbreak of military hostilities is a constant danger. Nationalism has reached soaring heights not just in China but throughout East Asia, in a spiral of mutual antagonism. The possibility of regional war is increasing, in an atmosphere similar to that of nineteenth-century Europe.

With crisis drawing ever closer, do we have a plan? It's easy enough to make a list of national policies to alleviate the situation, but the essential is to extirpate the roots of the crisis. And the origin of the crisis is nothing other than the mindset that accords utter supremacy to the nation, a mindset that entered China in the late nineteenth century and has since become the dominant way of thinking among officials and the common people. Nationalism has always been an integral part of modernity, yet when it becomes the highest value of statecraft, it can inflict destructive calamities on the world, as in the European World Wars.

To truly address the problem at its roots, we need a form of thought that can act as a counterpoint to nationalism. I call this thought the "new *tianxia*," an axial civilizational wisdom that comes from China's premodern tradition, interpreted anew along modern lines.

The Universal Values of *Tianxia*

What is *tianxia*? Within Chinese tradition, *tianxia* had two essential meanings: an ideal civilizational order, and a world spatial imaginary with China's central plains at the core.

The American sinologist Joseph Levenson (1920–69) argued that in China's early history, "the notion of the 'state' referred to a structure of power, while the notion of *tianxia* pointed to a structure of values."[2] As a value system, *tianxia* was a set of civilizational principles with a corresponding institutional system. The Ming dynasty scholar Gu Yanwu (1613–82) distinguished between "the loss of the state and the loss of *tianxia*." Here, the state was merely the political order of the dynasty, while *tianxia* was a civilizational order with universal application. It referred not only to a particular dynasty or state, but above all to eternal, absolute, and universal values. The state could be destroyed, but *tianxia* could not. Otherwise humanity would devour itself, disappearing into a Hobbesian jungle.

While today Chinese nationalism and statism have risen to tremendous heights, behind these ideologies lurks a value system that emphasizes Chinese particularism. As if the West had Western values and China had Chinese values, meaning that China cannot follow the West's "crooked" path but must follow its own particular path to modernity. At first glance, this argument looks very patriotic, giving pride of place to China, but in fact, it is very "un-Chinese" and untraditional. This is because China's civilizational tradition was not nationalistic, but rather grounded in *tianxia*, whose values were universal and humanistic rather than particular. *Tianxia* did not belong to one particular people or nation. Confucianism, Daoism, and Buddhism all are what the German-Swiss philosopher Karl Jaspers (1883–1969) called "axial civilizations" of the premodern world. Just like Christianity or the civilization of Ancient Rome, Chinese civilization took universal concern for the whole of humanity as it starting point, using the values of other peoples as a kind of self-judgement. After the modern period, when nationalism entered China from Europe, China's vision narrowed considerably and its civilization was diminished. From the grandeur of *tianxia*, where all humans

---

[2] Lie Wensen (Joseph Levenson), *Rujia Zhongguo jiqi xiandai mingyun (Confucian China and its modern fate)*, Zheng Dahua, trans. (Beijing: Zhongguo shehui kexue chubanshe, 2000), p. 84.

can be integrated into the cosmos, Chinese civilization narrowed to the pettiness of "this is Western, and this is Chinese." Mao Zedong once spoke of "China's need to make a greater contribution to humanity," arguing that "only when the proletariat liberates all of humanity can it liberate itself," revealing a broad vision of internationalism behind his nationalism. But all we find in today's China Dream is the great revival of the Chinese nation.

Of course, premodern Chinese people spoke not just of *tianxia* but also of the difference between barbarians (*yi*) and Chinese (*xia*). However, the premodern notion of Chinese and barbarian was completely different than the China–West, us–them binary discourse on the lips of today's extreme nationalists. Today's binary thinking is the result of the influence of modern racism, ethnic consciousness, and statism: Chinese and barbarian, us and the other, exist in a relationship of absolute enmity, with no space for communication or integration between them. In traditional China, the distinction between Chinese and barbarian was not a fixed, racialized concept, but was rather a relative cultural concept that contained the possibility of communication and transformation. The difference between barbarian and Chinese was determined solely on the basis of whether one had a connection to the values of *tianxia*. While *tianxia* was absolute, the labels of barbarian and Chinese were relative. While blood and race were innate and unchangeable, civilization could be studied and emulated. As the Chinese American historian Hsu Cho-yun (b. 1930) put it, within Chinese culture "there are no absolute 'others,' there are simply relational 'selves.'"[3] History has many examples of Chinese being transformed into barbarians, as in the case where Chinese were assimilated into the "southern barbarians" known as the Man people. Likewise, history provides many examples of the reverse process, with barbarians being transformed into Chinese, an example of which would be the western, nomadic Hu people's transformation into Hua, or those who have embraced *tianxia*. The Han people were originally a farming people, while the majority of the Hu people were a grassland people: during the periods of the Six Dynasties (222–589), the Sui-Tang (589–907), and the Yuan-Qing (1271–1911), farming China and grassland China underwent a dual-directional process of integration. Chinese culture absorbed much of the culture of the Hu people. For example, Buddhism was originally the religion of the Hu people; the blood of the Han people has mixed within it elements of barbarian peoples; from clothing to daily habits, there is not a single area where the

[3] See Xu Zhuoyun (Cho-yun Hsu), *Wozhe yu tazhe: Zhongguo lishishang de neiwai fenbu (Self and other: Distinctions between inner and outer in Chinese history)* (Beijing: Sanlian shudian, 2010).

people of the central plains have not been influenced by the Hu peoples. For example, in the earliest periods, Han people were accustomed to sitting on mats. Later they adopted the folding stools of the Hu people, and from folding stools they developed toward backed chairs: in the end they ended up changing their customs completely.

The reason that Chinese civilization did not decline over the course of 5,000 years is precisely because it was not closed and narrow. Instead, it benefitted from its openness and inclusiveness, and never stopped transforming outside civilizations into its own traditions. Employing the universal perspective of *tianxia*, China was concerned only with the question of the character of these values. It did not ask ethnic questions about "mine" or "yours," but absorbed everything that was "good," connecting "you" and "me" in an integrated whole which became "our" civilization.

However, today's extreme nationalists see China and the West as absolute, natural enemies. They use absolute distinctions of race and ethnicity to resist all foreign civilizations. Even in the academic world there is a popular "theory of the original sin of Western learning," according to which anything created by Westerners must be rejected out of hand. The judgements of these extreme nationalists regarding standards of truth, goodness, and beauty no longer display the universalism of traditional China. All that is left is the narrow perspective of "mine": as if as long as it is "mine" it must be "good," and as long as it is "Chinese" then it is an absolute good that does not need to be proven. This kind of "politically correct" nationalism seems like it is extolling Chinese civilization, but in fact it is doing just the opposite: it takes the universality of Chinese civilization and debases it into nothing but the particular culture of one nation and one people. There is an important difference between civilization and culture. Civilization is concerned with "what is good," while culture is merely concerned with "what is ours." Culture distinguishes the self from the other, defining the self's cultural identity. However, civilization is different, seeking to answer the question "what is good?" from a universal perspective transcending that of one nation and one people. This "good" is not just good for "us," it is also good for "them," and for all humanity. Within universal civilization, there is no distinction between "us" and "the other," only human values respected universally.

If China's goal is not simply to strengthen the nation-state, but rather to become once again a civilizational power with great influence on world affairs, then its every word and deed must take universal civilization as its point of departure, and in dialogues with the world it must have its own unique understanding of universal civilization. This understanding cannot be culturalist, and it cannot be littered with standard forms of self-defense like "this is China's particular national character," or "this concerns China's sovereignty, and no one else is allowed to discuss it." It must use the values of universal civilization to persuade the world and demonstrate its legitimacy. As a great power with global influence, what China must achieve today is not just its dream of rejuvenating the nation and the state, but more importantly the redirection of its nationalistic spirit toward the world. What China needs to reconstruct is not just a particularistic culture suited to one country and one people, but rather a civilization that has universal value for all humanity. A value that is "good" for China, particularly core values that touch on our shared human nature, must in the same way be "good" for all humanity. The universal nature of Chinese civilization can only be constructed from the perspective of all humanity, and cannot be grounded solely in the particular interests and values of the Chinese nation-state. Historically speaking, Chinese civilization was *tianxia*. To transform *tianxia*, in today's globalized era, into an internationalism integrated with universal civilization is the major goal of a civilizational power.

China is a cosmopolitan power, a global nation that bears Hegel's "world spirit." It must take responsibility for the world and for the "world spirit" it has inherited. This "world spirit" is the new *tianxia* that will emerge in the form of universal values.

A De-centered, Non-hierarchical New Universalism

When Chinese talk about *tianxia*, neighboring countries will react with a fear born of history,[4] worrying that China's rise heralds the return from the dead of the arrogant, self-important, imposing Chinese empire of yore. This concern is not baseless. Alongside universal values, the traditional *tianxia* also had a geographic and spatial expression: a "differential mode of association," to use an expression coined by sociologist Fei Xiaotong (1910–2005) based on China's central plains. *Tianxia* was organized through three concentric circles: the first was the inner circle, the central areas directly ruled by the emperor through the bureaucratic system; the second was the middle circle, the border regions that were indirectly ruled by the emperor through the system of hereditary titles, vassal states, and tribal headsmen; and the third was the tributary system, which established an international hierarchical order bringing many countries to China's imperial court. From the center to the border areas, from inner to

---

[4] Translator's note: Xu uses an expression (*chengyu*) to the effect that "anyone who has actually been bitten by a tiger will blanch at the mention of the word, while the rest of us talk about tigers without difficulty."

outer, traditional *tianxia* imagined and constructed a tripartite concentric world with China at the center, in which the barbarian peoples submitted to central authority.

Over the course of Chinese history, the process of the expansion of the Chinese empire brought sophisticated religion and civilization to bordering areas and countries, and at the same time was replete with violence, subjugation, and enslavement. This was true of dynasties like the Han, Tang, Song, and Ming, ruled by Han emperors, as well as the Mongol Yuan and the Manchu Qing, which had rulers from the border regions. In today's era of the nation-state, with our respect for the equality of peoples and their right to independence and self-determination, any plan to return to the hierarchical *tianxia* order, with China as its center, is not only historically reactionary but is in fact merely wishful thinking. For this reason, *tianxia* needs to pick and choose and revitalize itself in the context of modernity, so as to develop toward a new configuration: *tianxia* 2.0.

What is "new" about the new *tianxia*? In comparison with the traditional concept, its novelty is expressed in two dimensions: one, its de-centered and non-hierarchical nature; two, its ability to create a new sense of universality.

Traditional *tianxia* was a hierarchical concentric politico-civilizational order with China as its core. What the new *tianxia* should discard first is precisely this centralized and hierarchical order. What is "new" about the new *tianxia* is the addition of the principle of the equality of nation-states. In the new *tianxia* order, there is no center, there are only independent and peaceful peoples and states who respect one another. Nor will there be a hierarchical arrangement of power in terms of domination and enslavement, protection and submission; instead it will be a peaceful order of egalitarian coexistence, one that spurns authority and domination. Even more important is that the subject of the new *tianxia* order has already undergone a transformation: there is no longer a distinction between Chinese and barbarian, nor between subject and object. Instead it will be something like what the ancients said: "*Tianxia* is the *tianxia* of *tianxia* people." In the internal order of the new *tianxia*, Han people and the various national minorities will enjoy mutual equality in legal and status terms, and the cultural uniqueness and pluralism of the different nationalities will be respected and protected. And in the international, external order, China's relations with its neighbors and indeed every nation in the world, regardless of whether they are great or small nations, will be defined by the principles of respect for each other's sovereign independence, equality in their treatment of each other, and peaceful coexistence.

The principle of the sovereign equality of nation-states is in fact a kind of "politics of recognition" in which all sides mutually recognize each other's autonomy and uniqueness, and indeed recognize the authenticity of all peoples. The new *tianxia* that takes the "politics of recognition" as its base differs from the old *tianxia*. The reason that the old *tianxia* had a center was due to the belief that the Chinese people who inhabited the center had received the mandate of heaven, and their legitimacy to rule the world thus came from the transcendent will of heaven. This is why there was a distinction between the center and the margins. In today's secular age, the legitimacy of nations and states no longer derives from a universally transcendent world (regardless of whether you call it "God" or "heaven"), but instead from their own authentic nature. The authentic nature of every nation-state means that each has its own distinctive values. A healthy international order must first require that every nation show mutual respect and recognition to all other nations. If we say that the traditional *tianxia*, with the mandate of heaven as its core, was built on the hierarchical relationship of center and periphery, then in the new *tianxia*, in the secular age of the "politics of recognition," this relationship will be that of sovereign equality and mutual respect between all nation-states.

The new *tianxia* is a mutual overcoming of both traditional *tianxia* and the nation-state. On the one hand it overcomes the sense of centrality of traditional *tianxia*, yet maintains its universalist attributes; on the other hand, it absorbs the principle of the sovereign equality of nation-states, yet overcomes the narrow perspective placing national interest above all, using universalism to balance out particularism. The authenticity and sovereignty of the nation-state are not absolute, but subject to outer constraints. This form of constraint is the principle of universal civilization provided by the new *tianxia*. Its passive dimension emerges from its de-centered, non-hierarchical nature; its active dimension attempts to construct a new *tianxia* universalism, one that can be commonly shared.

While traditional *tianxia* was a universal civilization for all humanity, it was like other axial civilizations such as Judaism, Christianity, Islam, India's ancient religions, and the civilizations of ancient Greece and Rome: its universal character took form during a central time in a particular people's history, in which a sense of holy mission was expressed through the principle of "Heaven has given a responsibility to this people" to save a fallen world. In this way, a people's particular culture was elevated to become a universal human civilization. The universality of ancient civilizations emerged from a particular people and region who were able to transcend their particularity through communication with a transcendent holy source (either God or heaven), creating a transcendent and abstract universality. The universal value expressed by China's trad-itional *tianxia* found its source in the transcendent universality of the way of heaven, the principle of heaven, and the mandate of heaven. The diffe-rence between Chinese civilization and the West was that in China the holy and the secular, the transcendent and the real, did not have absolute boundaries: the universality of the sacred *tianxia* was expressed in the real world through the secular will of the common people. Nonetheless, China's *tianxia* was similar to other foundational civilizations in that they all took one people chosen by heaven as their center. As the people's spirit subsequently oriented itself toward the world, it expanded toward its neighbors and toward larger territories, establishing the universality of *tianxia*. Modern civilization, which the Israeli sociologist Shmuel Eisenstadt (1923–2010) has called the "second axial civilization," appeared first in Western Europe and then expanded toward the rest of the world. Like *tianxia* it had an axial character: it moved from the center to the margins, from a core people to every corner of the world.

What new *tianxia* wants to undo is precisely this axial civilizational structure, which is shared by both traditional *tianxia* and other foun-dational civilizations, all of which move from a core people toward the world, from the center to the margins, from a singular particularism to a homogenous universalism. The universal value that the new *tianxia* seeks is a new universal civilization. This kind of civilization does not emerge out of the variation of one particular civilization; it is rather a universal civilization that can be mutually shared by many different civilizations.

Modern civilization emerged in Western Europe, but in the process of its expansion toward the rest of the world, it experienced differen-tiation, stimulating the cultural modernization of various peoples and axial civilizations. By the latter half of the twentieth century, following the rise of East Asia, the development of India, the revolutions in the Middle East, and the modernization of Latin America, many variations of modern civilization had emerged, and modernity no longer belonged to Christian civilization. Rather, what emerged was a multivalent mod-ernity that was integrated with many different axial civilizations and local cultures. The universal civilization that new *tianxia* seeks is precisely this modern civilization that can be collectively shared by different nations and peoples. In his *The Clash of Civilizations and the Remaking of World Order*, Samuel Huntington (1927–2008) clearly differentiated between two different narratives of universal civilization: the first appeared within the binary analytical framework of "tradition and modernity," which was part of Cold War ideology. Such a framework saw the West as the standard for universal civilization, and deserving of imitation by all non-Western countries. The other narrative employed the analytical framework of plural civilizations, which understood the concept as the common values and accumulated social and cultural structures that could be mutually recognized by various civilizational entities and cultural communities. This new universal civilization takes shared mutuality as its founding characteristic. While it shares historical origins with the West, in its current development it has separated from and transcended the West, and is now shared by the entire world.

The new universality sought by the new *tianxia* is a shared universality, and in this sense differs from the universality of the old axial civilizations. The traditional *tianxia* and the old axial civilizations possessed universals that were distilled from the particularism of a given people, in communication with each of these people's transcendent worlds. But the universal character of the new *tianxia* is not founded on the basis of any one particularity, but on many particularities. As such it no longer possesses the transcendental character of traditional *tianxia*, nor does it need the endorsement of the mandate of heaven, the will of the gods, or moral metaphysics. The universality of new *tianxia* takes as its basic characteristic each civilization's and culture's "accumulated common knowledge." In one sense, this is a return to the Confucian ideal of the world of the "superior man": "The superior man acts in harmony with others but does not seek to be like them."[5] The different value systems and material pursuits of various civilizations and cultures are accommodated in the same world using harmonious methods, sharing the most basic consensus regarding mutual values.

The universality sought by the new *tianxia* transcends both Sinocentrism and Eurocentrism. It does not seek to create a civilizational hegemony on the basis of an axial civilization and national culture; it does not imagine that any particular civilization will represent the twenty-first century, to say nothing of representing humanity's vast future. The new *tianxia* rationally understands the inner limitations of all civilizations and cultures, and accepts that today's world is plural and multipolar, whether from the perspective of civilizational order or political alignments. Despite the discourse of power and the hegemony of empire, the true wish of humanity is not the domination of a single civilization or system, no matter how ideal or great it might be. What the Russo-French scholar Alexandre Kojève (1902–68) described as a "universally homogenous

---

[5] Translator's note: The "superior man," or *junzi*, is a key concept in the Confucian *Analects*, representing the end result of Confucian cultivation. The full quotation, in the Robert Eno translation available online, is "The *junzi* acts in harmony with others but does not seek to be like them; the small man seeks to be like others and does not act in harmony." See www.indiana.edu/~p374/Analects_of_Confucius_(Eno-2015).pdf, 13.23.

state" is always terrifying. The truly beautiful world is the one praised by the German Enlightenment intellectual Johann Herder (1744–1803), perfumed by the aroma of many different flowers. But for a pluralized world to avoid massacres between civilizations and cultures, one needs a Kantian universalism and an everlasting peaceful order. The universal principle of world order cannot take the rules of the game of Western civilization as its standard, nor can this principle be built on the logic of resistance to the West. The new universalism is one that all people can enjoy: the "overlapping consensus," in the American scholar John Rawls's (1921–2002) words, that has emerged from different civilizations and cultures.

In his essay, "How Does the Subject Face the Other?" the Taiwanese philosopher Qian Yongxiang (b. 1949) differentiates between three different kinds of universality. The first emphasizes the struggle between domination and subjugation, life and death, where one achieves the "universality of the negation of the other" through his conquest. The second uses avoidance to transcend the other, pursuing a kind of neutrality between the self and other and achieving a "universality that transcends the other." The third is produced out of the mutual recognition of the self and the other, based on respecting difference and actively seeking dialogue and consensus, a "universality that recognizes the other."[6] A universalism that takes either China or the West as its center belongs to the first category of dominating and "negating the other," while the kind of "universal values" that liberalism promotes disregard the internal differences that exist between different cultures and civilizations. Liberalism aims, in a "value-neutral" way, to transcend the particularism of both the self and other on its way to constructing a "transcendent universalism." However, behind both domination and transcendence lies a lack of recognition and respect for the uniqueness and pluralism of others. The "mutually shared universality" of the new *tianxia* is similar to Qian Yongxiang's third category: a "universality based on recognition of the other." It does not seek to establish the hegemony of one particular civilization among many different civilizations, cultures, peoples, and nations, nor does it belittle the particular paths taken by major civilizations. Instead, it seeks dialogue and the achievement of shared commonality through equal interactions among multiple civilizations.

---

[6] Qian Yongxiang, "Zhuti ruhe miandui tazhe: Pubian zhuyi de sanzhong leixing" (How does the subject deal with others? Three types of universalism), in Qian Yongxiang, *Pubian yu teshe de bianzheng: Zhengzhi sixiang de fajue (The dialectics of universal and particular: The exploration of political thought)* (Taibei: Taiwan yanjiuyuan renwen shehui kexue yanjiu zhongxin zhengzhi sixiang yanjiu zhuanti zhongxin, 2012), pp. 30–31.

John Rawls once envisaged an order of universal justice for constitutional states and a global order of the "law of peoples," the title he gave to his 1999 book on the subject. He argued that the constitutional state could establish a politically liberal internal order based on a "common understanding" arising out of the "overlapping consensus" drawn from different religious, philosophical, and moral systems. In international affairs, a globally just order could be constructed out of universal human rights. Here, Rawls perhaps errs in reversing the paths to be followed. A country's internal order of justice requires powerful common values with substantive content; it cannot use an expedient "overlapping consensus" as its base. But for many axial civilizations, the elements of international society that coexist with national culture, and the use of Western human rights standards as the core value of "the law of peoples," have appeared to be too substantive. Internally, the nation-state requires a thick common rationality, while international society can only establish a thin minimalist ethics. Such minimalist ethics can only take the "overlapping consensus" of different civilizations and cultures as its foundation: this is the de-centered, non-hierarchical shared universality that the new *tianxia* seeks.

Tianxia's Internal Order: Unity in Diversity as National Governance

Tianxia was the soul of premodern China, and the systemic body of this soul was the Chinese empire, which differs greatly from the form of today's nation-state. The systemic form of the nation-state is one nation for one people, a nation that establishes an internally unified market and institutional system, as well as a unified national identity and national culture. The methods of governance of an empire are more diverse and flexible: it does not demand uniformity between the inner regions of the empire and its border areas. As long as border regions maintain their allegiance to the central government, the empire can allow the peoples and regions under its administration to maintain their religions and cultures, and in the political realm maintain a sense of relative autonomy. All successful empires in history, including the Macedonian, Roman, Persian, or Islamic empires of the ancient past, as well as the modern British empire, shared similar characteristics in the realm of governance. The Chinese empire, whose 2,000-year history stretches from the Qin–Han period to the end of the Qing, has left us with an even greater supply of governing wisdom that deserves to be appreciated.

Even though China transformed itself into a modern European nation-state after the end of the Qing dynasty, the vast population which it governed, made up of peoples and ethnicities of different religions and cultures, as well as the vast and intersecting plains, highlands, grasslands, and forests which made up its territory, meant that China remained an empire, despite taking on the systemic form of a modern nation-state. From the Republic of China to the People's Republic of China, generations of central governments have sought to construct a highly unified administrative system and cultural nexus, and to create the Chinese people as a homogenized national group. Yet after 100 years, not only has systemic, cultural, and national unification *not* been achieved, instead, in the past ten years religious and ethnic problems in border regions such as Tibet and Xinjiang have become ever more severe, to the point that separatism and terrorism have emerged. Where does the problem come from? Why was it that under the traditional empire the minority peoples of the border regions could exist in relative peace, but in the framework of the modern nation-state multiple crises have arisen? Can the experience of governance under the empire provide guidance for today's modern nation-state?

In terms of its conceptualization of space, *tianxia* was a differential mode of association with the central plains at its center. The Chinese empire's style of governance employed a series of mutually supporting concentric spheres. In the inner sphere, where the Han people lived, it used the bureaucratic system developed by the first Qin emperor. In the outer sphere, the border regions inhabited by the minority peoples, it employed a variety of local forms of governance such as the systems of hereditary titles, vassal states, and tribal headsmen, which were based on the different historical traditions, ethnic characteristics, and territorial situations of each region. As long as the minority peoples were willing to recognize the governing authority of the central dynasty, the former could have considerable autonomy, maintaining the cultural customs, religious beliefs, and local politics that had been passed down through history. The "one country, two systems" concept proposed by Deng Xiaoping (1904–97) in the 1980s for Macau, Hong Kong, and Taiwan traces its origins to the wisdom of pluralistic governance of the premodern imperial tradition.

In Chinese history there were two different kinds of centralized monarchies: one was the ethnic Han dynasties of the central plains, which included the Han (206 BC–AD 220), Tang (618–907), Song (960–1279), and Ming (1368–1644); the other was the dynasties of the border peoples, including the Liao (907–1125), Jin (1115–1234), Yuan, and Qing (1644–1911). The Han were a farming people, and the territory under their control was essentially agricultural. Except for brief periods during the Western Han and at the height of the Tang, the Han people never achieved long-term, peaceful, stable rule over the nomadic peoples of the grasslands. The reason for this lay in the vast differences between the farming peoples and nomadic peoples in terms of lifestyles and religious beliefs. The Han people could successfully bring the ethnic groups of the south under direct imperial rule, because they, like the Han, were farmers who used the slash and burn method to work the land. Yet the Han could not use the magic of the civilization of the central plains to assimilate and conquer the nomadic peoples of the north and west. Indeed, only the central dynasties established by the border peoples were able to unify the agricultural regions and the nomadic regions into one empire, forming contemporary China's expansive territory. The Mongol Yuan dynasty lasted only a scant ninety years, and we'll not discuss the success of that rule. The Manchu Qing dynasty, by contrast, was a multi-centric, multi-ethnic unified empire that was very different from the Han dynasties of the central plains. The Qing successfully integrated farming peoples and grassland peoples, who to this point had had difficulty coexisting in peace, into an imperial order. For the first time, the central government's power successfully expanded to the northern forest and grasslands and the western highlands and basins, achieving an unprecedented unified structure.

While the Manchu people came from the deep forests of the Greater Khingan Range in today's northernmost Heilongjiang province, they possessed first-rate political intelligence. For many years they lived and developed among farming peoples and grasslands peoples; they had been conquered and had also conquered others. They had a deep understanding of the differences between two different civilizations, and once they entered the central plains and took the central government they set out to reconstruct a great and unified empire, and their accumulated historical experience of survival was transformed into a political intelligence employed to govern *tianxia*. The great unity established by the Qing was very different from the great unity established by the first emperor of the Qin. It was no longer founded on "unifying cart axles, the written language, and rules of conduct."[7] Instead, it built on a dual-track political and religious system that was situated within a multi-ethnic empire. In the eighteen provinces making up the home territory of the Han people, the Qing dynasty continued the historical system of Confucian rites, using Chinese civilization to govern China. In the border regions of the Manchu, Mongolian, and Tibetan peoples, they

---

[7] Translator's note: Although this passage is often taken to describe the unification efforts realized by the Qin, it in fact comes from the *Book of Rites*, which was written prior to the Qin unification.

used Lama Buddhism as a common spiritual link, and employed diverse, flexible, and elastic methods of rule in order to achieve historical continuity. As such, the conquering dynastic empires of the Mongolian Yuan and the Manchu Qing were very different from the Han Tang dynasties of the central plains: the former was not a *tianxia* unified in religious, cultural, and political terms, but was rather defined by the harmony of cultural diversity, a dual-form system of mutual coexistence.

The irreconcilable differences in lifestyle and religion between farming and nomadic peoples were reconciled, within the governing experience of the Qing empire, through this dual system. In today's China, both the Han farming people and the nomadic border nationalities are encountering a more powerful, more secular industrial civilization, which entered China through the economic and political conquests of the European seafaring peoples, and fundamentally transformed the Han farming people, so that they now resemble nineteenth-century Europeans, with their inexhaustible desire for material wealth, their unending pursuit of secular happiness, and their intense competitiveness. Moreover, with the opening up of the western and northern nomadic territories, this disruptive secularism was brought into the grassland and plateaus, in the same way the imperial powers had brought it into China. Yet we tend forget that nomadic and grassland peoples are different from farming peoples; their understanding of happiness is completely different from the secular Han. For a people with deep religious beliefs, true happiness is not found in the satisfaction of material desire or the pleasures of secular life; instead, it is found in the protection of the gods and the transcendence of one's soul. When the central government uses the unified vision of the nation-state to spread the universal principles of the market economy, the uniformity of bureaucratic management, and secular culture into the border regions, they encounter an intense backlash among some members of minority groups, who will staunchly resist secularization, much like the resistance found in certain parts of the Islamic world of Southwest Asia and North Africa.

From another perspective, a key difference between the modern nation-state and the traditional Chinese empire is that the nation-state wants to create a unified citizenry: the Chinese people. Comprising more than 90 percent of the population, the Han people are the dominant and mainstream ethnicity, and for this reason often consciously or unconsciously imagine their history and cultural traditions as representing those of the Chinese people, and as the mainstream ethnicity they will seek to assimilate other ethnicities under the name of the "state" or the "citizens." However, the modern meaning of "nation" is not what we mean by the common understanding of "people," a group of people possessing natural customs, habits, and religious traditions, such as the Han, the Manchus, the Tibetans, the Uighurs, the Mongols, the Miao, the Dai, etc. The idea of "nation" is, rather, intimately related to the concept of "state," producing a people that is fused with the nation-state. This notion of people incorporates natural historical and cultural traditions, but also possesses highly artificial elements that have emerged at the same time as and, indeed, been produced by the modern nation-state. This is the fundamental difference between modern citizens and historical people.

The "Chinese people" are not a "people" in way we normally understand the term, but are like the American people: a citizenry that appeared and was forged together with the modern state. Although the notion of the Chinese people takes the Han as its subject, the Han are not the equivalent of the Chinese people. Premodern China had the idea of the Han, but not the notion of the Chinese people as citizens. The Qing dynasty created a multi-ethnic state whose contours are roughly those of modern China, but it did not attempt to forge a uniform Chinese people. The emergence of the concept of the Chinese people comes after the late Qing period, first in discussions by politicians such as Yang Du (1875–1931) and intellectuals such as Liang Qichao (1873–1929). The Republic of China established in 1911 was a nation-state based on a "republic of five peoples." This meant that the Chinese people were not limited to the Han, nor could one use Han historical cultural traditions to narrate and imagine the past and future of the citizenry that was to be the Chinese people. Premodern China was a multiple China. There was the China of Han civilization, which took the central plains as its center; there was also the China of the minority ethnicities of the grasslands, forests, and plateaus. Together they made up premodern China's history. The 5,000 years of Chinese history is a history of the mutual interaction between the peoples of the plains and the borders, the farming peoples and the nomadic peoples. Within this history, Chinese became barbarian and barbarian became Chinese. Finally Chinese and barbarian melded into a common current, and in the Qing period transformed into a modern nation-state, and began to cohere as the body of citizens known as the Chinese people.

Forging a multi-ethnic citizenry is much harder than constructing a modern state. The problem is not the attitude of the mainstream ethnicity, but in the degree to which minority ethnicities identify with the citizenry. Professor Yao Dali (b. 1949), a well-known scholar of China's border areas, has pointed out: "On the surface, the extreme demands of minority ethnic nationalism and state nationalism seem to be completely antithetical, but in reality, they are most certainly the exact same thing. History often reminds us that hidden within state nationalism is the ethnic nationalism of a given state's main ethnic group."[8] From the first late Qing attempts at building a citizenry down to the present day, the Han have often taken as the equivalent of the Chinese people, and the Yellow Emperor imagined as the common ancestor of all the Chinese people. Hidden behind this citizen nationalism lies the true face of ethnic nationalism. The construction of a citizenry on the foundation of a single ethnic group is doomed to fragility, because once a country experiences a political crisis there will be a backlash from the suppressed ethnic minorities, creating problems of separatism. The disintegration of the Soviet empire is a recent example.

Fei Xiaotong developed a classical view of the Chinese people, calling it "unity within diversity." What he calls "unity" is the unity of citizens that make up the Chinese people; what he calls "diversity" refers to the mutually recognized cultural autonomy and rights to political self-governance that all minority nationalities and ethnicities possess. While the Manchu Qing empire did not set out to create a unified citizenry, they did have a number of important successes in maintaining this "unity within diversity": they realized diversity by employing the dual-track system of religion and governance, and they realized "unity" through a shared multi-ethnic dynastic identity. This "unity" was not based on an identification as a citizen, but instead on identity with a universal dynasty. Han scholar-officials, Mongolian dukes, Tibetan lamas, and southwestern tribal chieftains all recognized the monarch of the Qing dynasty. The sole symbol of the state, the Qing emperor was called different names by different peoples. Han people called him emperor, Mongolian dukes called him the Great Khan, the leader of the alliance of the grasslands, and Tibetans called him Manjusri, the living Bodhisattva. The core of the state identity of the Qing empire was a political identity whose symbol was monarchical power, behind which was not only violence but also culture. Yet this culture was multi-faceted: one monarch, multiple expressions.

The Chinese "unity" created by the Manchu Qing dynasty through identity with the monarchy is not suitable for the era the nation-state. Today, China requires a unified citizen identity. Yet the problems emerging in the border regions and among the minority nationalities illustrate that we have not yet found the appropriate equilibrium in our "unity in diversity." In the areas where we need "unity" we have been too "diverse." For example, in the application of the law to cases regarding

---

[8] Huang Xiaofeng, "Yao Dali tan minzu guanxi he Zhongguo rentong" (Yao Dali discusses ethic relations and Chinese identity), *Dongfang zaobao*, December 4, 2011.

ethnic minorities we have, for purposes of stability, been overly lenient, which has generated resentment and opposition among the Han living in the border regions.[9] In the areas where we need "diversity" we have been too "unified." For example we have lacked respect for the religious beliefs and cultural traditions of the ethnic minorities, and we have insufficiently implemented the right to autonomous rule in minority regions. These phenomena all exhibit a tendency toward Han chauvinism.

The tension that exists between diversity and unity is a shared concern of all multi-ethnic nations in the world today. Ethnic questions have their own complexity and democratic systems offer no simple solutions. According to some liberals, the so-called ethnic question is a false one. They believe that as long as you have genuine, universal self-governance for the minority regions, and a federal system replaces centralized political power, then the ethnic question will be solved at once. However, we know from Chinese and foreign history, and from past and present examples, that once a revolution occurs in a highly centralized country, followed by the introduction of democratic processes resulting from the weakening of the power of the centralized government, long-suppressed ethnic minorities in the border regions will seek to free themselves and demand independence. As such, the unified nation will face a crisis of disintegration. Both the Ottoman and Soviet empires collapsed under such conditions.

How, in the process of democratization, can a country prevent ethnic separatism leading to the breakup of the nation while, at the same time, rigorously implementing the cultural and political self-governance of minority peoples? Obviously, a model of unified national governance that puts too much emphasis on economic, political, and cultural integration will struggle to solve this intractable problem. And the successful experiences of premodern empires with a plural system of religion and rule can provide us with historical wisdom and guidance. In today's China, "constitutional patriotism" can, in the realm of the law, provide individuals of different nationalities and regions with the equal status and mutual respect due to citizens. As citizens, this will strengthen the national identity of each minority nationality and ethnicity. The transformation that still needs to be effected is to take traditional dynastic identity, based on the symbol of monarchical power, and transform it into a national identity based upon a modern nation-state with the constitution as its foundation. At the same time, we need to draw on the

---

[9] Translator's note: Ethnic minority groups were not required to follow the "one-child policy" by which China hoped to limit population growth. Certain Han Chinese found this unfair.

traditional empire's plural system of religion and governance, allowing Confucianism to serve as the symbol of the cultural identity of the Han people, while also protecting the religious, linguistic, and cultural uniqueness of the minority nationalities, recognizing their collective rights and providing them with systemic guarantees. "One country, two systems" should be used not only in relation to Hong Kong, Macau, and Taiwan. It should be expanded to become a guiding principle of governance for the autonomous border areas. It is only through such measures that the internal order of the new *tianxia* can be built, realizing a structure for the citizenship of the Chinese people that is both "unified" and "diverse."

New *Tianxia*'s External Order: Beyond the Sovereignty of the Nation-State

The nineteenth century through the present day has been the era of the establishment of distinct nation-states. National sovereignty above all else, national survival as a core interest, clear territorial boundaries from land to sea … in China, all of these tenets of nationalist consciousness, so different from traditional *tianxia* thinking, have already entered deeply into people's hearts, from the officials down to the common people. In Europe, those responsible for the violence finally absorbed the bloody lessons of two World Wars and began to weaken statism, moving toward a European union and emphasizing globalization. Yet the East Asian world (including China) has seen an unprecedented resurgence in nationalism and statism, with the potential for military conflicts to erupt at the drop of a hat.

Can the new *tianxia* act as an antidote to this deformed, surging statism? The American China-scholar and political scientist Lucien Pye (1921–2008) once said that China is a civilizational empire masquerading as a nation-state. If we accept this judgement, then today's China remains a traditional monarchical empire rather than a European state based on a single nationality insofar as it refers to China's diverse border regions and multiple nationalities. Yet from another angle, we can also say that today's China is actually a nation-state masquerading as a civilizational empire, because it uses the methods of the nation-state to govern a massive empire, and in international affairs and conflicts regarding its own interests it relies on a mentality that accords absolute primacy to national supremacy.

China's rise has made neighboring countries uneasy. They fear that the soul of the Chinese empire will be reborn in a different body, to the point of asking the United States, the greatest of the imperialists, to enter

East Asia in order to balance China's growing power. Recently, in an article entitled "The East-Asian Meaning of the Theory of the Chinese Empire," Korean professor Yông-sô Paek observed that:

China's pre-modern empire did not break up into different nation-states, and to the present day has still maintained its medieval imperial personality. This particularity has decided contemporary China's mode of existence. At the same time, if we say that the modern period is one of rapid transformation from nation-state to empire, then in a certain sense one can say that China's original imperial character not only will not disappear, but will in fact grow stronger.[10]

Why is it that even as China repeatedly states that its rise is peaceful, it cannot convince its neighbors? One important reason is that within China's terrifying imperial body lurks a frightening soul that values national supremacy above all else, an empire without consciousness of *tianxia*.

Behind the traditional Chinese empire was a *tianxia* consciousness for all humanity, a universal set of values that transcended the individual interest of any given dynasty. Its source was in the moral way of heaven and it served as a standard to measure right and wrong, constraining the behavior of rulers and deciding the legitimacy of a given dynasty's rule. But an empire without *tianxia* consciousness means that the imperial body no longer contains a civilizational soul with universal values to put people at ease. In its place, there is nothing but calculations regarding the interests of the nation-state. The concept of modernity that came from Europe has two dimensions: one is the technical dimension aiming to strengthen and enrich the nation; the other is the values dimension, with freedom, the rule of law, and democracy at its core. The former concerns itself with strength, the latter with civilization. However, if you look at China's report card after a half-century of imitating the West, it gets high marks in the technical dimension of strengthening, practically performing as a child prodigy. But as for civilizational values, it failed. It has even completely forgotten traditional *tianxia* discourse, to say nothing about the discourse of modern civilization. The spokespeople for China's foreign ministry often uses the following phrases to express China's national will: "This is a domestic political matter, we do not permit foreigners to meddle"; or "This regards China's sovereignty and core interests, how can we permit foreign countries to intervene?" In an international society that has already established measures of universal value, China remains a stranger to the discourse of universal civilization,

---

[10] Bai Yongrui (Yông-sô Paek), "Zhonghua diguolun zai Dongya de yiyi" (The meaning of Chinese imperialism in East Asia), *Kaifang shidai* 1 (2014).

and protects herself through the rigid discourse of national sovereignty. The traditional Chinese empire attracted many countries to its court over the years not because neighboring countries feared the empire's military force, but because they were attracted by its advanced civilization and institutions. This kind of civilizational attraction is precisely what is meant by a country's soft power.

The supremacy of national interest will only convince those on "my side" who stand to benefit; it has no way to convince "the other." The greatness of Confucianism came precisely from its capacity to transcend the interests of the individual "small person" and of the dynasty of a particular family. It is above the state, and possesses the universal values of *tianxia*, which is the greatest of "great selves," humanity's "great self." The Chinese intellectuals of the May Fourth period carried forward the *tianxia* spirit connecting the individual to humanity via the internationalist spirit of the modern era. The scholar and linguist Fu Sinian (1896– 1950) had a well-known saying that represented the psychology of the May Fourth intellectuals: "At a high level, I only acknowledge the existence of humanity. Of course, 'I' exist in my small world, but the things that mediate between me and humanity, like classes, families, regions, and the state, they're nothing but idols."[11] Even Liang Qichao, who was the first to bring the notion of the nation-state into China, and who during the late Qing furiously expounded on the absolute supremacy of the nation-state, during the May Fourth period abruptly awoke to the fact that "Our patriotism cannot embrace the nation and ignore the individual, nor can it embrace the nation and ignore the world. We must rely on the protection of the nation to develop to the utmost the innate abilities of one and all, so as to make a great contribution towards the entire global civilization of humanity."[12] The patriotic movement of May Fourth was thus grounded in internationalism. The students took to the streets not to struggle for narrow national interests, but rather for common principles of international society. Rather than using force to resist force, they used principle. This was the heart of the May Fourth patriotic *tianxia* consciousness. The concept of the nation-state came to China from Europe via Japan, and it melded with Darwinian ideas of the "survival of the fittest" so that by the late Qing it had penetrated deeply into people's hearts. Yet the May Fourth intellectuals were alarmed by

[11] Fu Sinian, "'Xinchao' zhi huigu yu qianzhan" (Review and future perspectives for "New Wave"), in Fu Sinian, *Fu Sinian quanji (The complete writings of Fu Sinian)* (Changsha: Hunan jiaoyu chubanshe, 2003), p. 297.
[12] Liang Qichao,"Ouyou xinying lu" (A record of my travel impressions of Europe), in Liang Qichao, *Liang Qichao quanji (The complete writings of Liang Qichao)* (Beijing: Beijing chubanshe, 1999), vol. 5, p. 2978.

the devastation of World War I, and they sought to use internationalism as a remedy. Today, when the nationalism of every country in East Asia is once again on the rise, fanned by politicians and public opinion, the question of how we can overcome the supremacy of the nation-state and find a new universalism for East Asia and the world has become a concern for all engaged intellectuals in East Asia. The world center of the twenty-first century has already moved from the Atlantic to the Pacific. The East Asia that stands on the western shore of the Pacific cannot be an antagonistic East Asia, but must be a community of common destiny.

East Asia's community of common destiny has already appeared, from the fifteenth to the eighteenth century, in the form of the China-centered tribute system. As explained by the famous world-systems scholar Andre Gunder Frank (1929–2005), in his *Re-orient: The Global Economy in the Asian Age*, this was an "Asian era" that took place before Europe's industrial revolution, in which Asia was the center of the world's economic system. The hierarchical tributary system was *tianxia*'s form of external order, as well as the outer extension of the corresponding concentric spheres that defined China's imperial order. In this twenty-first-century era of new *tianxia*, which requires a new shared universalism that is de-centered and non-hierarchical, the tributary system is of course no longer suitable. However, certain factors from the tributary system can be incorporated into the framework of interstate relations of the new *tianxia*, provided that they are de-centered and non-hierarchical. For example, the tributary system acted as a kind of complex ethical, political, and commercial network. It was entirely different from the unidirectional domination that defined the era of European imperialism, in which there were masters and slaves, exploiters and exploited, pillagers and pillaged. The tributary system put greater emphasis on the mutual interests and benefits shared between countries. It did not just emphasize commercial "interests," but rather saw commerce as having to conform to a notion of "justice" grounded in ethics: through commodity, capital, and financial commerce, warm neighborly relations could be established, and in this way a community of common destiny in East Asia was formed.

Historically, the Chinese empire used the mutual benefits of the tributary system to make alliances in many places, even turning enemies into friends, and maintaining long-standing relations of peace with neighboring countries. *Tianxia* has its own civilization, complete with an understanding of and a quest for a universal ethical order. The Chinese empire did not need enemies, and its practical goal was to turn enemies into friends, transforming the antagonism between enemies into relationships of equality and mutually beneficial trade. Its highest ideal was to cherish *tianxia* and establish a moral universe. The Chinese empire of the past had friends everywhere, yet today rising China has enemies all around. Some hawks in the military have even complained that "China is surrounded on all sides." Whether these enemies are real or imagined remains to be seen, but what is clear is that the form of thinking that places national supremacy above all easily creates enemies, even where there aren't any. Another dimension of the problem is that while "national supremacy above all else" is now a universal mindset shared by both officials and the common people, and the severity of China's domestic crisis indeed requires that a new shared national identity be constructed, contemporary Chinese nationalism has been emptied of its civilizational meaning, and there remains nothing left but an immense, empty symbol. External enemies need to be created to fill up this internal emptiness. Where there are no enemies, foes are imagined, and once the predators appear, the fragile "us" can be protected from the confrontational "other." In this way national and state identity is established. This has made China's relationship with its neighbors, and with the world, ever more tense. In the past Mao Zedong proudly proclaimed that "We have friends all over the world," yet today's China is just the opposite: we have enemies all over the world.

In today's East Asian societies, including China and Japan, nationalist sentiment is on the rise. The controversies surrounding various islands in the East and South China Seas have, in particular, become lightning-rods which could set off war with one rash incident. Is sovereignty clear in matters of oceans and their various islands? In the premodern East Asian world this was simply not a problem. Professor Takeshi Hamashita (b. 1943), a Japanese authority on the tribute system, has noted that:

In East Asian history, from the perspective of territorial cooperation, the sea was to be used by all. The sea could not be carved up and was to be used by all seafarers. Yet the Western perspective regarding the sea was completely different. They saw the sea as the extension of land, beginning with the Western traditions of the Portuguese and the Spanish. Yet Western regulations are not the only regulations, and indeed have caused much conflict since the beginning of the modern period. The conflicts regarding the seas in Asia are a product of these Western regulations.[13]

---

[13] "Binxia Wuzhi [Takeshi Hamashita] tan cong chaogong tixi dao Dongya yitihua" (Takeshi Hamashi discusses the transition from the tribute system to the integration of East Asia), in Ge Jianxiong, ed., *Shei lai jueding women shi shei? (Who decides who we are?)* (Nanjing: Yilin chubanshe, 2013), p. 124.

In historical East Asia, while the sea separated countries from one another, the waters were common to all and to be mutually enjoyed. The sea and its islands were collectively owned and enjoyed by all countries. This is the sea as understood by farming peoples. It is only in the modern period, when the seafaring peoples of a rising Europe sought to control the sea's resources out of commercial need, thus imposing hegemony across the world, was the sea looked upon as an extension of land, as something that belonged within the purview of national sovereignty. As such, the collective sea was cut up and every inch of every single island the subject of conflict. In the era of the sovereign nation-state, it was the logic of seafaring peoples that imagined the international order and decided the rules of the game of in relations between countries. However, when a struggle of sovereignty over the sea and its islands erupted, if one looked upon the notions of sovereignty possessed by the seafaring peoples from the perspective of the past, they would have no legitimacy whatsoever, because the historical sea did not possess modern sovereign borders. If you wanted to look at the matter from the perspective of who actually controlled the seas, this kind of international law was clearly grounded in a logic of power, which enabled and encouraged violence and wars over who had the right to practical control of the sea. Yet if we use a different mode of thought and employ traditional *tianxia*'s understanding of a commonly shared sea, then the "backward" intelligence of the farming people can in fact provide an entirely new method to resolve the conflicts created by the principles of the "advanced" seafaring peoples. In the proposal that Deng Xiaoping offered in the 1980s to resolve the Diaoyutai Island (known as Senkaku in Japanese) dispute, "Avoid Conflict, Collectively Develop," we see the intelligence of traditional *tianxia* playing an important role in contemporary international society. Yet to the present day, people only pay attention to the strategic meaning of the proposal. They lack an understanding of the Eastern wisdom that lies behind it, an intelligence that provides new principles for dealing with rules of the international games that are played in the ocean.

On the Possibility of an East Asian Community of Common Destiny

The construction of China as a civilizational nation was intimately related to the order of East Asia. Professor Yông-sô Paek has pointed out that:

[I]f China is not grounded in democracy, but instead seeks to legitimize its power by reviving the historical memory of a great unity, then what it will have done is to follow the modern model of modernization in which the motive force is nationalism. It will have been unable to create a new model that can overcome this limitation. As such, though China wants to lead an East Asian order, it finds it difficult to get neighboring countries to participate voluntarily.[14]

If China successfully implements democracy and the rule of law, becoming a civilized country like the United States or England, would this put neighboring countries at ease? Given China's power, size, and population, once it rises it will be a great power with the capacity to dominate. Even if it becomes an "empire of freedom," it will make neighboring countries fearful, particularly small ones. Korea and Vietnam are both independent countries who split off from the Chinese empire's tributary system. As such, they are particularly vigilant toward the country that was historically their suzerain. In no case will either of them be willing to become China's vassal state again, even if China turns itself into a civilized nation.

All of this means that the reconstruction of a peaceful order in East Asia cannot be as simple as some Chinese liberals have suggested: it cannot all be reduced to a question of China's internal political reform. The reconstruction of East Asia's peaceful order is a worthy cause in its own right. Its precondition is not that China must become a Western-style democracy. In fact, even if China is a non-democratic benevolent country, with a domestic order based on the rule of law, and a basic respect for international rules, then it is possible that it can participate in the reconstruction of East Asian order.

In his essay "Asia's Territorial Order: Overcoming Empire, Towards an East Asian Community," Professor Yông-sô Paek points out that, historically, East Asia has had three imperial orders: the first was the traditional tributary system with the Chinese empire at its center; the second was the Japanese Greater East Asian Co-Prosperity Sphere, which replaced China as the region's hegemon in the first half of the twentieth century; the third was the post-World War II Cold War order established in East Asia out of the conflict between the United States and the Soviet Union.[15] Recently, with the rise of China, American's "pivot" toward Asia, and Japan's attempts to act once again as a normal country, an imperialistic conflict for hegemony has again emerged in East Asia. This is why East Asia finds itself on the edge of war, with conflict possible at any moment. For this reason, as Professor Paek suggests, how to discard the centralism of empire and establish a community of common destiny in East Asia based on equality has become the common mission of all countries in the

---

[14] Bai Yongui (Yông-sô Paek), "Dongya diyu zixu: Chaoyue diguo, zouxiang Dongya gongtongti" (East Asian regionalism: Transcending empire, moving toward an East Asian community), *Sixiang* 3 (2006).
[15] Ibid.

region. A modern empire based on the supremacy of the nation-state, in which sovereignty dominates all, is grounded in a hegemonic logic that sees oneself as the only subject, while making neighboring countries into objects. How to learn peaceful coexistence and the recognition of each other's subjectivity is the goal of the new *tianxia*. Indeed, this goal is the new internationalism upon which the community of common destiny in East Asia will be constructed.

A new East Asian order of peace requires a new set of universal East Asian values. With the end of the Cold War, East Asia lost any sense of universal value, even of the oppositional kind. What remained between each country was nothing but interest-based alliances or antagonisms. The alliances were nothing but short-term plans based on expediency, lacking any deeply shared common values to ground them. The antagonism emerged from conflicts over interests: the fight for power in the realm of resources, trade, and the control of islands. Because the East Asian world no longer has universal values, alliances and conflicts are all defined by disorder, variability, and instability. Today's enemies are yesterday's allies, and today's allies may well be tomorrow's enemies. From the perspective of interests, there are no eternal enemies, nor are there eternal friends. This constantly churning "Three Kingdoms"[16] drama, these unending games, do nothing but increase the looming danger of war, turning East Asia into one of the world's most unstable regions.

The East Asian world today is reminiscent of Europe during the first half of the twentieth century, the heyday of national interests, when multiple countries gambled in games of confrontation, resulting in the eruption of two world wars. Europe after World War II saw the reconciliation of France and Germany, followed by the long Cold War period, finally achieving European integration at the turn of the century. The establishment of a common community in Europe was grounded in two universal values: the first was a historically shared Christian civilization, the second was the values of Enlightenment of the modern period. Without Christian civilization and the universalizing values of the Enlightenment, it would be very difficult to imagine a stable European union. Any community established solely on the basis of interests is always temporary and unstable. The only lasting and stable community is one in which universal values serve as a base of shared consensus. Even

[16] Translator's note: The reference is to the famous sixteenth-century novel, *The Romance of the Three Kingdoms*, attributed to Luo Guanzhong, which recounts the history of conflict and machinations in the wake of the fall of the Han dynasty.

if there are conflicts over interests, negotiation can lead to compromise and exchange.

To truly make East Asia into a community with a common destiny, one cannot employ interests to temporarily bind it together, nor can one regard the West as the other through which the self is recognized. This community should be historical and constructed. From a historical perspective, the notion of a common East Asian order is not a hollow imaginary community. The historical tributary system, the deeply interrelated movement of peoples, the sphere of culture defined by Chinese characters, and the civilizations of Buddhism and Confucianism that spread across East Asia: all of these provide the East Asian community with historical legitimacy. The Japanese philosopher and literary critic Karatani Kôjin (b. 1941) has pointed out that "even though nations that have emerged out of one common empire may have strong antagonisms, they still possess religious and cultural commonalities. Generally speaking, all modern countries emerged out of the breakup of world empires. As such, when they experience threats from other world empires, they will work hard to preserve the unity that once bound them in the old empire. This can be called 'Imperial Return.'"[17] Yet this is not a simple return. In the era of the nation-state it requires new elements of creativity, namely, the attempt to establish a de-centered, even anti-imperial, community of peaceful nations. East Asian universalism must be reconstructed and recreated on the basis of the region's historical inheritance. The new *tianxia* is just such a new universalistic program that embraces and transcends history. Developed out of the imperial tradition, it possesses cultural characteristics that are united and universalistic. At the same time it works to expel the centralism and hierarchy of empire, preserving internal religious, institutional, and cultural diversity. One might say that this is the rebirth of a de-imperialized empire, an internally peaceful, trans-ethnic, transnational community.

East Asia's community of common destiny requires a soul, a universal value that is waiting to be created. It also must have an institutional body. The community cannot rely simply on alliances between nations to form a peaceful union that transcends the nation-state. What is required even more is that the intellectuals and common people of each East Asian nation engage in dialogue, producing a "people's East Asia," which will be more able than the states themselves to overcome the barriers between various nation-states. This "people's East Asia" will overcome various old centralisms and hierarchies, for it will itself possess a natural sense of

---

[17] From Karatani Kojin's lecture at Shanghai University, "Shijieshi zhi jiegouxing fanfu" (The reversal of the structure of world history), presented on November 8, 2012.

equality, becoming the deep social ground from which the new universal values of East Asia will emerge.

The new *tianxia* emerges from the historical wisdom of premodern China, discarding and de-centering traditional *tianxia*. Rejecting hierarchy and placing mutually shared equality at its core, it attempts to establish a new and "commonly shared" universalism. Historical *tianxia* used imperial methods of governance to serve as its institutional body. Traditional empire is different from the modern nation-state, which seeks to homogenize and incorporate all into a single system. In traditional empire, the internal order honored diversity in the realm of religion and institutional governance, and the external order was an integrated political, commercial, and ethical network, one that placed the mutual benefits of the tribute system at its center, sharing in international trade. The traditional empire's *tianxia* wisdom can provide us insights today in the following ways: the overly singular and uniform logic of the nation-state cannot, internally, resolve the minority issues in the border regions, while externally it is not helpful in easing conflicts over political sovereignty with neighboring countries. To the unified logic of the nation-state should be added the flexible diversity and multiple-systems of empire, providing balance. In sum, in the core regions of China, "one system, different models" should be implemented; in the border regions, "one nation, different cultures" should be realized; in Hong Kong, Macau, and Taiwan, "one civilization, different systems" should be experimented with; in East Asian society, "one region, different interests" should be recognized; in international society, "one world, different civilizations" should be constructed. In this way, the internal and external order of the new *tianxia* can be established, creating the conditions for mutual coexistence, indeed the mutual benefit, not only for all of China's domestic ethnicities but for all East Asia's nations, creating a new universalism for a future world order.

7 Two Kinds of Enlightenment: Civilizational Consciousness or Cultural Consciousness

Translator's Introduction

This chapter, first published online in 2015, is in many ways a more scholarly version of Chapter 1, and treats the same themes: the many ramifications of the tension between culture and civilization. Taken together, these two essays illustrate two facets of Xu Jilin's life as a scholar and a public intellectual; he is both scholar and an engaging essayist. His deft handling of both styles illustrates an interesting aspect of China's directed public sphere and modes of communication within that sphere. Chinese readers expect public intellectuals to have scholarly credentials and to be able to strut their academic stuff from time to time; in this way they are like the French and unlike the Americans. Chapter 7 comes perhaps the closest to the sort of "scholarly" text that history professors must master on the way to becoming public intellectuals and hence is denser and more carefully documented than some lighter pieces in this volume. The chapter also participates in a major rereading of the May Fourth movement that has occurred in China and elsewhere over the past few decades.[1]

The May Fourth movement, of course, has become a founding narrative of modern China. Originally – and simplistically – characterized as the iconoclastic moment when "China turned away from its Confucian past," the May Fourth is now accorded a more textured complexity. In a chronological sense, the May Fourth "moment" in 1919 has been pushed back to encompass the thought of various reformers of the late Qing, and forward at least through the 1930s if not to Mao's "Talk at the Yan'an Forum of Literature and Art" in 1942. Earlier characterizations of major figures – as "total Westernizers," for example – of arguments – such as "problems versus isms" – and of causation – "May Fourth paved the way for Chinese acceptance of Marxism and hence the Chinese revolution" – are now accorded considerably greater complexity. Xu's discussion of

---

[1] Originally published as "Liangzhong qimeng: Wenming zijue, haishi wenhua zijue," first published online in May 2015 at www.aisixiang.com/data/88161.html. Later republished in Xu Jilin and Liu Qing, eds., *Zhongguo qimeng de zijue yu jiaolü (The self-consciousness and anxiety of the Chinese Enlightenment)*, no. 14 of *Zhishi fenzi luncong* (New Tianxia, Intellectuals series) (Shanghai: Shanghai renmin chubanshe, 2016). For more of Xu's work on the May Fourth movement see his essay translated as "Historical Memories of May Fourth: Patriotism, but of What Kind?" *China Heritage Quarterly*, no. 17 (2009), available online at www.chinaheritagequarterly.org/features.php?searchterm=017_may fourthmemories.inc&issue=017.

DuYaquan and the Xueheng group, of the impact of World War I on the original optimism of late Qing reformers such as Kang Youwei, Liang Qichao, andYan Fu, and of debates over cultural agency in the 1930s all illustrate the discovery of hitherto little explored "conservative" responses to the May Fourth, or perhaps their integration into a more nuanced historical narrative.

This essay may be too academic for the reader who prefers Xu's more polemical side, although there are hints of polemics as well, but it shows the strong basis in historical research on which Xu's reputation rests. His ability to produce nuanced and detailed studies such as this carries considerable weight in public intellectual debates. One might note as well that the Communist Party does not appear in Xu's rereading of the May Fourth movement, which is some indication of the "negative freedom" scholars and public intellectuals achieved during this period.

The New Culture movement, symbolized by the *New Youth* journal founded by Chen Duxiu (1879–1942), is one hundred years old as I write these words. This movement is also known as China's Enlightenment movement, as well as the May Fourth movement, but one hundred years on, what is enlightenment and what is cultural consciousness remain unresolved questions provoking many debates. What kind of enlightenment characterized the New Culture movement, and the intellectual enlightenment to which it gave birth? Was it a civilizational consciousness or a cultural consciousness? As the New Culture movement flowed into the mainstream of world civilization, what happened to China's cultural agency, the cultural identity of the Chinese people? These timely questions, which have been raised repeatedly in Chinese intellectual history over the past century, still confront Chinese intellectuals in the twenty-first century.

Civilizational Consciousness and Cultural Consciousness

In their path toward modernity, the historical paths followed by China and Germany are quite similar. The original Enlightenment movement occurred in France and Scotland, but just as the American scholar James Schmidt pointed out, "the question of 'what is Enlightenment' is without a doubt an authentically German question."[2] For England and France, the Enlightenment meant emerging out of medieval religious obscurantism, so that people relied on their own reason, which replaced God as the agent of history and the law-maker for the world. The Enlightenment was a process of "emerging from the cave" of ignorance

---

[2] Zhanmusi Shimite (James Schmidt), *Qimeng yundong yu xiandaixing: 18 shiji yu 20 shiji de duihua (What is Enlightenment: Eighteenth-century answers and twentieth-century questions)*, Xu Xiangdong and Lu Huaping, trans. (Shanghai: Shanghai renmin chubanshe, 2005), foreword, p. 1.

toward civilization. But for nineteenth-century Germany, the meaning of the Enlightenment was much more complex and contradictory. On the one hand, the German Enlightenment movement was a positive response to the Anglo-French Enlightenment, which is why Kant (1724–1804) said that Enlightenment meant "having the courage to use one's own reason." This was a civilizational consciousness modeled on the English and the French experiences, suggesting that if Germany was to be a European country it had to acknowledge eighteenth-century universal Western European civilization. On the other hand, as a late-developing country, the German reaction to Napoleon's (1769–1821) invasion was the rise of an extreme nationalism that sought to use the particular char- acter of the German will to combat universal civilization as represented by the British and the French, which in turn created another kind of Enlightenment consciousness. This "other Enlightenment," unlike the Anglo-French Enlightenment, did not use universal human reason to discover universal human nature and civilization, but rather argued that each nation, group, and individual possessed its own particular- ities. As Isaiah Berlin (1909–97) pointed out, "they had been ignorant of their own national spirit, and the process of becoming aware of their uniqueness was a process of enlightenment."[3]

In the Anglo-French context, the Enlightenment movement was the discovery of civilization as well as the development of their own cultures, so that culture and civilization were the same, and universal modern civilization occupied a place in the long-term stream of evolution of their own unique national cultures. Identifying with universal civiliza- tion meant identifying with the agency of their own national cultures. For this reason the question of "What is civilization?" was not problem- atic. But for Germany, within the Enlightenment existed an inner tension between civilization and culture. Enlightenment meant absorption into Western European universal civilization as represented by England and France, and this civilization was not the result of a natural evolution of Germany's own cultural tradition. Civilization came from outside, while culture was self, whence the origin of the tension between and resistance to culture and civilization. In modern German, civilization (*Zivilisation*) means that which belongs to the common values or common nature of all humanity, while culture (*Kultur*) emphasizes differences between nations and ethnic particularities. The expression of civilization is com- prehensive, including material, technical and institutional dimensions, as well as religious and philosophical aspects, but culture necessarily takes

---

[3] Yisaiya Bolin (Isaiah Berlin) *Eguo sixiangjia (Russian thinkers)*, Peng Huaidong, trans. (Nanjing: Yilin chubanshe), p. 147.

on spiritual form, and culture does not discuss abstract "man's" existential value, but rather the values created by particular nations and ethnic groups.[4]

In the German Enlightenment we find two different types of intellectual consciousness. One is civilizational consciousness, which hopes through enlightenment to overcome its uniqueness and become a universal country like England or France. What universal countries seek is not national authenticity, but a universal human nature that transcends nations. The other is cultural consciousness, which under external pressure from universal civilization seeks from within Germany's own historical, linguistic, and religious traditions to discover its unique authenticity, the national spirit that makes Germany German, and on this basis create a cultural identity. If we say that Kant, at the end of the eighteenth century, represented the banner of German civilizational consciousness, then Johann Gottlieb Fichte (1762–1814) in the nineteenth century symbolized the spirit of cultural consciousness. And the bridge between these two kinds of consciousness is Johann Gottfried Herder (1744–1803), who was born in the eighteenth century but represents the spirit of the nineteenth. Herder is important for having understood the agency of national culture during the Enlightenment, and also having self-consciously combined civilizational consciousness and cultural consciousness in one, representing a way to transcend the tension between civilization and culture.

The identities encoded in civilizational consciousness and cultural consciousness are not the same. Civilizational identity is universal, and what it seeks is a universal "good" appropriate to all humanity. Cultural identity is particular, and uses the notion of "ours" as a motive for self-protection. Civilization is concerned with "what is good"; culture is concerned only with "what is ours." Culture creates an "us" identity so as to distinguish between "us" and "the other," resolving questions regarding feelings about one's own cultural or historical origins, answering the questions "Who am I?" and "Who are we?" "Where do we come from and where are we going?" Civilization is different, and takes a transcendent perspective, that of nature or God or universal history to answer the question "What is good?" This "good" is not only good for "us," but is equally good for "you" or for "them" – it is good for the whole of humanity. In universal civilization, there is no distinction between "us"

[4] See Nuobeite Ailiyasi (Norbert Elias), *Wenming de jincheng: Wenming de shehui qiyuan he shehui xinli qiyuan de yanjiu (The civilizing process: Sociogenetic and psychogenetic investigations)*, trans. Wang Peili (Beijing: Shengghuo Dushu Xinzhi Sanlian shudian, 1998), vol. 1, pp. 61–63.

and "the other"; there are only universal values sanctioned throughout the world. The agent of civilization is humanity, it is universal, abstract human nature. By contrast the agents of culture are concrete individual nations or ethnic groups, the "us" produced by individual streams of history, culture, and religion. In the enlightenment movements of modern Germany, Russia, and China, because "good" universal civilization came from the West and not from their own historical and cultural traditions, the pursuit of the civilizational consciousness of "good" universal values produced a huge rift with the pursuit of cultural consciousness and of "our" national spirit. The conflict in Germany between rationality and romanticism, and the debates in Russia between Westernization and Slavism trace their roots to this.

China's ancient tradition was not only the Chinese culture of the central plains, it also had a universal civilization based on the consciousness of humanity. It was particular, making distinctions between Chinese and barbarian, and also universal, which is why we call it *tianxia*. The distinction between Chinese and barbarian is relative, while the idea of *tianxia* is absolute. The distinction between Chinese and barbarian is not an ethnic distinction, but a cultural frontier: as long as the eastern, southern, western, and northern barbarians accepted the culture of the central plains, then they could change from "the other" to "us," as an accepted member of the Han people. Consequently, Chinese culture is also Chinese civilization, the particular Chinese culture of the Han people of the central plain, and it is also an expansive, non-ethnic, transnational, universal civilization of all humanity. It is concerned not only with the unique values of the Chinese Han people, but also with the "good" that transcends distinctions between Chinese and barbarians and embraces universalism. Confucians, Daoists, and Buddhists all shared such *tianxia* concerns. "Ours" was "good" and "good" was "ours"; cultural identity and civilizational identity were one, undivided.

Two thousand years of cultural self-confidence was destroyed in late Qing times by the rise of Western civilization. The foreign enemies China had faced in the past were either like Buddhism, which had civilization but no real power, or like the northern nomadic peoples who had power but no civilization, and both Buddhist civilization and the nomadic peoples were assimilated into China. But the post-Opium War West had both power and civilization, both of which surpassed those of China, which sparked an unprecedented civilizational crisis. It turned out that outside of Chinese civilization, there had all along existed a "better" Western civilization, which also took the place heretofore occupied by China's universalism (*tianxia*), and comparatively speaking, Chinese culture lost its prize position as a universal civilization and was reduced to nothing more than a particular national culture. The emergence of all sorts of national studies in the late Qing and the rise of national consciousness all illustrated that knowledge of China had itself changed from its original identity as a universalistic civilization to a particularistic cultural identity. Even formulae like that of the powerful late Qing official Zhang Zhidong (1837–1909) – "to take Chinese knowledge as essence and Western knowledge as application" – discarded the concerns of traditional *tianxia*, as their goal was solely to safeguard Chinese culture. The formula could not be applied to the world at large, but was merely a nationalistic strategy to save China. When the throne of civilization passed to the West, and Chinese began "studying Western civilization" and "preserving Chinese culture," a rift appeared between civilizational identity and cultural identity. What kind of civilization should we identify with? How should we protect Chinese culture? What was the relationship between Western civilization and Chinese culture? These difficult questions confounded various thinkers and factions.

The New Culture movement occurred under just such intellectual conditions, and as we will see below, the May Fourth appears to have been a period of civilizational consciousness. Genuine cultural consciousness would only appear twenty years later during the 1930s, and was still unable to dissolve the tension and conflict between civilizational identity and cultural identity.

The New Culture Movement as Civilizational Consciousness

Zhang Hao (b. 1937), the well-known Chinese-American scholar of Chinese intellectual history, calls the period between 1895 and 1925 a "transformative age" during which the old culture gave way to the new. In fact, the twenty years of the late Qing–early Republican period (1895–1915) and the later ten years of the May Fourth–New Culture movement, were extremely different periods. Simply put, the late Qing/ early Republican period was a nationalistic era, beset by serious national crises and the rise of nationalist and statist consciousness. Consensus formed throughout society on the need to study Western civilization, but the understanding of Western civilization by Chinese of the late Qing was centered on wealth and power and Social Darwinism's natural selection and the survival of the fittest. Everything revolved around technical and institutional revolutions, and little attention was paid to the dimension of values in Western civilization. But the 1915 New Culture movement was an important turning point, and Chen Duxiu argued that in addition to technical and institutional revolutions, China needed a further

"moral awakening," which would bring about an intellectual enlightenment leading to a civilizational consciousness. This new consciousness
would allow China to move from a particular nationalistic standpoint to
a universalism in which traditional *tianxia* would receive a new life form
in the May Fourth period.

In the first period of the May Fourth, between 1915 and 1919, a sea
change occurred in the thought of Chinese intellectual groups, whether
the last of the late Qing scholar-official reformers or the first generation
of Republican enlightenment intellectuals. We might call this change the
"transformation of the strong country dream": from national strength
to civilizational consciousness. In the process of this transformation, the
world war in Europe (then called the "European War") was an extremely
important historical moment.

The Western thought encountered by Chinese intellectuals from
the late Qing forward was basically that of the capitalist civilization of
nineteenth-century Europe, with historical evolutionism as its core and
nationalism as its motivation, a mentality that had rapidly expanded
throughout the entire world. The strong preference expressed by late
Qing China for wealth and power was a product of nineteenth-century
European civilization. Intellectuals in pursuit of the strong-country
dream all believed that once China was like the West, endowed with the
power to compete in the struggle for existence and a perpetually unsatis-
fied Faustian spirit, it would then create a powerful modern nation-state.
But the tragedy of the European war awoke Chinese intellectuals from
their dream, and they started to think anew about civilizational choices.

Yan Fu (1854–1921), the late Qing intellectual who, through his
translations and writings, had offered a systematic introduction of
nineteenth-century European civilization to fellow Chinese intellectuals,
said to a disciple in a letter following the end of World War I:

> In my declining years, I witnessed the first seven years of the Chinese Republic and
> Europe's four years of unprecedentedly bloody war. And I sensed that 300 years
> of European progress had been reduced to a depraved ethos of self-serving
> slaughter of others. When I look back at the Way of Confucius and Mencius, their
> truths were as great as the great land and their benefits extended throughout the
> country. I am not the only one to say this. Even thoughtful Westerners agree.[5]

Yan Fu's disappointment is clear in his remark that 300 years of progress of European civilization had been reduced to "a depraved ethos of
self-serving slaughter of others"; this was a civilization in which he had

---

[5] Yan Fu, "Yan Fu zhi Xiong Chunru" (Yan Fu's letter to Xiong Chunru), in Yan Fu, *Yan
Fu ji (Yan Fu's writings)* (Beijing: Zhonghua shuju, 1986), vol. 3, p. 692.

previously invested his hope, it was the nineteenth-century civilization for which he had whole-heartedly yearned. The disappointment of this generation of late Qing intellectuals with Western civilization triggered their awakening from nationalism and materialism. After the war, Liang Qichao (1873–1929) toured Europe, and found that the rich areas of the past were now in ruins, and he wrote with feeling that "despite a century of material progress, which had surpassed by several times that of the preceding 3,000 years, humanity not only has not achieved happiness but has instead created many disasters."[6] In Western civilization, materialism and nationalism were linked by an inner logic, and the power of imperialism was rooted in the fleets and armaments of national power. In the foreword to the inaugural edition of *Xinqun* (New Society) magazine, founded by professors at the Zhongguo gongxue,[7] the authors examined the erroneous theories that had led humanity and China down diverging paths, and identified the chief culprit as nationalism. They quoted John Dewey (1859–1952) to the effect that nationalism had evolved as a European strategy employed in the particular context of certain religious wars, and had subsequently been mistaken for the basic principles of universal life, "thus giving birth to the tragedy of this great European war." The journal passionately called for the "destruction of national borders," saying that "we should not follow others and advocate nationalism."[8] At the outbreak of the European war, the educator and journalist Du Yaquan (1873–1933) advocated the use of peaceful "cooperationism" to counterbalance the wild violence of nationalism. He noted that "extreme nationalism feeds the greed and hostility of a nation's people."[9] The harm of nationalism was not only that it led to international conflicts and wars, it also destroyed the character of the people, inflating human nature's tendencies toward corruption and violence. Nationalism was never alone, Du noted, but was always linked to materialism and utilitarianism. This rethinking of nationalism also meant rethinking mainstream thought from the late Qing forward.

[6] Liang Qichao, "Ouyou xinying lu" (A record of my travel impressions of Europe), in Liang Qichao, *Liang Qichao quanji (The complete writings of Liang Qichao)* (Beijing: Beijing chubanshe, 1999), vol. 5, p. 2974.
[7] Translator's note: Zhongguo gongxue (China Public School) was a modern, Western-inspired college established in Shanghai in the early twentieth century. It is identified with many of the Guomindang revolutionary elite.
[8] "Xinqun fakanci" (Foreword to the first issue of "Xinqun"), cited in Liu Hongquan and Liu Hongze, eds., *Zhongguo bainian qikan fakanci (A century of periodical forewords in China)* (Beijing: Jiefangjun chubanshe, 1996), pp. 152–55.
[9] Du Yaquan, "Shehui xieli zhuyi" (Social cooperativism), in Du Yaquan, *Du Yaquan wencun (Extant writings of Du Yaquan)* (Shanghai: Shanghai jiaoyu chubanshe, 2003), p. 22.

Those who reflected most deeply on these questions were often the same people who had originally believed most deeply in the promise of Western civilization. Liang Qichao discovered that Social Darwinism, which he had previously taken as the gold standard for understanding the evolution of society, was the intellectual source for the European war. Now he saw Social Darwinism as of a piece with utilitarianism, individualism, and Nietzsche (1844–1900): "For private individuals, worship of power and money has taken pride of place; for the state, militarism and imperialism have become the most fashionable political policies. The recent world war traces its origins precisely to this."[10] After painful reflection, he rejected wealth and power and extreme nationalism, stressing that "in our patriotism, we cannot acknowledge the country without acknowledging the individual, and we cannot acknowledge the country without acknowledging the world."[11] At the same time Liang continued his reflections on the materialism and utilitarianism that fueled nationalism. He pointed out that the first victim of the rise of science was religion. If all phenomena in the universe resulted from the interaction of material elements: where was the soul or heaven? Under the protection of science, materialist philosophers had built a purely mechanical view of human life, reducing all internal and external life to the natural laws of material movements. Yet if there was no free will, where was responsibility for good and evil? Liang plaintively wrote:

Utilitarianism and power are all the rage. Since there's no heaven after we die, we might as well spend our few decades here on earth enjoying ourselves. Since there is no responsibility for good and evil, why not pursue our own desires by all possible means? Yet no matter how efficient we become in increasing our material capacities it cannot keep up with our ever increasing desires, nor is there any way to bring the two into balance. What to do? All we can do is to rely on our own strength in free competition, or in other words, let the strong consume the weak. Today's militarists and tycoons are all the products of this, and the Great War was our just reward.[12]

Liang Qichao's thoughts reflect the discovery of the social psychological basis created by the pursuit of wealth and power, beginning in the late Qing embrace of materialism and utilitarianism. The original strong country dream had lost its way as Europe destroyed the traditional civilization of the nineteenth-century, opening a new vista on the future.

---

[10] Liang Qichao, "Ouyou xinying lu" (A record of my travel impressions of Europe), p. 2972.
[11] Ibid., p. 2978.
[12] Ibid., p. 2973.

Sensitive Chinese intellectuals began looking for a new road to civilization outside of wealth and power. At the end of World War I, Du Yaquan published an article entitled "What is Chinese Enlightenment after the Great War?" in the magazine *Dongfang zazhi*, pointing out that World War I was a turning point between the old and new civilizations, the old civilization being modern civilization based on power and competition, and the new civilization being the future civilization based on justice and the public good. World War I and the chaos of China's early Republic illustrated the depths to which the old civilization had fallen. European competition over national interests led to international war; Chinese competition over individual power led to civil war. Du Yaquan believed that: "Having passed through this great conflict and this great sacrifice, there must be a great reform in our evaluation of material values versus spiritual values. All countries in the world must feel the weight of this great reform."[13]

The intellectual change prompted by the war is visible not only in representatives of the last scholar-official generation like Yan Fu, Liang Qichao, and Du Yaquan, but is also apparent in the new generation of Republican-period intellectuals, of which Hu Shi (1891–1962) is a representative example. In 1905, when he was still a young student at the Chengzhong Academy in Shanghai, Hu read Yan Fu's translation of Thomas Huxley's *On Evolution* and Liang Qichao's essays, and came to firmly believe in the evolutionary principles of natural selection and survival of the fittest, and he chose his name, Shi, which means "appropriate," as a result of these beliefs. He fell under the spell of Liang Qichao's magical pen and was an ardent nationalist and believer in wealth and power. When Liang published an essay entitled "Extending the Principles of Natural Selection and the Survival of the Fittest," the 14-year-old Hu excitedly wrote: "Today's world is a world of power. As people have already noticed, there is no justice in the world! ... In a weak posture, thrust into the flow of natural selection, we are unable to use blood and iron to struggle with other peoples, nor can we triumph through diplomacy. Given this, to hope not to be treated unequally by other countries or to avoid our ultimate disappearance is difficult! Alas! Have our people not heard the call to action?"[14] Hu's ideology of power politics remained until after the 1911 Revolution, when he left to study

---

[13] Du Yaquan, "Dazhan zhongjiehou guoren zhi juewu ruhe?" (The enlightenment of the Chinese people after the end of the great war), in Du Yaquan, *Du Yaquan wencun* (Extant writings of Du Yaquan), pp. 205, 208.

[14] Hu Shi, "Wujing tianze, shizhe shengcun, shishen qiyi" (Extending the meaning of natural selection and the survival of the fittest), in Ji Xianlin, ed., *Hu Shi quanji (The complete writings of Hu Shi)* (Hefei: Anhui jiaoyu chubanshe, 2003), vol. 21, pp. 2–3.

in the United States: "Those with power are strong, those without it are weak. This is the general rule of natural selection."[15] He believed that a true world patriot was one who loved his country most sincerely.[16] But with the expansion of his reading during his period of study abroad, Hu Shi was gradually influenced by internationalism, and discovered that there was a greater principle beyond patriotism. As the European War broke out, students on American campuses often debated nationalism versus internationalism. On one occasion, the internationalist students held a meeting to debate the question: "My country right or wrong? My country." Hu Shi, a skilled debater, spoke up and pointed out that the question itself was wrong, as it contained a double moral standard: civilized countries had a clear standard of justice regarding their own citizens, but always chose their own countries regardless of considerations of right or wrong when the question involved other countries. Hu Shi proclaimed, "in my view, we should hold to one standard of right or wrong whether at home or abroad."[17] Chinese embrace of great-power ideology was a reaction to the Western double standard of inner civilization and external great power, and sought to use civilization to resist civilization, great power to resist great power. At the outset, Hu Shi also was a firm believer in this logic. But after 1914, the cruel flames of war slowly convinced him of the disaster that the ideology of great power bequeathed to humanity, and he began to believe in universal principles beyond great power, in universal notions of right and wrong, good and bad. He began to turn a cold eye toward great-power ideology and the chivalry of nationalism:

Today's great blight is chivalrous nationalism, which argues that my country should lord it over other countries and that my race should lord it over other races. Anyone who can accomplish these selfish goals, even if it destroys other countries and exterminates other races, has no regrets ... Nationalism believes that power competition between countries is the basic law, and that "international law" means that the strong eat the weak. Those of us enamored of universalism must start with the basics. And what are the basics? A universal nationalism. Patriotism is a wonderful thing, as long as one knows that above the state there is a larger goal, and a larger community, what the ardent anti-imperialist scholar Goldwin Smith (1823–1910) called "the humanity above all nations."[18]

The true nature of chivalrous nationalism is great-power ideology, the belief that there is no principle greater than power, that power is

---

[15] Hu Shi, *Hu Shi liuxue riji (Hu Shi's diary while studying abroad)* (Haikou: Hainan chubanshe, 1994), p. 140.
[16] Ibid., p. 79.
[17] Ibid., pp. 134–36.
[18] Ibid., pp. 263–64.

indeed the greatest principle. In the blood of World War I, Hu Shi saw the scourge of great-power ideology, and thus sought to place a higher constraint on nationalism, which would be internationalism. Where is the value of internationalism? Hu Shi found it in humanism: "What is the great blight on today's world? Not humanism, but nationalism. That the strong eat the weak is the way of the beasts, not of humans. Mistaking the way of the beasts for the way of humans has become today's world ... There is no other way to save the world than to transform the way of humanity into the way of good, and replace power with justice."[19]

The intellectual transformation experienced by Hu Shi in the transition from the late Qing to early Republican times was a thought process followed by many Chinese intellectuals at the time. From a hot-headed, patriotic, angry youth who believed that might made right and that wealth and power were everything, Hu Shi slowly, because of the tragedy of World War I, discovered the negative aspects of nineteenth-century Western civilization. In late Qing and early Republican times, most Chinese had paid attention mainly to materialistic and nationalistic power, hoping to use strength to ward off strength and violence to constrain violence. After 1914, they began to see the frightening side of this, realizing that materialism, wealth and power, and narrow nationalism not only created the jungle order of the early Republic, but that they were destined to destroy humanity. Thus during the May Fourth period, young Enlightenment intellectuals began to take seriously the character of Western civilization: modern civilization with freedom as its core value. And at the same time, reformist scholar-officials looked back to Chinese tradition for civilizational resources to balance out the violence of Western civilization. Even if the civilizational path they were to follow was to diverge, at the time, both sides shared a common standpoint: to move away from the search for national wealth and power toward a consciousness of civilization.

The May Fourth Enlightenment movement began with questions about civilization. Chen Duxiu, in the founding issue of *New Youth* (then known under its original title *Youth Magazine*), published an article entitled "The French and Modern Civilization," in which he argued that all countries in the world, ancient, modern, Eastern, Western, could be considered civilized as long as they were countries that taught moral transformation. At the present time, Chen argued, only Europe possessed civilization, which meant Western civilization. France was the representative of modern civilization in Chen's eyes. Although German

[19] Ibid., p. 305.

science is advanced, Chen continued, "In the majority of Germans' minds, the love of liberty and equality has been squeezed out by love of national and racial strength. The French people, in contrast, have had the fondness for liberty, equality, and fraternity become part of their natures and customs."[20] In the opposing camps of World War I, Germany was the newly risen empire, having evolved from Bismarck's policies of blood and iron through Kaiser Wilhelm's (1859–1941) expansionist invasions, and Germany's path of rising through national wealth and power was something that most Chinese intellectuals had admired. But Chen Duxiu pointed out that liberty, equality, and fraternity were the soul of a properly managed civilization, while Germans displayed more a "love for a strong nation and a strong race," which was not a model for modern civilization. As a standard bearer for the May Fourth New Culture movement, Chen Duxiu astutely noted that the core of modern civilization is not national wealth and power, not material abundance, nor is it a Weberian institutional rationality or legitimacy, but is made up instead of the basic values of liberty, equality, and fraternity that emerged during the French revolution. Chen noted that when Western civilization entered China, the first thing that awakened the Chinese people was the technical dimension of science, where China was comparatively behind, which led to the Foreign Affairs and the Self-Strengthening movements which aimed at rapid Westernization. Next came a political-institutional awakening, when China discovered that her political institutions were not equal to those of the West, resulting in the 1898 reforms and the New Policies of the late Qing, when the government, beginning in 1905 finally attempted to implement many of the reforms suggested earlier. Then after the Republican state was set up, politics was manipulated by soldiers and factions, and most citizens still knew nothing about the state, and lacked citizens' consciousness, so that the thought and personality of the citizens under the Republic was no different than under a dictatorship. Chen Duxiu thus called for a third awakening, after the scientific and political awakenings: "Going forward, what our people should be most concerned about are ethical questions. If we cannot effect an ethical awakening, then we will find that what we formerly thought were awakenings were only partial, and we will remain as if in a haze. I predict that an ethical awakening will be the last of the final awakenings for my people."[21]

---

[20] Translation taken from Chen Duxiu, "The French and Modern Civilization," *Contemporary Chinese Thought* 31.1 (1999), p. 57.
[21] Chen Duxiu, "Wuren zuihou zhi juewu" (My final enlightenment), in Chen Duxiu, *Chen Duxiu zhuzuoxuan (Selected writings of Chen Duxiu)* (Shanghai: Shanghai renmin chubanshe, 1984), vol. 1, pp. 175–79.

Chen Duxiu's "final ethical awakening" is nothing other than civilizational consciousness: through cultural enlightenment, the people come to awaken to the path of national revival, which is not uniquely the pursuit of wealth and power, nor institutional or systemic rationality. The most important thing is to pursue the heart of modern civilization – the universal values of freedom and equality, which is the soul of a republican political body. As Chen insisted, "The establishment of a republican constitutional order is based on principles of independence, equality, and freedom."[22] Although freedom and equality had been discussed during the late Qing reform movement, they had never emerged as core values, but were lost under the central goals of wealth and power. To achieve the goals of wealth and power and community strength, the citizens' competitive capacities were elevated to the highest level, after which universal truth was reduced to one word, "competition." This was the universal consensus of public opinion in the late Qing. Competition relies on strength, be it military or intellectual. And in a discussion of strength in the context of World War I, Germany was the strongest, be it in terms of military preparations or science – although it finally lost to the alliance of free countries under England and France. Chinese intellectuals celebrated the World War I victory of "reason over power." The reason of the May Fourth period was no longer the reason of "competition," nor "the reason of "power" but was the reason of "freedom" and "equality."

In the first edition of *Weekly Critic*, Chen Duxiu answered the question of "what is truth and what is power" in a sweeping statement: "Whatever is in accord with equality and freedom is true; whatever relies on its own strength to invade other people's equality and freedom is power."[23] The understanding of truth during the May Fourth was very different from that of late Qing times, and was no longer the cold, unfeeling natural selection and survival of the fittest, no longer a technical, neutral competition of strength, but contained notions of universal values, and ethical principles based on human beings. Truth had once again been accorded a value content that brought it in line with Enlightenment thought. Freedom and equality became the common ideals of May Fourth intellectuals, the core content of modern civilization.

The hottest topic during the New Culture movement was the comparison of Chinese and Western civilizations. Chen Duxiu, Li Dazhao (1888–1927), and Hu Shi of *Xinqingnian*, as well as Du Yaquan of

---

[22] Ibid., p. 179.
[23] Chen Duxiu, "Meizhou pinglun fakanci" (Foreword to the first issue of "Weekly Critic"), in Chen Duxiu, *Chen Duxiu zhuzuoxuan (Selected writings of Chen Duxiu)*, vol. 1, p. 427.

Dongfang zazhi, all saw Chinese and Western civilizations as different, if not opposed, in terms of character and style. Chen Duxiu argued that Western nations took competition, the individual, the rule of law, and power as basic components, while Eastern nations emphasized harmony, family, feelings, and rituals.[24] Although Li Dazhao and Du Yaquan were in different camps, they both saw Western civilization as dynamic and Eastern civilization as passive. Their differences are seen in their conclusions: Chen Duxiu saw differences between Eastern and Western civilizations as differences between new and old, ancient and modern, seeing them in the light of evolution, with Western civilization representing a higher, newer civilization which would necessarily replace the old, obsolete Chinese civilization; by contrast, Du Yaquan maintained that Chinese and Western civilizations were "different in nature but not in process," and each contained flaws and could borrow from the other.[25] What is worth noting is that although the starting point of the great debate about Chinese and Western civilizations in the New Culture movement had to do with China's choosing a future cultural direction and path, the style of the debate was not "cultural" but "civilized." The opposing sides did not organize their debates from the perspective of the kind of national culture China required as a political entity, but rather began from the great perspective of universal civilization. From this vantage point, they compared the strengths and weaknesses of Chinese and Western civilizations, and located the path forward for Chinese culture within the comprehensive trends of universal civilization.

The May Fourth was not like the late Qing–early Republican period; it was an internationalist period, and regardless of whether the May Fourth intellectual was a cultural radical or a cultural moderate, they all carried forward the concerns of traditional Chinese *tianxia,* understanding the position of China's culture against the background of the evolution of the civilization of all humanity. Even people like Du Yaquan, who at first glance appears to affirm the plurality of civilizations, and views Chinese and Western civilizations as two distinct regional civilizations coexisting in space, finally employs the theory of unitary civilization to support his viewpoint concerning the possibility of mediation between civilizations. Du Yaquan in particular pointed out that the meaning of "old and new" changes with the times. During the 1898 reforms, proposals to imitate Western civilization were new, while proposals to maintain Chinese

---

[24] Chen Duxiu, "Dong-Xi minzu genben sixiang zhi chayi" (Basic differences in thought between Eastern and Western peoples), *Qingnian zazhi* 1.4 (1915).
[25] Cang Fu (Du Yaquan), "Jing de wenming yu dong de wenming" (Quiet civilization and active civilization), *Dongfang zazhi* 13.10 (1916).

customs were old. But after World War I, which revealed the flaws in Western materialism and nationalism, existing Western civilization no longer was in accord with the new era, and lost its utility. "If Chinese people want to use new and old as standards and base these on the historical era, then they must take proposals to create a future culture as new, and those to maintain modern culture as old."[26]

Du Yaquan's notion of creating a new civilization was a blend of Chinese and Western civilizations, but Li Dazhao, who held the same point of view, clearly fixed his hopes on the rise of a third civilization: "With Eastern civilization between decline and stagnation, and Western civilization exhausting itself in materialism, the crisis of the old world seems destined to fail in the absence of the rise of a third, new civilization. Russian civilization can surely mediate the succession of Eastern and Western civilizations."[27] Later on, Li Dazhao turned toward the Russian Marxist road, but his earliest point of departure was not nationalism but internationalism, and he searched for China's path within the broad trends of world civilization.

Evolutionism dominated the mainstream historical vision of intellectuals of the two generations of the late Qing and May Fourth periods. The choice of China's future path would not be determined by China's own particular national circumstances. Instead, China needed to catch up with the rest of the world, seeking commonalities despite differences. World trends were changing and China could not remain outside of those trends. The young Chen Duxiu saw French civilization as the leader of world civilization, but Du Yaquan argued that after World War I, world trends had changed: "China, as a representative of Asian society, cannot but experience a certain self-awakening and self-confidence in light of the adverse trends in world development."[28] This self-awakening and self-confidence were a "civilizational awakening" and not a "cultural awakening." Even if Chen Duxiu and Du Yaquan had awakened to world-leading currents with different civilizational contents, they remained internationalists, not nationalists, or to put it another way, they were nationalists emerging from a posture of internationalism. They situated China's national revival on the map of world trends, and China, as an Eastern country, was in no way exceptional. It was world universal

---

[26] Cang Fu (Du Yaquan), "Xinjiu sixiang zhi zhezhong" (A compromise between new and old thought), *Dongfang zazhi* 16.9 (1919).

[27] Li Dazhao, "Dong-Xi wenhua zhi yidian" (Differences between Western and Eastern cultures), *Yanzhi* 3 (1918).

[28] Cang Fu (Du Yaquan), "Zhanhou Dong-Xi wenming zhi tiaohe" (The reconciliation of Eastern and Western cultures after the war), *Dongfang zazhi* 14.4 (1917).

civilization, and not China's particular culture, that would determine China's future path of development.

May Fourth period intellectuals, full of the concerns of universalism, were preoccupied more with future prospects of the civilization of humanity than with the future of China's culture. After World War I, Liang Qichao traveled in Europe, and the subtitle of his volume *Reflections on a European Voyage* was *The Awakening of the Chinese People*. This awakening was a civilizational awakening, not a cultural awakening, and he summed up a series of arguments in a section entitled "The Great Responsibility of the Chinese People to World Civilization," in which he said "the greatest goal in human life is to make a contribution to all of humanity." Nation-building is merely a means in the evolution of the whole of humanity; we should not see achieving wealth and power for our own country as the goal, it is more important for our country to contribute to all of humanity. For this reason, China had a "huge responsibility" in its future, which was to "use Western civilization to enrich China's civilization, and use China's civilization to repair Western civilization, so that the two transform to become one new civilization."[29] This new civilization would be neither Western nor Chinese, but a universal civilization for all humanity. This humanitarian consciousness seeking to "commit to heaven and earth," to "open a way of peace for ten thousand generations" is found throughout the Confucian philosopher Liang Shuming's (1893–1988) *Eastern and Western Cultures and their Philosophies*. With great verve, Liang tours Chinese, Western, and Indian civilizations, viewing them, from a perspective of cultural relativism, as completely different in spatial terms, each possessing its own direction of development for its civilizational system. Yet at the same time, in chronological terms he adopts a monist historical view and argues that universal world history was moving from Western civilization to Chinese civilization and would arrive finally in India as its ultimate resting place. Once they had opened their eyes to the notion of civilization, May Fourth period intellectuals seem to have felt an urgent need to seek out the inner logic of universal civilization, and on the map of the world situate the geographical space and historical character of different civilizations. On this point, May Fourth intellectuals were very similar to Liang Shuming, whose inner being worked on world time and for whom different ages occupied different time zones in world history. In Liang's point of view, Western civilization was the civilization of humanity as a lively youth; Chinese civilization was a civilization of a mature humanity, and Indian

---

[29] Liang Qichao, "Ouyou xinying lu" (A record of my travel impressions of Europe), p. 2986.

civilization was a civilization of an elderly, most enlightened humanity. The current crisis from which Chinese civilization was suffering was the result of having matured too early, and having precociously entered the state of adulthood without having experienced the youth of Western civilization, which is why China had to study Western civilization. But for Western civilization, its final resting place would be in the East, and it needed to abandon its youthful vigor and embrace the harmony of middle age.[30] It is only from this standpoint of historical time that we can understand why from the point of view of May Fourth intellectuals, China was a historical people in a Hegelian sense. Chinese civilization belonged not only to the Chinese, but to all humanity.

Cultural Consciousness after the Japanese Invasion

While the New Culture movement plunged into a universalist comparison of civilizations, looking for the solution for China's cultural future from the perspective of universal civilization, one question had been obscured in the rush to embrace humanity: Where was China's cultural agency? What was a Chinese person's cultural identity?

In the intellectual transformation that occurred between 1895 and 1925, there were two generations of Enlightenment intellectuals. The first was the new wave from within late Qing scholar-officials, such as Kang Youwei, Liang Qichao, Yan Fu, and Zhang Taiyan (1869–1936). The second was the first generation of Enlightenment intellectuals: Chen Duxiu, Li Dazhao, Hu Shi, and Lu Xun. In the New Culture movement, the first new-wave generation was already "old," and was seen by most young people as made up of old-style figures, or "half new–half old," in the way that some people criticized Du Yaquan: "If you say he's old, he still seems new, but if you say he's new, that doesn't quite fit."[31] The May Fourth was a period when new intellectuals dominated public opinion, broadly discussed Chinese and Western civilizations, looked at China from the perspective of the world, and predicted China's future on the basis of world trends. Yet even in the face of a momentum that swept everything before it, a new cultural consciousness sprouted among older enlightenment figures such as Kang Youwei (1858–1927), Yan Fu, Liang Qichao, and Liang Shuming's father, the scholar and philosopher Liang

---

[30] See Liang Shuming, "Dong-Xi wenhua jiqi zhexue" (Eastern and Western cultures and their philosophies), in Liang Shuming, *Liang Shuming quanji (The complete writings of Liang Shuming)* (Jinan: Shandong renmin chubanshe, 2005), pp. 488–540.

[31] Du Yaquan, "Xinjiu sixiang zhi zhezhong" (A compromise between new and old thought).

Ji (1858–1918). When surrounded by conservative scholar-officials in late Qing times, they had actively promoted Western learning, but in the early Republican period, and especially after the impact of World War I, they began to turn their attention to the "national soul," the "national character," to "building the national spirit," and to reflections on the question of maintaining China's cultural agency in the process of importing Western learning.

What is the national soul? Kang Youwei said: "Every country builds itself on something. From its politics, moral teachings, and customs it penetrates into the hearts of the people, becoming the people's thoughts, sinking into their skin, molding the habits of the group. Over time it grows stronger, even if we are so accustomed to it that we forget it's there. This is what we call the national soul."[32] He argued that since the founding of the Republic, in the frenzy of nation-building no one had questioned the value of China's politics, moral teachings, and customs but simply excised and discarded them. Similarly, no one questioned the value of European and American politics, moral teachings, and customs, but simply obeyed and accepted them. So while China's body remained, her soul was gone. For this reason, Kang promoted the Confucian religion and established the Confucian Religion Society in 1912, in the hope of calling back the departed national soul. Where Kang talked about the national soul, Yan Fu and Liang Qichao talked about the national spirit. In 1913 Yan Fu published his "Reflections on Ancient Times," in which he criticized the worship of the West from late Qing times forward: "Most of your infatuation with other peoples is based solely on material civilization. You have not realized that the order of nations is determined first by the character of the nation and its people, and material matters are of a lesser importance. The character of China's nation and people is deeply rooted, who else can compare?"[33] The Yan Fu of the early Republican period had not abandoned his ideals of wealth and power, but as the American historian of Chinese thought Benjamin Schwartz (1916–99) noted, at this point his pursuits in terms of social legitimacy diverged from his views on the value of freedom and equality.[34] The young Yan Fu

---

[32] Kang Youwei, "Zhongguo dianwei wu zai quanfa Ou-Mei er jinqi guocui shuo" (The theory that the chief reason for China's crisis lies in imitating Europe and America and abandoning her national essence), in Tang Zhijun, ed., *Kang Youwei zhenglunji (Kang Youwei's political writings)* (Beijing: Zhonghua shuju, 1981), vol. 2, pp. 890, 913.

[33] Yan Fu, "Sigu pian" (On thinking about ancient times), in *Zhongguo xiandai xueshu jingdian, Yan Fu juan* (Modern Chinese academic classics, Yan Fu volume) (Shijiazhuang: Hebei jiaoyu chubanshe, 1996), p. 601.

[34] See Shi Huaci (Benjamin Schwartz), *Xunqiu fuqiang: Yan Fu yu Xifang (In search of wealth and power: Yen Fu and the West)*, Ye Fengmei, trans. (Nanjing: Jiangsu renmin chubanshe, 1990), p. 211.

criticized the formula "Chinese essence-Western utility" as "cow essence-horse utility," and pointed out that the West had its own utility, wherein "freedom was the essence and democracy the utility."[35] But in the early Republican period, he saw that Chinese enthusiasm for Western learning was concentrated on vulgar materialism, and that the Republican government put in place since the 1911 revolution was disastrous, and his faith in Western values of freedom began to waver. He came to believe that Weberian institutional rationality need not be linked to the values of universal freedom, but could also be constructed on the basis of China's particular "national character." Having witnessed the eclipse of materialism and great-power ideology, Yan Fu came to believe that a metaphysical "national character" was more important than this-worldly wealth and power, which constituted a reaffirmation and development of the "deeply rooted" Chinese civilization. "The existence of any nation must be built on its national spirit."[36] In his view, this national spirit was "the Chinese people's special characteristics of loyalty, filial piety, integrity, and righteousness. This is the spirit on which the country was built."[37]

In late Qing times, as China discovered the outside world, Liang Qichao felt deeply the differences between China and the West, and his concern was how to seek out similarities within the differences and quickly find a way for China to become a "country of the world." Yet in the early Republican period, his attitude came to be that of Kang Youwei and Yan Fu, and underwent a subtle change. In 1912, Liang published "On the National Character," arguing that a country had to be established on a foundation which, even if unnamed, was in fact the national character. Nations have characters in the same way that people have characters. How is national character manifested? Liang Qichao mentioned three elements: language, religion, and customs. He particularly noted: "National character can be improved but not created; it can be reformed but not discarded. China's national character is excellent and can compete and survive on the world stage, but the basis of our national character, handed down over several thousand years, is precarious to the point of falling into the abyss, which is what I am afraid of."[38]

[35] Yan Fu, "Yuanqiang" (The origin of strength), in *Zhongguo xiandai xueshu jingdian, Yan Fu juan* (Modern Chinese academic classics, Yan Fu volume), p. 547.
[36] Yan Fu, "Dujing dang jiji tichang" (We must actively encourage people to read the classics), in *Zhongguo xiandai xueshu jingdian, Yan Fu juan* (Modern Chinese academic classics, Yan Fu volume), p. 603.
[37] Yan Fu, "Daoyang Zhongguo minguo liguo jingshen yi" (Propagate the spirit of establishing the Republic of China), in Wang Shi, ed., *Yan Fu ji (Yan Fu's writings)* (Beijing: Zhonghua shuju, 1986), vol. 2, p. 344.
[38] Liang Qichao, "Guoqing pian" (On the national character), in Liang Qichao, *Liang Qichao quanji* (The complete writings of Liang Qichao), vol. 5, pp. 2554–55.

National character, national souls, national spirit are all different words to describe the same thing – a unique national spirit or civilizational base possessed by a particular modern state. In the Anglo-American pragmatic tradition, there is no metaphysical theory of the national spirit, which comes rather from the continental romantic tradition, a reaction against the French Enlightenment movement. The Enlightenment movement inherited Christian universal ideals, and molded a universal modern civilization on the basis of secular universal rationality. But Italians like Giambattista Vico (1668–1744) and Germans like Johann Georg Hamann (1730–88) and Johann Gottfried Herder strongly doubted the Enlightenment movement's arguments concerning the universality of human nature and the unity of civilization, arguing that universalism had erased everything that made man most human and had given him most of his personality. Herder argued that not all cultures were inter- changeable, since they belonged to particular communities that, linked together by common traditions of language, historical memory, customs and habits, national religions and feelings, bonded the members of the community together.[39] The national soul and national spirit emphasized by Kang Youwei, Yan Fu, and Liang Qichao in the early Republican period were very similar to the national spirit and national culture of the European romantic tradition. These reforming scholar-officials, who in late Qing times had preached universalism in the process of learning from the West how to build a universal people and state, hastened to embrace Herder-style cultural nationalism, and once again stressed the multiplicity of world cultures, when they discovered that the technical, rational processes at the core of wealth and power would destroy China's own moral and civilizational traditions. Their faith in the foundation of universal civilization began to waver, and they once again promoted the historical particularity of China's civilization.

In fact, Zhang Taiyan was the earliest to mention cultural multipli- city. In late Qing times, when Kang Youwei, Yan Fu, and Liang Qichao were deeply drawn to the notion of the universal historical evolu- tion of humanity, Zhang Taiyan raised instead the idea of "national essence": "Use the national essence to stimulate the race-nature, and increase the enthusiasm for patriotism."[40] "National essence" meant,

---

[39] See Yisaiya Bolin (Isaiah Berlin), "Fan qimeng yundong" (The Counter-Enlightenment), in Feng Keli, trans., Yisaiya Bolin, *Fan chaoliu: Guannianshi lunwenji* (Against the current: Essays in the history of ideas) (Nanjing: Yilin chubanshe, 2002), pp. 1–28.

[40] Zhang Taiyan, "Dongjing liuxuesheng huanyinghui yanshuolu" (Remarks at the wel- coming ceremony for the Tokyo foreign students), in Jiang Bin, ed., *Gegu dianxin de zheli: Zhang Taiyan wenxuan (The philosophy of reforming the ancient and establishing the new: Selected writings of Zhang Taiyan)* (Shanghai: Yuandong chubanshe, 1996), p. 142.

first, anti-Manchuism, and second, anti-Westernization. The Taiwanese historian Wang Rongzu's (b. 1940) comparative research illustrates that if we can call Kang Youwei a universalist, then Zhang Taiyan was a cultural pluralist, China's Herder, even if the origin of his thought came from Zhuangzi's (370–287 BC) Daoist doctrine of the equality of things.[41] Zhang opposed the notion of universal principle and evolutionary history, and argued that Chinese civilization had its own written language, institutional system, and significant people and events, different from the West, which made up its national essence and religion. In the early Republican period, cultural pluralism was taken up by Zhang's enemies such as Kang Youwei and Liang Qichao, becoming the basis for their theories of the national character and the national soul.

In 1915, Liang Qichao developed his thoughts on national character further in the foreword he wrote to the first issue of the *Dazhonghua* journal. At the start of the essay he pointed out that the decline in China's popular will had reached an extreme. The results of reformist policies promoted in and around the court over the past twenty years, resulting in new studies and new policies, had alienated all of society. To mobilize the people and effect their salvation, the national spirit had to be revived: "China has never disappeared over the course of thousands of years, this is an iron-clad historical fact, as solid as a mountain, for which there must be an unchanging reason, which the people of my country should reflect upon and awaken to. The foundation of a country relies on the national character, and if the national character declines, so too does the country." Liang Qichao noted three ways in which countries had disappeared over the course of human history. One was when there was no national spirit at the outset, meaning that the country could not be established; another was when the country encountered a stronger enemy before the national spirit could be established, and perished halfway; and the third was when that national spirit existed but the country chose the path of self-destruction. China was an ancient country with a venerable civilization, and had achieved full development. Thus in its case the greatest threat was that of "having national spirit but choosing the path of self-destruction."[42] The country was not the same as the dynasty, Liang argued. A dynasty can perish, but as long as the national spirit is preserved, the loss of the country can be avoided. National character

---

[41] See Wang Rongzu, "Zhang Taiyan wenhuaguan" (Zhang Taiyan's views of culture), in *Zhang Taiyan yanjiu (Studies of Zhang Taiyan)* (Taibei: Li Ao chubanshe, 1991).

[42] Liang Qichao, "Dazhonghua fakanci" (Foreword to the first issue of "Dazhonghua"), in Liang Qichao, *Liang Qichao quanji* (The complete writings of Liang Qichao), vol. 5, pp. 2823–25.

is civilization, as well as *tianxia*; it is the soul of why a country becomes a country. The loss of a country is not like the passing of a dynasty, but is a disintegration of the order of civilization or *tianxia*.

During the New Culture movement, we find the intellectuals of the Xueheng group who, like the first generation of Enlightenment scholar-officials, were culturally awakened and sensitive to questions of China's agency. Leaders of the Xueheng group, including the historian Chen Yinke (1890–1969), the sinologist and poet Wu Mi (1894–1978), and the scholar of foreign literature Mei Guangdi (1890–1945), were unlike Kang Youwei and Liang Qichao in that they had received a systematic, excellent education in famous schools in the United States. They were distressed by the domestic popularity of people like Chen Duxiu and Hu Shi with their half-baked knowledge of Western learning. In their view, the most essential part of Western civilization was the humanist tradition of ancient Greece, while what Hu Shi and company had brought in, mechanistic theories based on science, or melodramatic romanticism originating in Rousseau, were the dregs of Western civilization. At the same time, they argued, ancient Greek humanism as praised by the American humanist Irving Babbitt (1865–1933) contained many internal similarities with rational, moderate Confucian civilization. Although they too were engaged in comparison between Chinese and Western civilizations, the Xueheng intellectuals were not looking to the future, but rather returning to the rational traditions of ancient Greece and pre-Qin China, seeking cultural awakening in the common features of Chinese and Western classical civilizations. They argued that one should not belittle Chinese Confucian culture, saying that "if we wish to absorb Western culture, we must explore and develop the thoughts and feelings of our people."[43] In the 1920s, of all of the members of the new studies camp, Chen Yinke and Wu Mi worked toward a clear cultural consciousness of their own nation. When the scholar and poet Wang Guowei (1877–1927) killed himself by jumping into Kunming Lake and everyone was trying to divine the reasons for his death, they insisted that Wang was not a martyr to the Qing, but rather a martyr to Chinese culture. In his eulogy to Wang Guowei, Chen Yinke said: "Whenever a culture declines, those who have been molded by this culture suffer, and the suffering is greatest for those who have most embodied this culture."[44] Instead of explaining Wang Guowei, Chen Yinke in his remarks is describing himself and the fact that he had taken Chinese culture as his own responsibility, and

---

[43] Wu Xuezhao, *Wu Mi yu Chen Yinke (Wu Mi and Chen Yinke)* (Beijing: Sanlian shudian, 2014), p. 41.
[44] Ibid., p. 91.

had decided to devote his life to Chinese culture. As Wang Guowei was lowered into his grave, Wu Mi said: "My scholarship is not a tenth of that of Wang Guowei, but I vow to make the preservation of the spirit of Chinese culture, moral and ritual teachings my own responsibility."[45] This cultural awakening appears even more clearly when, sometime later, Chen Yinke penned a review of the second volume of Feng Youlan's (1895–1990) *History of Chinese Philosophy*: "Those who truly hope to construct an intellectual system and make original contributions must absorb and import foreign theories without forgetting the original role of our people. These two opposite yet complementary attitudes are the true spirit of Daoism as well as the old path of New Confucianism. This is clearly illustrated by the history of 2,000 years of intellectual contact between China and other peoples."[46]

We might see Chen Yinke as a vanguard of cultural consciousness during the New Culture movement, as he "absorbed and imported foreign theories without forgetting the original role of our people," which is the most correct expression of cultural awakening. Chen Yinke described himself as "devoted throughout my life neither to ancient nor modern studies. My thought was grounded in the culture of the period of the Xianfeng (1850–61) and Tongzhi (1861–75) emperors[47], somewhere between Zeng Guofan (1811–72), the stern Confucian general who defeated the Taiping rebels, and Zhang Zhidong (1837–1909), the late Qing official responsible for Westernizing reforms." Although Chen inherited the intellectual traditions of Zeng Guofan and Zhang Zhidong, his thought was different from the "Chinese essence-Western utility" formula of the late Qing. In late Qing times, opening to and understanding of Western learning was limited, and Zhang Zhidong used the traditional division of essence and function, limiting Western learning to an instrumental, practical dimension. But Chen Yinke lived in an era when China was open to the entire world, and culturally awakened people like Chen now possessed a fairly deep understanding of Western knowledge, in no way inferior to Hu Shi and other complete Westernizers. They thoroughly understood the similarities and differences between East and West, as well as the advantages and disadvantages of each, and their willingness to "absorb and import foreign theories" represented their continued openness to Western learning, their refusal to divide things into essence and function. Chen's attitude was, as long as something was good, we

---

[45] Ibid., p. 74.
[46] Ibid., p. 143.
[47] Translator's note: Chen Yinke was born in 1890, so he is making a point about the intellectual world of the family in which he grew up.

should do our best to absorb it. Yet such absorption occurred on the basis of an awakening of cultural agency that would selectively evaluate Western knowledge on the basis of "the original role of our people." Whether in matters of comparisons between civilizations or cultural reconstruction, there was no need to cling blindly to national traditions, but neither could one dispense with one's own consciousness of agency.

Wang Guowei, Chen Yinke, and Wu Mi, professors at the Qinghua National Studies Institute, were marginal characters who "did not fit in" with the mainstream New Culture movement, nor did their work coalesce into an influential shared body of thought. The great transformation in the thought of society as a whole did not occur until after the September Eighteenth incident in 1931 when Japan orchestrated a military confrontation leading to the establishment of Japanese control in Manchuria. If we say that World War I prompted a shift in the May Fourth movement from infatuation with French culture toward the search for a new, third culture, then the September Eighteenth incident gave rise to a strong nationalistic consciousness in China, and with the fall of Manchuria and the crisis in north China, the intellectual world changed course. In the stormy German movement at the end of the eighteenth century, Herder represented the German mainstream, which was a moderate cultural nationalism developing against the backdrop of internationalism. When Napoleon invaded in the nineteenth century, following Fichte's call, Germany turned toward a political nationalism with a strong sense of ethnic agency. The emergence of this ethnic subjectivity required the emergence of "the other," particularly the emergence of foreign enemies. Comparisons of Eastern and Western civilization receded, and universalistic concerns yielded to basic nation-state consciousness. The life or death of the Chinese nation was no longer to be defined by the universal flow of world history, but was rather to be discovered from within China's own historical traditions.

The question of cultural awakening came to the surface during the great debate over Chinese culture in 1935. In January of 1935, a group of ten professors, including Wang Xinming (1892–1961), Tao Xisheng (1899–1988), and He Bingsong (1890–1946), published an article in the officially supported *Chinese Culture Rebuilds* magazine entitled "A Proclamation on Rebuilding China's Culture," in which they announced that: "In the cultural realm, we cannot see today's China"; "in the cultural realm, China is disappearing; China's political form, its social organization and intellectual content and style have all lost their special characteristics." The ten professors pointed out: "If China's culture is to raise its head, her politics, society and thought must all possess Chinese characteristics, and we must devote ourselves to China's own cultural reconstruction."[48] This proclamation set off great waves in the intellectual world, drawing both praise and criticism, and led to a great debate on China's culture. Among the opposing camp there were great generals like Hu Shi and the noted scholar Chen Xujing (1903–67) who were in favor of complete Westernization, but compared to the May Fourth period, the overall atmosphere had changed, and theories grounded in defense of China's own culture gained even more sympathy from intellectuals and public opinion.

The question was, what did "China's own" mean? The proclamation was not clear on this point, ambiguously stating that "China's own culture will be built in this time and this place." The ten professors had all been baptized in the spirit of the New Culture movement, and were all new-style intellectuals with solid Western educations, and while they wanted to rediscover the specificity of Chinese culture and draw clear lines between China and the West, they were not proposing a return to tradition. Their notion of "China's own culture" was a new culture which neither clung to the past nor forgot its roots. They particularly stressed a creative spirit grounded in "the needs of this time and place": "This creativity is a creativity that will strive to catch up."[49] From the "civilizational awakening" of the May Fourth to the "cultural awakening" of the 1930s, there is a thread of "cultural creativity" that connects the two generations, a belief that cultural reconstruction is not a simple factual identity, but is rather a process requiring the creation of structures. During the May Fourth period, Li Dazhao and Du Yaquan tried to blend Chinese and Western civilizations to create a "new third civilization" for the twentieth century, and in the 1930s, those invested in China's own culture hoped to create a "new culture" based on "the needs of this time and place" that neither clung to the past nor forgot its roots." But the creation of the "third civilization" by Li Dazhao and Du Yaquan in the New Culture movement had a certain foundation, which was to carry out a blending of Chinese and Western civilizations which were opposed in nature but complementary in function. This was a realistic cultural creation. By contrast, those invested in the China's own culture project of the 1930s abandoned the tradition of Chinese and Western civilization, and employing an instrumentalist standard of cultural construction based on "the needs of this time and place," they fell into the trap of voluntarism. Cultural voluntarism is a historicism that denies universalism. As Leo Strauss said concerning historicism, "the

---

[48] Wang Xinming et al., "Zhongguo benwei de wenhua jianshe xuanyan" (Proclamation concerning the construction of China's own culture), *Wenhua jianshe* 1.4 (1935).
[49] Ibid.

only standards that can break with existing reality are wholly subjective standards. Aside from individual choice, they have nothing else to rely on ... The peak of historicism is nihilism."[50] Itô Toramaru (1927–2003), the Japanese scholar of modern Chinese literature, called it "dynamic nihilism": a realism that believes in no values, the only truth being the free will of the individual or the nation.[51] Beginning from nothing, it valiantly moves toward a dynamism that will create a new world. While on the surface those invested in China's own culture were grounded in "the needs of this time and place," in fact they were exactly like Fichte, and what they ultimately worshipped was the nihilistic free will of the nation.

In the great debate on China's own culture, although the total Westernizers and the champions of Chinese culture appear to be completely antagonistic, in fact they shared, behind their opposition, a common theoretical presupposition: cultural instrumentalism. Both groups saw culture as a tool to bring about national salvation and revival, rather than intrinsic national values. Behind Hu Shi's complete Westernization was the theory of evolution and the victory of the strong over the weak. He said: "In the process of this cultural movement where only the fittest survive, there is no completely reliable standard to guide our cultural choices."[52] Culture no longer possessed intrinsic values, only utility. And as for the ten professors advocating China's own culture, they were like their opponents Hu Shi and Chen Xujing, in that for them, culture was not the fruit of internal feelings and deep life experience, nor was it the object of a reassuring life identity, even less was it connected to feelings of origins, home, or belonging. Culture was merely a tool, an effective means to satisfy humanity's needs. For this reason, the relationship between nationalism and culture no longer concerned questions of values, identity, and community belonging, but was rather an instrumental relationship of effectiveness. Whatever was useful to a people or a nation was thus an "effective" culture, even if in terms of innate values it was not a "good" culture. And as for "China's own culture" that was to be created, its innate values were unimportant as long as they were effective in forming a modern nation-state, which would afford them the credibility to serve China's future core culture. Clearly, this is a false

[50] Lieau Shitelaosi (Leo Strauss), *Ziran quanli yu lishi (Natural right and history)*, Peng Gang, trans. (Beijing: Shenghuo, Dushu, Xinzhi Sanlian shudian, 2003), p. 19.
[51] See Yiteng Huwan (Itô Toramaru), *Lu Xun yu zhongmolun: Jindai xianshi zhuyi de chengli (Lu Xun and theories of the end: The establishment of modern realism)*, Li Dongmu, trans. (Beijing: Shenghuo, Dushu, Xinzhi Sanlian shudian 2008), p. 117.
[52] Hu Shi, "Shiping suowei 'Zhongguo benwei de wenhua jianshe'" (A critique of the so-called "construction of China's own culture"), in Hu Shi, *Hu Shi wenji (Hu Shi's writings)* (Beijing: Beijing Daxue chubanshe, 1998), p. 450.

cultural consciousness, one that has been emptied of any true national cultural content, a counter-cultural "own culture."

In the 1930s debate on China's own culture, the liberal camp included some with cultural consciousness, but they were cultural nationalists unlike Hu Shi and Chen Xujing. Representative figures include Zhang Junmai (or Carson Chang, 1886–1969) and Zhang Dongsun (1886–1973), both of whom were prominent intellectuals. Zhang Junmai was a dualist who accepted both mind and matter, culture and politics. In terms of political institutions he was an Anglo-American constitutionalist, but in terms of ethics, morals, and personal philosophy, as early as the late May Fourth period he advocated returning to Song–Ming Neoconfucianism, which prompted the great debate over science and metaphysics. After the September Eighteenth incident, he often plaintively remarked that "China's intellectual world has vague circles of American, English, French, German and Russian influence," but China had already lost its "intellectual sovereignty."[53] The Zhangs criticized Hu Shi's scientific standpoint and argued that "complete Westernization" or "basically Westernized" both amounted to "forgetting oneself" and losing cultural agency and one's own nation. Zhang Dongsun said: "We must restore the health of the Chinese subject, only after which can we absorb other people's cultures ... When a nation loses its agency, it absolutely cannot adopt another nation's civilization, because it will simply be conquered by that nation."[54] Zhang Junmai particularly appreciated Tao Xisheng, one of the ten professors who authored the proclamation on China's own culture, who talked about "the self discovering the self." Zhang argued that "the creation or revival of a culture can never, in any age, leave the self aside. If the nation's self does not know itself, then it cannot even imitate others, to say nothing of being creative."[55]

Zhang Junmai was also concerned with the utility of culture, but in his understanding culture was more an object of values rationality than a mere consciousness of utilitarian rationality. From a cultural

---

[53] Zhang Junmai "Sixiang de zizhuquan" (Intellectual sovereignty), in Zhang Junmai, *Minzu fuxing zhi xueshu jichu (The academic foundation of the national renaissance)* (Beiping: Zaisheng zazhishe, 1935).

[54] Zhang Dongsun, "Xiandai de Zhongguo zenyang yao Kongzi?" (What does modern China want with Confucius?), *"Zengfeng" banyuekan* 1.2 (1935), cited in Luo Rongqu, ed., *Cong "Xihua" dao xiandaihua: Wusi yilai youguan Zhongguo de wenhua quxiang he fazhan daolu lunzheng wenxuan (From "Westernization" to modernization: Selected essays on China's cultural trends and developments since the May Fourth)* (Beijing: Beijing daxue chubanshe, 1990), p. 406.

[55] Zhang Junmai, "Jinhou wenhua jianshe wenti – xiandaihua yu benweihua" (The question of cultural construction moving forward: Modernization and our own culture), *Zaisheng zazhi* 4.1 (1935).

standpoint, Zhang Junmai was a German-style romantic, and for him, culture was the sense of belonging felt by the individual or the group, a search for historical roots. For a nation or an individual, culture was not external, not a tool that could be taken up at will, but was innate to human nature, to history, to the subject's life choices. Zhang Junmai's romantic understanding of culture determined his core position in nationalist thought, and for this reason was very close to Isaiah Berlin's understanding of cultural nationalism: nationalism means that people first belong to a certain unique group, and this group's unique culture, history, language, religion, institutions, and lifestyle all mold their particular goals and values.[56]

Zhang Junmai argued that self-confidence came from China's nationalism, which was different from European nationalism. European nationalism had developed straightforwardly with the emergence of modern nation-states, while China "already possessed its own version but then added choices, and with confidence, created a new culture."[57] The most important part was the need for "intellectual sovereignty," or consciousness of national culture, employing one's own intellectual power, respecting the existing culture of one's country, not following Western thought blindly. Creation is honorable, imitation is not. From this we can see that Zhang Junmai's nationalism in the 1930s inherited the cultural nationalist tradition of the Germans Herder and Fichte, as he sought, through the reconstruction of national culture, to allow the nation to achieve spiritual rebirth as it faced an existential crisis, and built a national community with a core identity of national spirit.

Fichte's *Addresses to the German Nation* presented the German revival from a universalist perspective. In his view, the question of the German revival was also a question of how humanity could proceed from an unhealthy state (i.e., egoism) to a healthy state (i.e., rational self-consciousness). In this process, universalism would turn into a patriotism that constructed rational monarchy as a religion.[58] Fichte particularly emphasized that the German nation's unique ethnicity, history, language, and culture formed the nation's original nature and national

---

[56] See Yisaiya Bolin (Isaiah Berlin), "Minzu zhuyi: Wangxi de beihushi yu jinri de weili" (Nationalism: The neglect of the past and the power of the present), in Bolin (Berlin), *Fan chaoliu: Guannianshi lunwenji* (Against the current: Essays in the history of ideas), p. 407. Editions of this volume to which I have access do not include this essay.

[57] Zhang Junmai, "Zhonghua xin minzuxing zhi yangcheng" (The development of a new Chinese nationalism), *Zaisheng* 2.9 (1934).

[58] See Liang Zhixue, "Guanghui de aiguo zhuyi pianzhang" (On the brilliance of patriotism), Preface to Feixite (Johann Gottlieb Fichte), *Dui Deyizhi minzu de yanjiang (Addresses to the German nation)*, Liang Zhixue et al., trans. (Shenyang: Liaoning jiaoyu chubanshe, 2003), pp. 3–6.

spirit. This was a mysterious and sacred belief in this original nature and was an eternal part of the life of the nation-state, the location of their heaven. This nation, with its eternal outer shell, was worthy of sacrifice on the part of the citizens. And to ensure that citizens possess exalted patriotic sentiments, the most important thing was to provide national education for the citizens, allowing them to become new citizens of the rational monarchy.[59]

In his introduction to Fichte, Zhang Junmai played down the universalist narrative thread undergirding his patriotism, and instead stressed the unique historical background of his text: that the German nation was in crisis because of a foreign invasion. In this way, Fichte's sense of universal humanity, which supported his nationalism, became, in Zhang Junmai's interpretation, a special nationalist feeling. In fact, in Liang Qichao's *A Record of My Travel Impressions of Europe*, written in the 1920s, we can discover a nationalism grounded in universalism similar to Fichte's in Liang's call to "use Chinese culture to complement Western culture." But when we arrive at Zhang Junmai's generation of intellectuals, and especially after the 1930s, the nationalist narrative exists only to bring about national salvation, and universal consciousness of internationalism has been greatly diminished.

"Good" Civilization and "Our" Culture

The historical development of modern Chinese intellectual history from the May Fourth civilizational consciousness to the cultural consciousness of the 1930s reveals the inner complexity and tensions within Chinese culture. On the one hand, Chinese culture is universal, like Judeo-Christianity, Islam, Hinduism, Buddhism, or ancient Greek culture. It is an ancient civilization with significance for all humanity. Yet on the other hand, this universal character developed out of the unique historical and cultural traditions of the Han people, which means that Chinese culture is also unique, possessing its own sense of cultural agency. This contradiction did not emerge only in modernity; over the course of some 3,000 years of Chinese history, Chinese culture possessed a double nature containing both universalism and distinctions between Chinese and barbarians. *Tianxia* referred to a universal civilization without borders or frontiers, with the culture of China's central plains at its center. The distinction between Chinese and barbarians divided groups into "us" and "them" on the basis of their cultural levels, and represents

---

[59] See Feixite (Fichte), *Dui Deyizhi minzu de yanjiang* (Addresses to the German nation), lectures 7–9.

a clear, indisputable sense of Chinese cultural agency. But because the civilizational subject of the universal *tianxia* civilization and the cultural subject that divided the world into Chinese and barbarians were both the same Han people, the tension between civilizational and cultural agency remained latent in traditional times, and did not become a real problem.

The situation changed in the modern period. When the Chinese people for the first time encountered a Western civilization which was stronger or more civilized, then *tianxia* was transformed into the vision of modern civilization with the West at its center, and the distinction between Chinese and barbarians became a modern nationalism with ethnic consciousness at its core.[60] Consequently, *tianxia* and the distinction between Chinese and barbarians came to experience an unresolvable tension: the civilizational subject of modern civilization was no longer China, but the West, while the cultural subject of modern nationalism was the Chinese nation-state that suffered from Western domination and awaited enlightenment. The civilizational subject and the cultural subject experienced a historical dislocation. Did China need a civilizational awakening or a cultural awakening?

The New Culture movement was a movement of civilizational awakening. Extreme anti-traditionalists like Chen Duxiu and Hu Shi believed that Western civilization represented humanity's universal history, which China could not remain outside of. The only difference between them was whether universal civilization was represented by French civilization (Chen Duxiu) or Anglo-American civilization (Hu Shi). By contrast, Li Dazhao and Du Yaquan placed their hopes for humanity's universal civilization in a "third civilization" that would result from the mixing of Chinese and Western civilizations, and Liang Shuming went even further, painting a universal evolutionary portrait of Chinese, Western, and Indian civilizations. Regardless of the differences in their positions, they shared a common standpoint regarding civilizational consciousness. Since May Fourth intellectuals had all been deeply influenced by traditional *tianxia* and modern theories of universal evolution, they all envisioned China's future culture in light of humanity's evolution and universal history. In affirming the unique value of Chinese culture within universal civilization, May Fourth intellectuals had a hard time imagining a Chinese cultural subject disconnected from universal world history, since China's cultural subject was within the universal world civilization.

---

[60] See Xu Jilin, "Tianxia zhuyi, yixia zhi bian jiqi zai jindai de bianyi" (Universalism, distinctions between Chinese and barbarians, and their evolution in the modern period), *Huadong shifan daxue xuebao* 6 (2012).

During the New Culture movement, Xueheng members like Chen Yinke and Wu Mi, who had a thorough understanding of Western culture, had already learned that there was not one, unified Western culture, and that within Western culture there were many historical and cultural traditions. They further insisted that Chinese Confucian civilization contained many inner similarities with ancient Greek civilization. Thus while China was absorbing modern civilization, it could not forget the value of its national culture. This cultural consciousness had only a faint footprint in the May Fourth era, with almost no impact in the intellectual world, but against the backdrop of the great social changes of the 1930s, cultural consciousness rose to the top to become mainstream social thought. Two important background factors meant that when Chinese intellectuals, who were infatuated with all sorts of foreign doctrines, sought to make choices in the context of China's future culture, they urgently required a standpoint with a clear cultural agency. First was the re-emergence of the Chinese–barbarian distinction during the national crisis following the Mukden Incident in September of 1931, when Japan launched its initial invasion of Manchuria. Second was that with the deepening of understanding of Western culture, sharp divisions arose between various "isms": scientism versus humanism, rationalism versus romanticism, liberalism versus socialism. But the cultural consciousness that replaced civilizational consciousness not only did not provide a solution, it instead exacerbated the tensions between universalism and the distinction between Chinese and barbarians, between civilizational agency and cultural agency. Did China ultimately need a sense of universal civilization or a sense of unique cultural agency? If we say that Chinese culture is also a world civilization, then how were the displaced culture and civilization to be unified again?

As recounted above, civilization and culture respond to the different questions. Civilization seeks out what is "good" in the universal experience of humanity, while culture looks for the particular expression of what is "ours." From the perspective of Westernizers, whatever was "good" for the universal civilization of humanity should also be China's, since Chinese culture could not cling to its own standards; but from a nativist perspective, the cultures of various nations and ethnicities were not commensurate or comparable. For these figures, there was no universal civilization, and what was "ours" was also "good." In the century since the New Culture movement, China's intellectual world has wavered between a Hegelian, monist, historical view and a postmodern cultural relativism, leaving the question of cultural agency in an awkward position. The conflict between civilization and culture has never been resolved.

Is there a way out of the antimony between civilizational consciousness and cultural consciousness? Germany's Enlightenment movement in the late eighteenth century has left us a historical indication that can lead us out of our historical dilemma. Although both Kant and Herder were classical humanists, Kant was from the eighteenth century and Herder from the nineteenth. Kant represents eighteenth-century German civilizational consciousness, having inherited the French rationalist tradition, and he reflected on the common fate and civilizational future of all humanity. By contrast, although he lived at roughly the same time as Kant, the romanticist thinker Herder represented the cultural consciousness of the nineteenth century. Rationalists believe that material structures and values exist in the world, and that man can discover these through his own reason, arriving at a universal, perfect solution. By contrast, romanticism believes that a nation's culture must rely on its own natural endowment to create itself, and that this creation does not occur in the framework of universal rationality, but instead in the environment of the unique history of each nation.[61] Herder founded the German cultural nationalist tradition, yet this cultural nationalism was not really in conflict with universalism – in fact it was just the opposite. It constituted an indispensable part of universal civilization. Herder believed that a perfect world was constructed out of many pluralities. Each individual is unique, each nation is unique, and the world is a vast garden made up of these multiplicities. There is no nation chosen by God as the world nation. Isaiah Berlin described Herder's thought as follows:

A man should speak the truth he believes to be true. All people believe that their truths are absolutely correct. This diversity makes up our kaleidoscopic world, but no one can see the whole world, no one can see all the forests. Only God can see the entire universe. Since we belong to particular groups and live in particular regions, humanity cannot see the entire universe. Each age has its own particular ideals.[62]

Herder's notion of a unique national culture is not based on rejection of or resistance to the universal civilization of humanity, but is instead a cultural consciousness within universal civilization. All national cultures have their uniqueness, and they make up the diversity of the entire world, yet they all share in a world civilization, so that universality exists within specificity, not on top of it. Herder is a cultural nationalist, but at the same time is a universalist, and reflects on the unique character of national culture against the great backdrop of world civilization. He

---

[61] See Yisaiya Bolin (Isaiah Berlin), *Langman zhuyi de genyuan (The roots of romanticism)*, Lü Liang et al., trans. (Nanjing: Yilin chubanshe, 2008), pp. 107, 127.
[62] Ibid., p. 70.

contemplates the common future of world civilization that exists within the pluralism of national cultures. Isaiah Berlin, who agreed completely with Herder, put it this way: We are the descendants of two worlds. On the one hand we have inherited romanticism, and thus refuse monism and believe in man's creativity, yet on the other hand we still believe that there are universal values and that we belong to defined traditions.[63]

Early German romanticists, as represented by Herder, were not really cultural relativists, as they were misunderstood to be by people at the time. Instead they were genuine cultural pluralists. Cultural relativism argues that different cultural values have no comparable common measures, and thus none is absolutely true or false. And "good" is relative and limited, and only "good" for particular nations. There is no "good" for all humanity. But cultural pluralism accepts universal values within the streams of different histories and cultures; universal values can take on different cultural forms and concrete expressions. Separated from their roots in national cultures, universal values are rootless. Taken a step further, cultural relativism become Nietzschean nihilism. But cultural pluralism can coexist with universal Enlightenment values. Isaiah Berlin argues that different cultural values are equal – equally true, equally final, equally objective. There is no hierarchy of values. But regarding human nature, no matter how complex or capricious a person might be, as long as we can still refer to him as a person, then he must still bear the marks of "humanity." Which means that different cultures do share common values. Even if the differences in national cultures are great, the core elements are overlapping, and the core values and ultimate goals are wide open, and pursued in common by all of humanity.

On this hundredth anniversary of the New Culture movement, there are two real questions that we have not resolved: first, how to interiorize "good" civilization so that Chinese people can identify with it as their "own" culture? And second, how to elevate "our" culture to the level of the universal civilization of humanity?

Some of my friends with universalist concerns argue that whatever is "good" should be "ours" and there should be no distinction between "ego" and "other." If Christianity can save China, then why shouldn't we accept it as a mainstream Chinese value? I reply that even the best foreign civilization must be transformed to become "our" culture, because "our" space is not a vacuum. Foreign civilizations must exchange and blend with existing, native culture, realizing the nativization of foreign civilization by which it becomes "ours" and part of Chinese culture. Historically,

---

[63] Ibid., p. 140.

Buddhism was a foreign religion, and had Chan not transformed "good" Buddhism into "our" Buddhism, then it would not be a part of Chinese culture. In the post-Song period, the most impressive cultural creation was the combination of the three teachings of Confucianism, Daoism, and Buddhism. With regard to universal civilization, people always use rationality to judge whether something is "good" and worthy of being accepted. Yet in the context one's own culture, people use their feelings to judge whether something is "ours" and should be identified with. If a foreign civilization stops as a level of "good" that is defined by a redemptive, utilitarian wealth and power, it remains an external "good" that is different from one's self, meaning that it has not yet taken root in the soil of the national culture, and that it can be removed at any time. But once it enters into the historical traditions of the nation, and becomes part of the inner life of the Chinese people, it changes from external object to internal subject, and becomes part of "us" that we cannot live without. In this way, external universal civilization can be transformed into our own national culture, with a sense of home, origin, and belonging.

Although "our" culture is worthy of identity at an emotional level, this is not self-evident from a rational perspective, and whether it is good or bad must be judged against the backdrop of universal world civilization. Some militants for China's own culture simplistically equate "ours" with "good," as if only "our" culture accords with China's particular national characteristics, so there's no point in discussing what is "good." If we say that internationalists use universality to dismiss particularity, and replace culture with civilization, then these nationalists use particularity to erase universality and use culture to replace civilization in the same way. Chinese culture is not only a unique national culture, but is also universal culture that influences all humanity. Values that are "good" for China, especially core values that relate to basic human nature, should also be "good" for all humanity. Universal civilization is not only "good" for "us," but is also valuable for "others." The universal nature of Chinese civilization can only be built from the perspective of all humanity, and cannot be reduced to China's particular values and interests.

How, from within the particular nature of "our" historical and cultural traditions and current experience, can we refine a universal "good" in the modern sense? And from another angle, how can we transform the universal "good" of world civilization into something suitable to the particular "us" born and raised in China's native soil? This is the core question in the reconstruction of China's cultural agency. This agency is both the subject of our national culture, and also the subject of humanity's civilization. Only when the subjects of culture and civilization are reunited, and no longer split asunder and in opposition, can

China emerge from its century-long antimony, and rebuild the national self-confidence, becoming once again a world nation that is responsible to humanity.

Civilizational consciousness or cultural consciousness? A century has passed since the New Culture movement, a century of divided consciousness. Will the next century be a new age where civilizational and cultural awakenings occur together? Everything depends on our consciousness.

8   Li Shenzhi: The Last Scholar-Official, the Last Hero

Translator's Introduction

The life of Li Shenzhi (1923–2003) was cleaved painfully in two by the suppression of the Tian'anmen demonstrations in 1989. Prior to 1989, Li had been an establishment intellectual loyally serving the Communist regime in a variety of capacities: international editor and deputy director of the Xinhua News Agency; advisor to Zhou Enlai and Deng Xiaoping; director of the United States Research Institute, and vice-director of the Chinese Academy of Social Sciences. After 1989, Li's revulsion at the violent suppression led him to embrace liberalism, and he became, in the eyes of many, "China's Havel," courageously speaking out against what he saw as China's long history of autocratic despotism and for the embrace of liberal ideals, a stance for which he was and is much admired in some quarters.

Xu's text is a kind of eulogy, originally published in 2004 in the Hong Kong magazine Ershiyi shiji *(Twenty-First Century), a journal widely read in China. The tone is one of sadness, first because Xu knew and admired Li and shared many if not all of his ideas and ideals, but more broadly because Xu paints Li's death as the passing of the tradition of moral idealism embodied in the Chinese scholar-official ideal. Admiration for "Chinese tradition" is hardly rare in Chinese intellectual circles, although liberals are in general less drawn to the glories of the Confucian past than are other groups. Yet Xu seems to identify with Li – or at least to empathize with him – and the text can be read as a call for moral re-engagement based on a combination of Confucian and liberal principles, which is perhaps why Xu chose to publish the text in Hong Kong. In any event, the language of the text is quite different from that of the other essays in this volume, both because of its eulogistic overtones and its Confucian inflection – and its implicit call for action. At the same time, Xu's identification with Li Shenzhi acknowledges a fact not often acknowledged: both are members of the CCP. What may seem like a contradiction to the Western observer is less so for Chinese intellectuals, for whom service to the state remains something approaching a moral imperative, and serving the state without serving the CCP comes perilously close to dissent, which renders service impossible.*

As a historian, Xu also uses the figure of Li Shenzhi to raise questions about China's modern history and the role therein of ideas, ideals, and intellectuals. He praises Li Shenzhi as someone who ultimately kept the faith in the progress of history despite his disappointment that the revolution had "devoured its children." His embrace of communism gave way to an embrace of liberalism, but his

191

emotional attachment and fiery optimism remained the same. As already noted, Xu traced the source of Li's attachment and optimism to the ethic of service practiced by the Confucian scholar-official over the centuries, and more particularly to the vision of Wang Yangming, who preached the unity of knowledge and action, by which he meant active engagement in the world, and not detached study of abstract principle. It was Xu's evocation of this world, his personal identification with specific figures from China's Confucian past, that persuaded me to include the essay in this volume.

The meaning of Xu's eulogy is layered, as the text can be read in many ways. To some extent, Xu is bemoaning his fate and those of his fellow intellectuals, condemned by secularization to a life of merely "academic" concerns. This is a somewhat familiar trope but presented with unusual depth here. From another angle, Xu's text can be read as a liberal appropriation of the Confucian tradition – as we see in other essays in this volume – an effort to provide liberal principles with a moral substance not found in a defense of "market principles." There are references in Xu's text to the limits of modern rationality, the hubris of reason, likewise suggested in earlier essays in this volume. Belief in the "unity of heaven and man" might serve as an antidote or a corrective to these limits. Indeed, it is possible to read Xu's text as questioning the limits of secularism, something of relevance to liberals everywhere today. At the same time, Xu raises timely – and timeless – questions about the sweep and direction of history, which Li Shenzhi embraced, to Xu's admiration, and about individual choices and decisions. In many ways, the Li Shenzhi presented here is the personification of the ideals, tribulations, and enduring challenges facing Chinese intellectuals, many of which are relevant to intellectuals around the world. At the same time, as Xu muses about the choices made by Li Shenzhi, Gu Zhun, Hu Shi, and Lu Xun, the reader cannot help but wonder if he is not musing about his choices and those of his peers in China today.

It has been a year since Mr. Li Shenzhi died. His death, like his life, was a spectacle, and became a cultural event. Anyone who inspires a cultural event must be a symbol of some kind of spirit. What did Li Shenzhi, this towering, venerable figure of the Chinese thought world, symbolize?

In the year since he died, the debates about Li have not died down. Many people see Li Shenzhi as the propagator of liberalism; some have even constructed an orthodox genealogy of Chinese liberalism[1] consisting of Liang Qichao (1873–1929), the late Qing reformer and creator of modern Chinese journalism, Hu Shi (1891–1962), symbol of the May Fourth movement, Gu Zhun (1915–74), a trained accountant and committed Marxist who "rediscovered" market principles after being convicted and imprisoned as a rightist, and Li Shenzhi. Li Shenzhi was a liberal, everyone acknowledges this, but the question is whether

[1] Originally published as "Li Shenzhi: Zuihou de shidafu, zuihou de haojie," *Ershiyi shijie* 4 (2004). Also available online at http://blog.sina.com.cn/s/blog_5107c26901009gzo.html. He Jiadong, "Weiliao de xinyuan" (The unfinished goal), in Ding Dong, ed., *Huainian Li Shenzhi (Remembering Li Shenzhi)* (self-published, 2003), vol. 1, p. 65.

liberalism has an orthodoxy. While he was alive, Li Shenzhi did not like to call himself "the representative of contemporary Chinese liberalism." In the autumn of 1999 he visited Hong Kong to give a talk at the Chinese University of Hong Kong's Chinese Culture Research Center. I was working there at the time, so I was at the reception. Someone in the audience asked him if he was the symbol of contemporary Chinese liberalism and he flatly denied it. At least in a public setting, he did not want to be simplistically reduced to an ideology. Many people have recalled that Li Shenzhi liked to call himself "China's last scholar-official." In terms of the past binary division of traditional and modern, "scholar-official" and "liberal" seem to be in strict opposition. Which symbol comes closest to Li Shenzhi?

The saddest fate for someone who has died is to become the stereotype or the symbol of an ideology. My guess is that the reason that the wise Li Shenzhi called himself an "old-fashioned" "scholar-official" rather than a more fashionable "liberal," is because he had foreseen just such a fate. Liberalism was surely his final political ideal, but not the symbol of his personality. On a spiritual level, the role that Li Shenzhi embodied was that of the literati tradition, beginning with Confucius (551–479 BC) and Mencius (372–289 BC) in the Warring States period (475–221 BC), and carried forward by high-minded Confucians throughout the ages.

The outstanding expression of the spirit of the Chinese scholar-official was his worrying over the rise and fall of *tianxia*; the scholar-official's will was set on moral practice grounded in the idealism of the Way and the unity of knowledge and practice. Chinese history since pre-Qin times, a vast span of two to three thousand years, involves what was basically a scholar-official's society. Over the course of this period, despite the many damages inflicted by unenlightened rulers, eunuchs, factions, and the masses, scholar-officials who took the Way as their mission remained the central players on this stage, laughing or crying in any number of comedies or tragedies; they were responsible for the dynasty, and for *tianxia*. In the late Qing–early Republican period the scholar-officials were transformed into modern intellectuals, but even as they donned Western suits and leather shoes, their soul remained that of the scholar official. Intellectuals such as Lu Xun (1881–1936), modern China's most famous writer, Hu Shi, Chen Duxiu (1879–1942), iconoclastic thinker and co-founder of the Communist Party, and Chen Yinke (1880–1969), one of the twentieth century's most famous historians – they were all like this. Yet at the end of the twentieth century there occurred a historic change: scholar-officials as a spiritual group finally disappeared over the historical horizon following the rise of industrial-commercial society, the disintegration of ideology, and the professionalization of intellectuals and their confinement to the academy.

The age of the scholar-official is gone. While the streets bustle with people hustling after profits, while a generation of vulgar Confucians fills its pockets by peddling ideas, Li Shenzhi, at twilight, like the bald eagle, sounded his final cry. The fading figure of the Chinese scholar-official, how empty, lonely, and despairing he appears!

An Old-Style Communist Party Member

When talking about Li Shenzhi we must remember that before anything else, he was a Communist Party member.

What does it mean to be a Communist Party member? Whenever I hear a student vow that he is going to "solve his Party question" before graduation in the same way that he would talk of earning his Cambridge Advanced English certificate, I sigh for a Communist Party that has been invaded by opportunists. The Party has been secularized, and with secularization comes the loss of ideals. When people like Li Shenzhi joined the Party, they were motivated not by fame and fortune, but by a heart of heroism. From the first, May Fourth, generation of old Party members, to the young cadres mobilized by the December 9, 1935 student movement, all of them displayed the idealism of the scholar-official spirit. They supplied the Party with its charisma and brilliance. In Li Shenzhi's remembrance of Kuang Yaming (1906–96), the well-known revolutionary and, later, university president under the Communist regime, we find the following passage:

The reason that I always thought that the Communist Party could carry out the Chinese revolution, in addition to the objective conditions and the political line, was because most of the old generation of Communist Party members were heroic characters. They had the essence of traditional Chinese culture in their bones, they felt the burden of the famed scholar Gu Yanwu's (1613–82) assertion that "the fate of the world rests with the scholar-officials." They expressed their ideals and integrity in Confucian sayings such as: "The people are my siblings, and all living things are my companions," from Zhang Zhai's (1020–77) "Western inscription."[2] "The determined scholar and the man of virtue will not seek to live at the expense of injuring their virtue. They will even sacrifice their lives to preserve their virtue complete."[3] Like Confucius, they made up their minds that "The commander of the forces of a large state may be carried off, but the will of even a common man cannot be taken from him."[4] This is why they fought, why they never gave up, why they never rested until they achieved their goal.[5]

[2] Online translation available at http://facultysites.vassar.edu/brvannor/Phil210/Translations/Western%20Inscription.pdf.
[3] Online translation available at http://ctext.org/analects/wei-ling-gong.
[4] Online translation available at http://ctext.org/analects/zi-han.
[5] Li Shenzhi, "Zuo xuewen shouxian yao zuoren: Kuang Yaming xiansheng yinxiang" (To be a scholar one must first be a person: The impression left by Kuang Yaming), *Yanhuang chunqiu* 6 (1997).

Li Shenzhi was just this kind of Communist Party member, and even if later on "the revolution devoured its children," he never regretted his initial passion. In 1998, I visited him at his home while on a work trip to Beijing. We talked about the revolution, and about the choices he had made when he was young. I wrongly believed that the intellectuals that joined the revolution were young hotheads with average grades. Li Shenzhi was almost angry at my ignorance: "What are you talking about? Those on the front lines during the December 9th movement[6] were those with the best grades, who were the most respected by their classmates. The useless ones with no talent had all joined the Three People's Principles Youth Corps[7] to suck up to the Nationalists." I asked him, "If you could go back in time sixty years, would you still make the same choice?" He looked down and thought for a minute, and in a low voice answered:

There was no other choice to make at the time. We wanted to resist Japan, the Nationalists weren't resisting Japan and the Communists were. We wanted democracy. The Nationalist Party was a dictatorship and the Communist Party was against dictatorship. We were carrying the ideal of the liberation of freedom and democracy as we embraced the CCP. As long as you had blood in your veins, as long as you had any conscience at all, there was no other choice to make.

And it's true. Those that flocked to Communist base areas like Yan'an were, like Li Shenzhi, the best of China's youth, the hot-blooded elite of that generation's scholar-officials. In the hopes of realizing their democratic liberation, they were full of the spirit of self-sacrifice and martyrdom. Li Shenzhi calls these CCP members "old-style CCP members."[8] And old-style is good! The old-style CCP members were the idealists of the CCP, twentieth-century scholar-officials who took spreading the Way as their personal mission.

New-style CCP members enter the Party in pursuit of personal interests. The Party is a tool for them to climb the official ranks and make money. But for old-style CCP members, the loves and hatreds of

---

[6] Translator's note: A student movement, starting in Beijing in December 1935, demanding that China's government take action against Japan.

[7] Translator's note: The Three People's Principles Youth Corps, or Sanqingtuan, was created by the Nationalist Party in 1938 in the hopes of mobilizing the nation's youth for the fight against Japan, and improving recruitment of new members into the Nationalist Party.

[8] Li Shenzhi, "Huainian Wen Qize tongzhi: yige laopai gongchandangyuan" (Remembering comrade Wen Qize, an old-style Communist Party member). Many of Li's most recent writings had not been published at the time of this writing. In this essay, unless otherwise indicated, quotations from Li were found on the website www.sinoliberal.com, which as of 2017 appears to no longer be in operation, but may be available via DACHS – Digital Archive for Chinese Studies – www.zo.uni-heidelberg.de/boa/digital_resources/dachs/.

their lives were poured into the Party. Their pride in the Party and fervor for their ideals are hard for later generations to understand. That they invested the feelings born of their red-blooded youth and their tragic love for their country is something that no one can disparage or deny. Their devotion recalls the filial piety of Nezha, the Chinese folk god who cut off his flesh to give to his mother and removed his bones to give to his father. In the words of the Tang-dynasty poet Li Bai (701–62), "such devotion is indelible."[9]

Without such indelible devotion, there would be no elderly Li Shenzhi; both the young man and the old were fueled by the same idealism.

Historical Idealism

The greatest source of Li Shenzhi's suffering was that "the revolution devoured its children." Its idealism was subverted, and the utopianism of the revolution came to play the role of the cannibal. The "old-style CCP members" could not avoid the tragedy inflicted on the historical tradition of the scholar-officials: They fought the trends of the time by residing in the Way of the scholar-official, and were punished for their loyalty. Even when the pain subsided its ravages demanded reflection, and the elderly Li Shenzhi followed the example of Gu Zhun, moving, toward the end of his life, from idealism to empiricism, from revolutionary utopia to liberalism. But did he really abandon idealism, and become a cold-blooded empiricist like the famed Scottish Enlightenment thinker David Hume (1711–76)?

I have read and compared the writings of Gu Zhun and Li Shenzhi many times, and to my mind, Gu Zhun's resolve and his theoretical rigor in his later years led him to make certain sacrifices: once the revolution was over he resolutely said goodbye to idealism. Gu Zhun was ice; Li Shenzhi was fire. The fire's flame is inseparable from the fuel of intense emotion, but if the emotion lacks the conviction of ideals calling it forward, then how long can it burn? While Gu Zhun claimed to have exchanged his idealism for empiricism, Li Shenzhi doubted him, arguing that "Gu Zhun is really an idealist who continues his search against all odds.[10] So I would say that

---

[9] Translator's note: This phrase is taken from a poem, "Shang Anzhou Li Changshi Shu" (Letter to Secretary Li on the route to Anzhou), by the Tang-dynasty poet, Li Bai (701–62).

[10] Translator's note: Xu uses a line from Qu Yuan's "Lisao" (On encountering trouble), "And I wanted to go up and down, seeking my heart's desire." The translation is from David Hawkes, *The Songs of the South: An Ancient Chinese Anthology of Poems by Qu Yuan and other Poets* (London: Penguin Classics, 1985), p. 30.

what he has abandoned is despotism, and what he is looking for is liberalism."[11]

The idealism that Li Shenzhi is talking about here is no longer revolutionary utopia, but instead the new road to truth that he discovered in his later years – liberalism. Why did Li Shenzhi not see liberalism as a natural product of his empirical reasoning, but instead proclaim it as a new dawning of idealism? In his study of a century of revolutionary thought in China, the Chinese-American historian Zhang Hao (b. 1937) noted the widespread existence of an attitude of "historical idealism" in the thought of progressive intellectuals:

The most important feature of this thought was to dispense with the traditional cyclical view of history and to accept the basically Western notion of straight-line historical development, the idea being that history moved from the past toward an ideal future in a predestined arc of development. In the course of this development, the present era is one of historical transformation. For this reason, at the core of this view of history is a special consciousness of crisis ... Under the weight of this attitude, intellectual concerns naturally concentrated on how to move from a pessimistic present to an ideal future.[12]

Behind Li Shenzhi's search for liberalism we find precisely this kind of historical idealism. From the time of his youth, his sense of time was that of a direct flow, based on the theory of historical evolution: "Down to the present day, humanity's notion of time is that it is a flow moving forward, not backward."[13] Even if this notion of time is related to Christianity, at a more basic level it is a product of "modernity." In the Enlightenment idea of historical progress we find a belief that the march of history has a purpose, that there is a process of straight-line progress in an ideal direction according with human rationality. Or as Sun Yat-sen put it in Li Shenzhi's favorite quotation attributed to him: "The flow of history is mighty; he that follows it triumphs and he who opposes it perishes." If we say that in the past Li Shenzhi had taken revolutionary utopia as the final term of history, then in later years, after painful reflection, Li rediscovered the light of idealism. In his view, the history of the past two or three hundred years had proven that liberalism provides the best, most

[11] Li Shenzhi, "'Gu Zhun riji' xu" (Preface to the "Diary of Gu Zhun"), in *Gu Zhun riji (The diary of Gu Zhun)* (Beijing: Jingji ribao chubanshe), 1997.
[12] Zhang Hao, "Zhongguo jin bainian lai de geming sixiang daolu" (The path of revolutionary thought in China over the past hundred years), in Zhang Hao, *Zhang Hao zixuanji (Self-selected essays by Zhang Hao)* (Shanghai: Jiaoyu chubanshe, 2002), p. 296.
[13] Li Shenzhi, "Zhongguo chuantong wenhua jiushi zhuanzhi zhuyi" (China's traditional culture is nothing but authoritarianism), available online at www.shz100.com/article-11098-1.html.

universal global values.[14] He also interpreted twentieth-century Chinese history as a history in which high-minded people pursued mainstream thought – which he identified as liberal ideals: "China's modern history is actually a history in which liberal ideals suffered many tribulations."[15] Here we can see that even if contemporary Chinese liberalism is a historical denial of revolutionary utopia, at the same time both are products of modernity, and at base both share a common historical premise: that the Enlightenment understanding of the end points of history meant that history possessed its own objective laws and final destination, and that what people should do is to discover the one correct road from among the many possibilities that would lead them to the opposite shore. Yet this is in clear contradiction with the view of history of the British empiricists so much admired by Chinese liberals. In other words, after liberalism arrived in China, its historical role was redefined, and re-explained as part of a straight-line view of historical development, which in the process took on the character of a kind of historical idealism that shared a structure with revolutionary utopianism.

Li Shenzhi was not aware that the Enlightenment thought of his youth would lead him to search everywhere for the "sole correct" historical route toward the ideal world. In his heart of hearts he always nourished an enthusiasm for an ideological utopia, hoping that he could identify the packaged solution or "ism" that would provide definitive answers to China's problems. After having lived through a confused period, Li Shenzhi happily discovered the foundation for his new world – liberalism. The fire of his passion for historical idealism finally reignited in Li's later life.

The winding Yellow River eventually empties into the sea. Once history had set its sights on a new final destination, then for Li Shenzhi all questions could be readily solved by placing them on the scale of liberal values and weighing them once again. He asked: "What was the 'May Fourth' spirit? It was precisely the Enlightenment – the use of the spirit of rationality to destroy the despotism and obscurantism that had shackled Chinese thought for thousands of years. The thought of the leaders of the May Fourth movement was moving toward the liberalism and individualism that for 300 years had already constituted the mainstream of thought in the world."[16] In this way, he offered a reinterpretation of the

---

[14] Li Shenzhi, "'Beida chuantong yu jindai Zhongguo' xu" (Preface to "The Beijing University tradition and modern China"), in Liu Junning, ed., *Beida chuantong yu jindai Zhongguo (The Beijing University tradition and modern China)* (Beijing: Zhongguo renshi chubanshe, 1998).

[15] Li Shenzhi, "'Gu Zhun riji' xu" (Preface to the "Diary of Gu Zhun").

[16] Li Shenzhi, "Chongxin dianran qimeng de huoju: jinian wusi bashinian" (Reignite the torch of the Enlightenment), available online at www.modernchinastudies.org/us/issues/past-issues/66-mcs-1999-issue-3/499-2012-01-01-10-06-23.html; English-language

May Fourth spirit based on its essential nature, instead of as a prelude to an inevitable socialist revolution, seeing it as a legitimate historical proof of the final destination of liberal values.

Riding on the mighty river of this forward-moving time, the values of Chinese traditional culture also came into focus. Many of his friends were puzzled when in the early 1990s, the same Li Shenzhi who embraced the Chinese philosophical notion of "the unity of heaven and man," one of the central insights of traditional Chinese thought, also, on the eightieth anniversary of the May Fourth movement, denounced traditional culture as a simple despotism. How can we explain the changes in his thought during this period? To my mind, this all has to do with his conversion to liberalism in the 1990s. From that point forward, his judgements and reflections on many questions took as their criteria the idea of the ultimate achievement of liberal values. On an axis of time that could only move forward, Li evaluated all forms of thought in terms of friends and enemies. He argued: "At present there is only one enemy, and it is precisely the despotism that has endured in China for 2,200 years."[17] And thus he returned to the May Fourth, to the anguished mood of that period's violent denunciation of tradition.

Yet even if Li's anti-traditional stance was virulent, it was not comprehensive. What he hated were political ideologies that provided legitimacy for imperial despotism, the ideology, cloaked in Confucian ethics, that had hidden the inner core of Legalist authoritarian rule, creating the despotism and the servile personality that reigned, dynasty after dynasty. But there were things in traditional culture that were not taken over by politics, for which Li always maintained a great respect. In late 1999, when talking about Chen Yinke, he said with great feeling:

Over the course of the twentieth century, much of China's traditional culture has declined or even disappeared. This was deeply appreciated by Chen Yinke, which is why he was seen as a "cultural relic." And this is especially true for the Tongzhi (1861–75) and Guangxu (1875–1908) reign periods, which most people see as a time of repeated foreign invasion and the decline of national fortunes, but which Chen praised as "the beginning of an especially prosperous age." In fact, as a member of the famous Chen lineage from Yining, Jiangxi, from a poor family with a spotless reputation, the people around him during his youth were dignified and courteous, and their literary and cultural style truly embodied the essence of Chinese traditional culture. I'm thirty-three years younger than Chen, and in terms of morality and talent cannot hold a candle to him. Yet when I think about

---

translation available in Li Shenzhi, "Reignite the Torch of the Enlightenment," *Contemporary Chinese Thought* 33.2 (Winter 2001–2): 14–29.

[17] He Jiadong, "Weiliao de xinyuan" (The unfinished goal), p. 63.

a model of the older generation and the lingering influence of former worthies, even today I cannot but behold Mr. Chen and others like him with awe and admiration. I think of them but cannot approach them, I hate to part with them, especially since Mr. Chen was immersed in that life from when he was a boy. Yet what Mr. Chen did not foresee is that even as a great part of traditional Chinese culture has disappeared, the darkest, most reactionary part of that culture – despotism – has survived, and has become all the more severe, finally developing into the most savage mass dictatorship that put even Chen to death.[18]

In Li's elegiac description, the elegance and courtesy, the cultural and literary styles of traditional scholar-officials are refined to the point to inspire envy. Unfortunately, the good parts of the tradition largely disappeared in the twentieth century, and only the blackest despotism remained! The suffering Li Shenzhi could only rail against that tradition, the cultural tradition that even today remains problematic. In fact, behind the passion of his words we find a sentimental attachment to Chinese culture. The depth of his hatred grew out of the depth of his love. His anger did not allow him to parse the various aspects of traditional culture – rational, emotional, superficial, and subconscious – that are all mixed together in complex and contradictory ways. He did not take the time to examine whether there might be differences between traditional despotism and revolutionary utopianism, whether traditional culture might possess the potential to achieve a modern transformation. As he wrestled with the big questions and the intellectual reflexes of mainstream ideologies, he essentialized and simplified traditional culture, reducing it to despotism. In the face of the mighty wave of globalization, traditional culture had become a historical stumbling block on the way to the ideal liberal world.

If we take the essential spirit of May Fourth to be that of liberalism, then what figure best represents the May Fourth? This is another question that had to be rethought. Li Shenzhi said that "For sixty years I always took Lu Xun's judgements as my judgements." Yet on the eightieth anniversary of the May Fourth, Li continued: "I discovered that Lu Xun could not represent the entirety of the May Fourth. In fact, Hu Shi comes closer to representing the totality of the May Fourth."[19] Li argued that this was because throughout his life, Hu Shi upheld Chinese democracy, law, and constitutional rule, and especially because he exhibited a tolerant spirit rarely seen in the context of traditional Chinese culture.

---

[18] Li Shenzhi, "Duli zhi jingshen, ziyou zhi sichao: lun zuowei sixiangjia de Chen Yinke" (Independent spirit, free thought: On the thinker Chen Yinke), available online at www.aisixiang.com/data/29091.html.

[19] Li Shenzhi, "Huigui 'Wusi,' xuexi minzhu" (Looking back on the "May Fourth," studying democracy), available online at www.douban.com/group/topic/1275200/.

By contrast, Lu Xun was solely devoted to individual liberation. Later, Li said to a young friend, in a tone of unusual discomfort: "It is no small matter to compare Lu Xun and Hu Shi. As one who has been there I can tell you that our generation was misled."[20] Even if Hu Shi clearly pointed out the liberal direction of history, questions still remain concerning the path to follow from the dark past to the ideal present. The path of gradual, step-by-step reform proposed by Hu himself? At the time, Gu Zhun criticized Hu Shi's call to "talk less about isms and more about problems" as lacking in idealism. Li Shenzhi's difficulty seems to be the same: once he has turned Hu Shi's emphasis on problems into an "ism," he fails to find the needed idealistic spirit to carry out the "ism" he identified in Hu Shi's thought, to say nothing of the lack of a warrior's personality and the idealistic spirit of struggle and sacrifice. On this point, warriors like Lu Xun still hold a certain power for Li Shenzhi, even after his professed change of heart in later years. In the summer of 2001, when an interviewer asked him to identify China's greatest intellectuals, he immediately replied: "Lu Xun and Gu Zhun were the best!"[21]

So what we need to understand is how the elderly Li Shenzhi could, in a rational if "heartbroken" manner, come to understand that Lu Xun had "misled" him for sixty years, while continuing on an emotional level to identify with Lu Xun rather than Hu Shi? How could his mind and his heart be this divided?

Moral Idealism

In his analysis of revolutionary thought in modern China, Zhang Hao emphasized that the intensification of historical idealism can produce a sort of heroic spirit, a personality ideal that has been extremely influential in twentieth-century China. The point of departure for this intensification was traditional Confucian moral idealism, which taught that man lived for lofty moral ideals, to which he must unconditionally devote his life through politics.[22] This heroic spirit, defined by the moral idealism particularly displayed by Chinese scholar-officials, was deeply engraved in the hearts of the "old-style Party members" and absorbed into their

[20] Shao Jian, "Lilao, qing yunxu wo yong zheyang de fangshi jinian" (Mr. Li, please permit me to remember you this way), in Ding Dong, ed., *Huainian Li Shenzhi* (Remembering Li Shenzhi), vol. 1, p. 465.
[21] Zhu Jing, "Li Shenzhi yinxiang" (The impression left by Li Shenzhi), in Ding Dong, ed., *Huainian Li Shenzhi* (Remembering Li Shenzhi), vol. 1, p. 336.
[22] Zhang Hao, "Zhongguo jin bainian lai de geming sixiang daolu" (The path of revolutionary thought in China over the past hundred years), in Zhang Hao, *Zhang Hao zixuanji* (Self-selected essays by Zhang Hao), p. 304.

blood. Even at the end of his life, when the focus of Li's moral idealism had shifted from revolutionary utopianism to liberalism, he maintained the martial posture of his youth, inherited from Lu Xun, and threw himself into the battles necessary to achieve his new ideals.

In twentieth-century Chinese history, moral idealism belonged not only to the revolutionaries, but also to some liberals. The Chinese-American historians Zhang Hao and Lin Yusheng (b. 1934) note that the Taiwanese philosopher Yin Haiguang's (1919–69) liberalism contained a strong moral dimension. Zhang Hao argued that the "central theme of Yin's life was that of idealistic spirit, which required a combination of high-level consciousness of values, moral courage, and passion for life."[23] Lin Yusheng also noted that while Yin did not build new theories, in his thought he affirmed liberal values, which he lived in concrete practice. He gave moral dignity to the Chinese movement for freedom and democracy.[24] Li Shenzhi can be seen in a similar light. The reason is that both Yin Haiguang and Li Shenzhi were children of the May Fourth and belonged to the post-May Fourth generation, and the May Fourth Enlightenment movement, both in terms of content and spirit, was strongly influenced by the moral idealism of the Confucian cultural tradition. Zhang Hao argues that the May Fourth was marked by a number of inconsistencies, of which the most important was that it was both rational and romantic.[25] Both revolutionaries and at least some liberals shared this fervent moral idealism, the source of which has much to do with the turbulent romanticism of the May Fourth.

The New Enlightenment movement of the 1980s was in many ways a re-enactment of the May Fourth, in that it was both a rational movement as well as an emotional period of *Sturm und Drang*. In fact the emotional aspect was stronger than the rational side. If we put it in the context of the history of Chinese scholarship, the 1980s were like the Song dynasty, everyone full of ideas and discussing everything under the sun, like traditional scholar-officials hoping to make the world a better place. Beginning in the 1990s, there was a huge change in scholarly trends, and a gradual shift from this kind of moral engagement and toward more academic scholarship. There were fewer thinkers and more scholars; more than a few of those involved in the Enlightenment left the public

---

[23] Zhang Hao, "Yitiao meiyou zouyuan de lu" (The unfinished path), in Zhang Hao, *Zhang Hao zixuanji* (Self-selected essays by Zhang Hao), p. 332.

[24] Lin Yusheng, *Relie yu lengjing (Ardor and calm)* (Shanghai: Weiyi chubanshe, 1998), p. 235.

[25] Zhang Hao, "Chongfang Wusi: lun Wusi sixiang de liangzhixing" (Revisiting May Fourth: On the dual nature of May Fourth thought), in Zhang Hao, *Zhang Hao zixuanji* (Self-selected essays by Zhang Hao), pp. 252–57.

square and returned to the academy, where scholarly research replaced moral arguments, and we arrived at a situation like that of the Qing dynasty, which was often criticized for intellectual sterility. Although China was peaceful and prosperous, important moral questions had not been resolved, and instead revealed their dimensions ever more acutely. Moral arguments and scholarship parted ways; debates between Han-style and Song-style learning never ceased. On the one hand, the Qing-style scholars developed rapidly, helped by the state system and their strength in specialization. On the other hand, the Enlightenment camps that had flourished in the 1980s suffered internal divisions. Three lofty academic Confucians of the age each took a different road and came to symbolize a different spirit. Indologist and historian Ji Xianlin (1911–2009) was the greatest "national studies" scholar of his generation, widely acknowledged as the paragon of Qing-style studies who was devoted to academics for academics' sake, knowledge for knowledge's sake, and became the model for today's scholarly Confucian. Wang Yuanhua (1920–2008) was a writer and public intellectual and along with Li Shenzhi was an Enlightenment leader: people talked about "Wang in the south and Li in the north." Although after bitter reflection both came to accept basic liberal values, their paths to enlightenment differed.

Wang Yuanhua was greatly touched by the impulsive scholarly winds of the 1980s; he cared only about "isms" and didn't ask about problems. So even in the 1990s he continued to advocate "scholarly thinking and thoughtful scholarship," continuing the rational tradition of the May Fourth. He was like the Qing scholar Dai Zhen (1727–77), in that both accorded equal weight to truth and scholarship; Wang further sought to add "science" to "morality" and to transform Enlightenment ideals into weighty scholarly principles. In addition, Wang Yuanhua came to rethink Enlightenment itself, looking at how the Enlightenment contained the seeds of its own negation, producing the tragedy of modern utopianism. His goal was to arrive at a new way to protect the goals of the Enlightenment by transcending the Enlightenment mentality. By contrast, Li Shenzhi continued the turbulent tradition of the May Fourth, and felt that the academic personality of the 1990s was listless and had lost critical passion. To wake people up and move them forward, he took up the banner of liberal ideology, and through his personal moral practice sought with all his might to put an end to the bloody road that had snuffed out the ideal world. So as to better distinguish friend and enemy, Li Shenzhi starkly divided Enlightenment from despotism, as stark a division as light and darkness. Wang Yuanhua had personally experienced the complexity and urgency of Enlightenment thought, which on occasion revealed the tragedy of rationality. But Li Shenzhi's understanding of the

Enlightenment was idealized, full of naïve optimism. Wang's reflections, Li's enthusiasm: same vision, different paths. This was not only a parting of the ways of two great Enlightenment thinkers but marked a division in the efforts of the Enlightenment intellectuals who followed in their wake.

Yet the intellectual pursuits and moral practice involved in the Enlightenment movements of May Fourth and the 1980s were united. The two took separate paths in the 1990s: what was explored in scholarship no longer had any practical direction, and increasingly became a kind of elite knowledge divorced from public life. And intellectuals could not identify with the existing ideological banners that sanctioned moral practice because of their scholarly emptiness. This dilemma continues to trouble Enlightenment scholars to this day.

What kind of spiritual symbol does Li Shenzhi represent in this sort of post-Enlightenment atmosphere? If we say that "Qing-style academicians" reigned in the 1990s, then the forceful spirit represented by Li Shenzhi might be called "overthrowing the Qing to restore the Ming,"[26] since what he earnestly desired was to return to the radical Wang Yangming (1472–1529) style of the late Ming period. To call Li Shenzhi a Chinese scholar-official is too general; to be more precise, no matter how you look at him he was, like Wang Yangming, the sage of his generation. Wang Yangming preached "innate moral knowledge," the idea that practice is knowledge. He called himself "the madman" and set out to eradicate hypocrisy and vulgarity. But why stop at Wang Yangming? Li Shenzhi even more resembles the martial stance of the extreme Taizhou school, an offshoot of Wang Yangming's teachings, under the leadership of Wang Gen (1483–1541). Note how the Republican period scholar Ji Wenfu described another Taizhou leader, Wang Xinzhai (n.d.): "He wanted to be a colossal scholar of indomitable spirit, who could shore up the universe with his body. He solemnly placed himself in the role of a master or even of a superior man. He was open-hearted and candid, and never played to the gallery."[27]

Under great pressure from the imperial autocracy, the Taizhou group renounced working with the elite and instead sought to teach the people, hoping to improve the social atmosphere through their own moral practice. After Li Shenzhi retired from his "imperial court," he devoted his later years to mass enlightenment and moral practice. In his last few

---

[26] Translator's note: "Overthrow the Qing and restore the Ming" was a slogan attributed to certain secret societies during the Qing dynasty. Such sentiment was supposedly based in peasant nationalism. Xu's use of the phrase is humorous, although the humor is untranslatable.

[27] Ji Wenfu, *Zuopai Wangxue (Studies of the left-wing Wang Yangming)* (Shanghai: Shangwu, 1934), p. 43.

years he hoped to edit a citizenship reader for the people, and repeated
that his greatest wish was to be teacher in citizenship education. He was
disappointed with elites, whether they were political elites or intellectual
elites. His dream was to transcend the academy and speak directly with
the masses. Like the May Fourth generation, Li in his final years was particularly attentive to transparency of language. In the fall of 1996, when
Li Shenzhi came back from the United States, I sent him an essay I had
written criticizing trends in postcolonial cultural thought. He wrote me
a long letter in return, and particularly noted my use of terms like "text"
and "discourse," saying that leaving them in English "is neither necessary
nor always understandable." He noted seriously:

Please indulge an old man's fancy as I say something to my dear young friend: use
simple language that everyone can understand. Speak straight from the heart, and
as long what you say is true and what you think gets to the heart of things, then
it will be a good essay. There's no need to add foreign touches. To tell the truth,
I too have read some foreign theory, and they don't use as many neologisms
as the Chinese do. My hope is that all of you can become great specialists that
establish the foundation for contemporary Chinese thought. But to get there,
you need to pay attention to how Hu Shi and Lu Xun wrote, and imitate them.[28]

In his study of Hu Shi, Lin Yusheng noted that Hu's liberal views were
constructed on the basis of common sense. Common sense is usually
the result of experience, but also possesses its own truth, based in a language reflecting either a new ideology or a common political culture.[29]
But common sense is often reductive and non-reflexive, and in terms of
scholarship lacks the ability to recognize the complexity of an issue or to
engage in self-examination. In the China of the 1990s, we should have
critically reflected on liberalism both from a perspective of scholarship
and of moral practice; because of the lack of an institutional platform
for liberalism and the lack of civic culture, delivering Enlightenment
discourse "in plain language" was another pressing need. This is all the
more true in the context of the moral practice of "speaking truth." Li
Shenzhi particularly emphasized "speaking truth" in his final years. The
famous writer Ba Jin (1904–2005) also advocated "speaking truth" in
the 1980s, but this was the fruit of personal regrets. For Li Shenzhi,
"speaking truth" was not only the moral practice of an individual conscience, but was also an important, tangible, critical strategy. He greatly
appreciated Vaclav Havel's (1936–2011) "living in truth," which he saw
as authorizing the extension of power to the powerless in society, and
as an anti-political politics. In his preface to *Havel's Selected Writings*, he

---

[28] Li Shenzhi, unpublished letter to the author, September 1996.
[29] Lin Yusheng, *Relie yu lengjing* (Ardor and calm), p. 206.

sought to approach Havel and to understand the existentialist strains in Havel's thought with which Li was not familiar. Still, at an important level, Li continued to read Havel as a philosophy of the mind like that of Wang Yangming. For Havel, "speaking truth" of course is a matter of the responsibility of an individual conscience, and the reason why lies are everywhere around us is that people today have abandoned their responsibilities, becoming alienated from their everyday existence. For this reason, Havel does not seek an answer in the idea of total social liberation, but hopes instead that people can return to their individual existence and take up their human responsibilities. Li Shenzhi interprets Havel's understanding of the consciousness of existence as being the same as in Wang Yangming's philosophy of the heart/mind, where "innate knowledge is the same as heavenly principle."[30] On the basis of this "creative misunderstanding," Li seeks to awaken the innate moral capacity uniting the minds of the Chinese people with heaven, hoping to build a new liberal world without lies.

If this had produced nothing but a series of moral proclamations, then it would not be Li Shenzhi. In fact he was like the Taizhou scholars of the late Ming period, who emphasized action, believing that knowledge and practice were one. Havel's goal in "speaking truth" was to move citizens to act; he wanted a citizen's politics. But Li Shenzhi still believed in the modeling function of elite actors, and in the power of the moral practice of the scholar-official. Once when he was in Hangzhou, a young person asked him: "What force will push China forward?" Without thinking, Li answered: "First, there needs to be a bunch of intellectuals who stand up, like Chen Duxiu in the May Fourth period, great intellectuals who will come out and speak!"

In his last few years, after he had a stroke in Germany, he perhaps felt that he was not long for this world, and he became very anxious. He seems to have had a premonition that he could not wait for the realization of the ideal world, and full of despair and the resulting moral compulsion, he could not wait to tell the truth. He said repeatedly: "We're all almost 80 years old, we're almost gone. What are we afraid of? I can understand young people, they've got a career to pursue. But we should speak more truth."[31] Like historical scholar-officials such as the righteous official Hai Rui (1514–87), the activist Ming scholars of the Donglin

---

[30] Li Shenzhi, "Wuquanzhe de quanli he fanzhengzhi de zhengzhi" (The power of the powerless and anti-political politics), published as a preface to *Haweier wenji* (Havel's selected writings), Cui Weiping, trans. (self-published, 2003).

[31] Ren Bumei, "Yu Li Shenzhi xiansheng de yici duihua" (An exchange with Mr. Li Shenzhi), in Ding Dong, ed., *Huainian Li Shenzhi* (Remembering Li Shenzhi), vol. 2, p. 647.

Academy, and the radical late Qing reformer Tan Sitong (1865–98), the aging Li Shenzhi displayed an unusually strong martyr spirit of a moral idealist in his words. He believed that a man's soul does not die. The universe is always advancing, and man is the heart of the universe, having the same value as the heart of the universe.[32] As long as he follows the flow of history and the principles of the universe, man's heart/mind will represent heavenly principles, and his soul will obtain immortality.

Whoever came in contact with Li Shenzhi felt his radical spirit. He himself said: "I'm hot-tempered." He often overwhelmed people with his passion, which sometimes overcame reason; his was a moral force. He who possesses a moral force is a true hero and not every age has its heroes. The twentieth-century Chinese historian Qian Mu (1895–1990) argued that we find heroic scholar-officials only in the Warring States period (475–221 BC), the Three Kingdoms period (220–80), and in the Tang (618–907) and Ming (1368–1644) dynasties. If we add the May Fourth to this, this gives us only five generations of heroes. Heroic characters aren't produced out of nothing; there has to be a base, an inspiration. Heroes of the Warring States period modeled themselves on the nobility of the Zhou dynasty. Heroes of the Three Kingdoms period took the disciples of the great hereditary families as their model. The heroes of the Tang period based themselves on Buddhists, and heroes of the Ming period on the spirit of heaven and earth that we find in Wang Yangming. But most of the heroes of the May Fourth period came from political people, dressed in the armor of new evolutionism.[33] From where did Li Shenzhi draw his heroic spirit?

As a transmitter of the May Fourth spirit, we can naturally trace the origins of his heroism. First would be the idealistic spirit of the "old-style CCP members." Most of the heroes of the May Fourth eventually converted to communism, bringing their fiery spirit into the Party. Although in later years Li Shenzhi converted to liberalism, he never lost his basic heroic nature. He believed that history followed an objective course, that the universe had its progressive laws. As long as he understood the direction of truth and grasped the rudder of history, then everything the individual did would be to the benefit of heaven and earth, and would bring everlasting peace. As I mentioned above, Li's acceptance of the heritage of Wang Yangming – in fact, his worship of Wang Yangming – is hard for an outsider to understand. At the entrance to his study was a

---

[32] Li Yu, "Diaonian Li Shenzhi xiansheng" (Mourning Li Shenzhi), in Ding Dong, ed., *Huainian Li Shenzhi* (Remembering Li Shenzhi), vol. 2, p. 393.

[33] Qian Mu, "Zhongguo zhishi fenzi" (Chinese intellectuals), in *Guoshi xinlun (A new national history)* (Taibei: Dongda chubanshe, 1980), pp. 161–76.

scroll on which was written "No noise, no scents. Only study," a phrase from Wang Yangming. A friend saw it and sighed, saying "that's impressive." Then half-jokingly he said to Li Shenzhi, "When you study, can you rise to see the workings of the Way in heaven, and descend to observe the affairs of men? Might I ask how many people on earth possess such powers?" Li laughed and quietly shook his head in agreement.[34]

In his early nineties, Li Shenzhi published an article in the intellectual journal *Dushu* about Feng Youlan's *History of Chinese Philosophy*, originally published in the 1930s, in which Feng (1885–1990), a leading twentieth-century Chinese philosopher, sought to harmonize Western and Chinese philosophical histories. In his review, Li criticized Feng from a Wang Yangming perspective: "The mainstream of Chinese philosophy is the theory of the universe and the theories of mind and human nature that correspond to it. It is not Mr. Feng's ontological theory, which is based on Western logic." In comparing Feng Youlan's "moral realm" with his "realm of heaven and earth,"[35] he noted, in a style that is worth remembering:

Precisely because the feelings and understandings of people in the realm of heaven and earth are superior, what they do and what they are exceed those of people in the moral realm. "Death is the only true difficulty." From time immemorial, in China and elsewhere, how many people have lost their virtue and ruined their actions because they could not transcend the dilemma of birth and death? Moreover, people in the realm of heaven and earth not only remain unaffected by the division of dreams and wakefulness but also by the division of life and death. As such they can naturally strengthen their capacity to know good and their will to do good at a basic level … If those in the moral world only do good out of a sense of social responsibility, then people in the realm of heaven and earth should do so out of a self-awakened desire to engage the heart/mind for heaven and earth. In modern terms, this means that their thoughts and actions should encourage humanity and history to conform to the laws of development, so as to follow the great trends in universal evolution.[36]

A few years later, Li Shenzhi opened the door and left, going himself to inhabit the realm of heaven and earth whose existence he had long felt. From the position of his limited life, he looked past life and death, penetrating into the timeless. His lungs full of heroic spirit, his belly

---

[34] Lin Mengxi, "Zixu gaocai lao geng gang" (Old bamboo is even stronger), in Ding Dong, ed., *Huainian Li Shenzhi* (Remembering Li Shenzhi), vol. 1, p. 119.

[35] Translator's note: Feng Youlan divided human life into four universes, or realms: the natural realm, the instrumental realm, the moral realm, and the realm of heaven and earth. These were hierarchical, with the natural field at the bottom and the field of heaven and earth at the top.

[36] Li Shenzhi, "Rongguan Zhong-Xi, tongshi gujin" (Link East and West, unify ancient and modern), *Dushu* 12 (1991).

full of forthright remonstrance, all of it "to give his heart to heaven and earth." When the novelist Ba Jin (1904–2005) talked about "speaking truth," what propped him up was moral faith in humanism, which hardly transcends life and death. When Li Shenzhi "spoke truth," his basis was the realm of heaven and earth. When a hero does not fear death, what does he not dare say?

The last scholar-official, the last hero. Today we live in a peaceful secular world without scholar-officials, without heroes. In this age without passion, without idealistic spirit, we find false martyrs who chase after fame, scholars who feign bravery by wrapping themselves in the banner of various ideologies, and great cynics who seek only material gain. Some may be on fire, but most are fakes and hypocrites. And even if there are heroes, the noble spiritual basis of the past is gone, all that's left is barren land.

When the scholar-official spirit and moral idealism sing their final arias and the turbulent movement of a generation sinks beneath the horizon, maybe rationalism is our only rampart, a reflective rationality that continues and transcends enlightenment. Li Shenzhi's internal limited transcendence is perhaps our best souvenir of him.

Glossary

1898 Reforms – Also known as the "Hundred Days Reform," occurred when the young Guangxu emperor (r. 1875–1908), following the counsel of Kang Youwei (1858–1927), attempted to introduce a series of thoroughgoing reforms of China's government, military, and economy, similar to those carried out years earlier in Meiji Japan. The short-lived effort was brought up short by a coup led by more conservative members of the imperial court.

Big Five Religions – Refers to the five religions sanctioned by China's Republican and Communist constitutions: Buddhism, Daoism, Islam, Protestantism, and Catholicism.

Chen Duxiu (1879–1942) – An important intellectual figure during the May Fourth period, who iconoclastically denounced Confucianism and other Chinese traditions and eventually co-founded the Chinese Communist Party in 1921.

China model – The notion, particularly popular since China's rise to great-power status in the twenty-first century, that China's particular form of government and economy can serve as a model for the rest of the world. The idea has historical antecedents: China historically saw herself as the center of the world, and Mao Zedong viewed his version of sinicized Marxist rule as a model, at least for the Third World.

Civilization – A major theme in Chinese history, both traditional and modern. The traditional Chinese equivalent of "civilization" was *tianxia* ("all under heaven"), which expressed the belief that China's moral and political order was superior to all others. This belief was dashed by the arrival of the West in the nineteenth century, whose material and moral civilization reduced China to the status of a near-colony and forced China to endure a "century of humiliation." China's return to great-power status over the past few decades has encouraged some Chinese to believe that China's traditional civilization will return to its past prominence.

Daoism – An indigenous Chinese philosophy/religion, with roots in the pre-imperial era. In contrast to Confucianism, with its emphasis on morality and service, and Legalism, with its emphasis on laws and political acumen, Daoism stressed nature and the pursuit of immortality through ritual and cultivation.

Deng Xiaoping (1904–97) – An early Communist Party member who is best known for having engineered a fundamental redirection of the People's Republic following Mao Zedong's death in 1976. Deng's policies of "reform and opening" are largely credited for creating today's China, a great power focused on wealth and power rather than revolution.

Dong Zhongshu (179–104 BC) – A Han dynasty scholar who played a central role in the transformation of Confucianism from a philosophy into an ideology of state power.

Enlightenment – In this volume, Enlightenment can refer either to the European Enlightenment, to the May Fourth movement from 1915 to 1925, or to the "New Enlightenment" of the 1980s, when Chinese intellectuals turned their gaze to the West once more after the death of Mao Zedong and the failure of the Maoist revolutionary impulse. The notion is closely related to "civilization."

Foreign Affairs movement – Also known as the "Westernization movement," it refers to efforts in the 1860s and 1870s to learn from the West without fundamentally transforming Chinese politics or society. The Hundred Days Reform of 1898 was the first attempt to break away from this paradigm.

Fukuyama, Francis (b. 1952) – An American political scientist best-known in China for his book *The End of History and the Last Man* (1992), which for many Chinese symbolized American arrogance in the post-Cold War world. The Chinese New Left reacted particularly strongly, identifying it with neo-liberalism and the Washington consensus.

Gu Yanwu (1613–82) – A well-respected Confucian scholar known, among other things, for his reflections on political structures and state power. These reflections were prompted by the Manchu victory in 1644 over the Chinese Ming dynasty (1368–1644), a dynasty Gu refused to serve out of Confucian loyalty to the Ming.

Han – the name of China's first lasting dynasty (206 BC–AD 220), Han also refers to the Chinese ethnicity.

Hu Shi (1891–1962) – One of the Chinese intellectuals most identified with the May Fourth movement and the New Culture movement, particularly the "liberal" (i.e., non-revolutionary) currents of the movement. Hu championed language reform and scientific scholarship, as well as "pragmatic" politics focused on "problems" instead of "isms." Long despised on the mainland, Hu's thought and legacy have been re-examined by Chinese intellectuals beginning in the 1980s, and he has achieved a certain popularity in recent years.

Kang Youwei (1858–1927) – One of the most important intellectual figures of the late Qing–early Republican period, Kang embraced Confucianism as well as Western civilization, eventually imagining a new age when the two would be combined and finally transcended. He played an important role in the 1898 reform, was forced into exile after the failure of that movement, and was active in diaspora circles for many years, seeking to influence Chinese politics from outside. He returned to China with the fall of the dynasty, and, disappointed with the nature of China's Republican government, championed without success a return of Confucianism as China's national religion.

Laozi – Reputed founder of Daoism and author of the *Daodejing* (The Classic of the Way and its Power). The possibly legendary figure would have lived in the sixth century BC.

Legalism – A philosophy associated with the first emperor of China, Qin Shihuang (259–210 BC), which emphasized political rule through strict laws rather than moral example. Xu Jilin and other contemporary scholars argue that traditional China was more "Legalist" than Confucian, meaning that Confucianism functioned as moral ornamentation while emperors and courtiers ruled through Machiavellian *realpolitik*.

Li Dazhao (1888–1927) – An important May Fourth intellectual and eventual co-founder of the Chinese Communist Party, with Chen Duxiu.

Liang Qichao (1873–1929) – Originally a disciple of the late Qing reformer Kang Youwei, Liang was, like Kang, forced into exile after the failure of the 1898 reforms. He subsequently made major contributions to the evolution of modern China as a journalist and an interpreter of the West.

Lu Xun (1881–1936) – A major figure in the May Fourth movement, Lu Xun is widely acknowledged as modern China's finest writer of fiction and essays. Although claimed by the Chinese Communist Party as a "revolutionary," he was in fact an independent, complex thinker.

Mandate of Heaven – The notion that the Chinese emperor rules because he has been so mandated by the "heavens," and that the mandate is justified by the moral character and behavior of the emperor. In other words, the mandate could be revoked, which was the explanation of all changes of dynasty in traditional China. The notion is connected as well with traditional Chinese concepts of civilization (*tianxia*).

Mass Line – The notion, elaborated by Mao Zedong during the Yan'an period in the 1930s and 1940s, that Party rule was legitimized via popular authority as understood and reshaped by the Party. In this form of "democracy," the Party interacted with the people, understood their concerns and needs, and crafted policies to reflect that understanding.

May Fourth (1919) – "May Fourth" refers to student demonstrations, in Beijing and elsewhere, on May 4, 1919, in reaction to China's betrayal at the Versailles Conference marking the conclusion of World War I. China had joined the war in the hopes of seeing German concessions in China returned after the war, but the concessions were instead transferred to Japan. "May Fourth" also refers more broadly to the "New Culture" movement, an iconoclastic condemnation of China's tradition that marked an important turning point in China's cultural and political history.

New Left – A group of intellectuals in contemporary China, called the "new left" by their critics in an effort to discredit them by linking them to the "old left," seen as representatives of the Maoist tradition. In fact, most members of the New Left have either studied abroad or been otherwise influenced by Western ideas. Their "leftism" is an effort to locate alternatives to neo-liberalism from within the socialist tradition in China as elsewhere.

Rawls, John (1921–2002) – An American political thinker, identified with the social justice school among Anglo-American liberals. His work and thought were important influences on Xu Jilin.

Sun Yat-Sen (1866–1925) – Acknowledged by both Communists and Nationalists as the father of China's Republican Revolution, Sun was a major figure in Chinese politics from late Qing times until his untimely death in 1925. After attempting to organize rebellions in China in the 1890s, he spent many years in exile, where he developed his political philosophy known as the "Three People's Principles."

Tianxia – Literally translated as "all under heaven," *tianxia* was the functional equivalent of the notion of "civilization" in traditional China. In terms of physical territory, China was at the center of *tianxia*, but the notion went beyond territory to suggest compliance with a moral, cosmic order which sought a resonance between humanity and the gods via the proper behavior of the emperor, the son of heaven. *Tianxia* was a relatively open concept in that it could be learned, even by non-Chinese.

Wang Hui (b. 1959) – Professor of Chinese Language and Literature at Tsinghua University in Beijing, Wang Hui is a major public intellectual in contemporary China and a leading figure of the New Left. Although originally trained as a literary scholar, Wang now writes on a wide range of topics, ranging from history to economics to international affairs.

Wang Shaoguang (b. 1954) – Professor Emeritus of Government and Administration at the Chinese University of Hong Kong, Wang is a prominent member of China's New Left, with considerable influence in certain government circles. His research often targets questions of central interest to the government.

Wang Yangming (1472–1529) – A major figure in the history of Confucianism, Wang is best known for preaching a form of Confucian cultivation that stressed the power of intuition and humanity's inborn capacity for sagehood. He is most often contrasted with Zhu Xi (1130–1200), whose approach to cultivation was much more structured. "Extending knowledge" in Zhu Xi's program required years of patient study.

Yan Fu (1854–1921) – An important intellectual figure in the late Qing–early Republican period, Yan, who studied in England, was first known for his translations of important Western texts such as Huxley's *Evolution and Ethics*, Smith's *The Wealth of Nations*, Mill's *On Liberty*, and Spencer's *Study of Sociology*, in the process making available to China's educated elite many of the central ideas of Western civilization.

Index

Academy of Chinese Culture, The, xii
Ai Weiwei, xix
Arendt, Hannah, 49n63, 49–50, 53, 53n69
Atatürk, Kemal, 11

Ba Jin, 205, 209
Babbitt, Irving, 177
Beijing consensus, xix, xxi, 48n58, 79, 79n35
Bell, Daniel, 73
Bellah, Robert, xxix, 18
Berlin, Isaiah, 2, 7, 80, 90, 93, 157, 183, 187–88
Berman, Harold, 16
Bernstein, Eduard, 15
Bismarck, Otto von, 10, 167
Bonaparte, Napoléon, xxii, xxv, 157, 179
Buddhism, xxix, 2, 13, 17, 19, 100, 114–15, 119, 121–23, 125, 129–30, 141, 153, 159, 184, 189, 211

Callahan, William, ix
Chang, Carson, *see Zhang Junmai*
Cheek, Timothy, vii, xiv
Chen Duanhong, 48, 50
Chen Duxiu, xvii, xxvi–1, 156, 160, 166–70, 172, 177, 185, 193, 206
Chen Huanzhang, 120
Chen Shuibian, 52
Chen Xiaoming, 65
Chen Xujing, 180–82
Chen Yinke, 177–79, 186, 193, 199
China and the World, xii
China Dream, xix, 7, 128, 130
China model, xix, xx, xxi, xxii, 8–10, 41, 60, 63, 76, 78–81, 93
Chinese Communist Party, xxiii, xxiv, xxx, 28, 46, 48, 191, 195
Chinese exceptionalism, xxi, 78, 92
Chinese values, 61–62, 68, 74–75, 85n49, 85–86, 90, 93–94, 129

Christianity, xxix, 5–6, 14, 17, 19, 87, 100, 114, 119, 121–23, 125, 129, 134, 184, 188, 197
Cicero, 49
civil religion, xvii, xxix, 13, 16, 18–19, 114
communism, xii, xxx, 64, 113, 191, 207
Confucian Religion Society, 120
Confucianism, v, xvii, xxi, xxii, xxviii, xxix, xxx, 5, 13–14, 17, 19, 72, 95, 111, 114n3, 113–26, 129, 145, 147, 153, 178, 189, 211–14
Cui Zhiyuan, 42, 66
Cultural Revolution, 1, 39, 63–64, 86, 114

Dahl, Robert, 51
Daoism, xxix, 17, 19, 114, 119, 121, 123, 125, 129, 178, 189
Davies, Gloria, vii, xvii, xviii, 20
democracy, 21–22, 24–27, 29–41, 47, 52, 55, 57, 62, 67–68, 80, 82, 89–91, 107, 119, 121, 124, 146, 150–51, 174, 195, 202
Deng Xiaoping, xiii, xx, xxiv, 40, 63, 78, 82, 139, 150, 191
Derrida, Jacques, 15
Descartes, René, 109
Dewey, John, 162
Dong Zhongshu, 98, 117
Du Yaquan, xxvi, 66, 156, 162, 162n9, 164, 164n13, 169n25, 168–70, 170n26, 170n28, 172, 172n31, 180, 185

East China Normal University, i, ix
Eastern Europe, xii, xxi, 11
Eisenstadt, Shmuel, 3, 135
England, 7, 10, 36, 50, 70, 90, 92, 151, 156–58, 168, 214

fascism, xxv, 6, 58
Fei Xiaotong, 17, 132, 143
Feng Youlan, 208

215